Sociology for CHILDHOOD STUDIES

ALAN YEO AND TINA LOVELL

Hodder & Stoughton

Dedication

To all the children, parents (especially mine), early years workers and students who have informed my practice and taught me things down the years. They have on many occasions shared their wisdom, insight and experience and I am eternally grateful.

T.L.

With much love to my Dad, and to my children Sam, Lorna, Francis and Sophia.

A.Y.

Order queries: please contact Bookpoint Ltd, 39 Milton Park, Abingdon, Oxon OX14 4TD.
Telephone: (44) 01235 400414, Fax: (44) 01235 400454. Lines are open from 9.00–6.00, Monday to Saturday, with a 24 hour message answering service.
Email address: orders@bookpoint.co.uk

A catalogue record for this title is available from The British Library

ISBN 0 340 697792

First published 1998

Impression number	10 9 8 7 6 5 4 3
Year	2003 2002 2001 2000 1999

Typeset by Wearset, Bolden, Tyne & Wear.
Printed in Great Britain for Hodder & Stoughton Educational, a division of Hodder Headline Plc, 338 Euston Road, London NW1 3BH by J. W. Arrowsmith Ltd., Bristol.

Contents

How to use this book

This book was written because there seemed to be no other sociology or social policy textbook which covered all the topics of central concern on Childhood Studies courses, and in which the material selected was specifically orientated towards children and the young. This focus of attention on childhood and children, youth and the young, has been very conscious, in both the text and in the stimulus material selected. *Sociology for Childhood Studies* should, therefore, be of interest to those teaching or studying on a range of Childhood Studies courses, from BTEC National and CACHE/NNEB, to HNC and early degree levels. It is hoped that the book will also be of interest to those involved in sociology GCSE and 'A' level courses, especially as age status and related issues seem to have grown in importance in 'A' level syllabuses in recent years. Additionally, students on other caring professions courses, such as GNVQ Health and Social Care courses, and nursing and social work training courses, will also find the book relevant and, it is hoped, illuminating.

As will be readily seen, the book consists of text and activities. The activities are made up of extracts from articles, books or statistics, and are followed by questions to address, or suggestions for discussion and debate. The intention of the 'stimulus material' is to stimulate, and act as a trigger for thought and discussion. It should be stressed that, although answers can be straightforwardly wrong, in many cases there are no simple 'right' answers. In the social sciences as elsewhere, 'explanations' always involve a number of factors, and this should be reflected in discussion and answers.

1

Introducing Sociology

Key points

- most human behaviour has to be learnt
- it isn't 'instincts' which determine human behaviour
- every society's culture shapes the personalities of its members

Children in solitary confinement

In 1938, an illegitimate five year-old girl named Anna was unexpectedly discovered in a lonely American farmhouse. She had been locked up by her mother for years in solitary confinement. Since birth, she had had almost no contact with any other human being. She was unable to either walk or talk, and her physical health was poor. Five years later she died, but by that time she had learnt to keep herself reasonably clean, feed herself (though only ever using a spoon), dress herself (though she needed help in fastening her clothes), and had finally begun to speak and even to construct a few complete sentences.

In 1939, 9 months after the discovery of Anna, another illegitimate American child was discovered in almost total isolation. Isabelle was about 6 and a half and seemed to have lived alone in a dark room with her mother, who was a deaf mute. She too did not speak. At first, the specialists were unsure whether or not she was also deaf. When they had established that she wasn't, they thought she was brain damaged. Like Anna, Isabelle was in poor health and initially very fearful of and hostile towards strangers.

Despite the specialists' suspicions of brain damage, a carefully thought-out programme of training was launched. After a week of continuous effort, Isabelle made her first attempt at speech. Following a short period of gradual progress, she suddenly began to make rapid gains. She was speaking in complete sentences within about 2 months. Less than a year after she began her training she could identify written words and sentences, could write well, could count to 10, and could retell a story. Seven months later still, she had a vocabulary of about 2000 words and was asking complicated questions. She was then about 8 years-old and had completed in just 2 years the learning which would normally have taken 6. Moreover, she had completed the appropriate learning stages in the usual sequence – but very much more rapidly. By 14 years-old, her teachers were able to say that she was participating in school activities just like any other child, and was a bright, energetic and cheerful schoolgirl.

Is human behaviour instinctive?

Unable to stand, walk, talk, feed themselves, even apparently not able to discriminate sounds – sad cases such as Anna and Isabelle offer a powerful illustration of how much of our basic behaviour has to be learnt from other human beings. If we are deprived of that contact, we fail to develop many of the behaviours we think of as characteristically human, such as standing upright and developing speech.

For some non-human species, such as bees, spiders or ants, very little of their behaviour has to be learnt for they inherit much of their behaviour from their parents via their genes. This unlearnt behaviour can only be slightly changed. So all bees of a particular type behave in a very similar way, not because they've learnt to but because they are genetically pre-programmed to do so.

Animals which have inherited in their genes particular patterns of behaviour don't need to learn that behaviour from others of their species. For instance, a bird which belongs to a species which migrates is biologically compelled to migrate. It has to go. Such complex, genetically pre-programmed patterns of behaviour are sometimes called **instincts**.

It is very difficult to think of any human equivalent. Human beings do inherit genetically a number of **reflexes** – the body's standard automatic responses to a **stimulus**. A healthy baby will turn its head when gently stroked on the cheek, extend a leg when the sole of the foot is stroked, automatically suck when something is put in the mouth, or grasp when an object is put in the hand. Instincts, however, involve more complex behaviour – often the stringing together of a series of acts in a complex sequence – and humans don't seem to inherit *any* such fully developed instincts which compare in any way to other species.

Even the so-called 'maternal instinct' in humans is pretty weak compared to the instinctive behaviour of bees or ants. Women still seem to need to learn *how* to mother their children and bring them up, and many throughout history have chosen not to. Others have not loved them when they arrived, or have preferred to have others nurse or care for them. Still others have abused, deformed or killed their children. So if women do have a maternal instinct – which would mean that they are biologically 'obliged' to love, look after and protect their children – it seems sufficiently weak that millions of women throughout history have been able to overcome it.

Put simply, it seems that very little of our behaviour, other than more or less simple reflexes, is unlearnt, or just comes naturally. In the main, human behaviour has to be learnt.

ACTIVITY

Unlearnt behaviour among animals

If a bird such as a yellowhammer or corn bunting is hatched and reared, completely apart from any others of its species, its very first song is exactly the same as that of such birds raised normally in the wild. When a male moth emerges from its cocoon, it flies immediately towards a female moth, attracted by the odour she produces. The first time that a squirrel encounters a nut, without ever having seen another squirrel do it, it tries to bury it. Young spiders without any previous experience weave webs as well constructed as those of older spiders.

(Perrott, 1972)

The instinctive behaviour of bees

When a worker bee has found a rich source of nectar she flies in circles round the hive, alerting the other collectors. They identify the plant from the scent which clings to the body of the scout, but how will they discover the location?

The news is given by dances performed by the bees which indicate both direction and distance. If the food source is within about 85 yards they dance in a circle; if the supplies are more distant, they perform a 'tail-wagging' dance (wriggling movements of the abdomen), which also takes into account the direction of the wind and therefore time and energy needed to reach it. They actually navigate their direction from the ultra-violet radiation of the sun, which is invisible to humans.

However, despite these truly remarkable achievements, it would be quite wrong to think of bees' behaviour as intelligent in the human sense. Even the most complicated behaviour of bees derives from fundamental instincts from which they are incapable of deviating in the slightest.

(From H. Wolterek, 1965)

1 Make a list of any behaviours, simple reflexes or emotions you think humans *don't* have to learn. Then, consider whether you think that each of those items you have listed would be found in all human societies. Are there any that wouldn't be? Would they be exactly the same in different societies?
2 In two columns, list what you think are any similarities and differences between the behaviours of the species in the extracts and the behaviour of humans.

The importance of culture

As human beings don't have instincts which force them to behave in certain ways, they have to learn how they are expected to behave from other human beings. This process of learning is called **socialisation**, and refers to *the process of learning the culture of the society in which we live.*

A **society** is a grouping of people who share the same culture. A society could range from a few dozen members, such as a tribe of Amazonian Indians, to millions, as in Britain. As social scientists use the term, **culture** is much broader and more inclusive than in popular speech. It doesn't just refer to 'high' culture, such as Shakespeare or Beethoven, but to *the entire way of life of members of a particular society*. So the term 'culture' includes everything that one learns as a member of a human society. It includes the knowledge and beliefs of members of the society, the **social norms** and **laws** – that is the ideas about how people should behave – the values, the attitudes, the language and literature, the religion and the traditions. Indeed, everything that people learn as they grow up in their society. When we look at other societies, especially those very different to our own, we see how our behaviour is largely the result of our socialisation, of our being brought up in a particular society with its particular culture.

In some societies it is possible for an individual to learn almost the entire culture of their society. However, in a society as large and as complex as that of Britain, no-one learns the whole of the culture. For instance, you may not know how to set a table for a six-course dinner, and your parents may not have heard of the bands you like. Millions of bits of information – some of it factual, some of it ideas about how we are expected to behave – are contained within our culture. Which bits of our culture we are expected to learn – the relevant bits of the culture for us – depends upon the various social positions we occupy, our **social statuses**.

We each occupy many social statuses or positions at any one time. I may be teacher, female, black, Methodist, British, middle aged, mother, wife. You may be male, white, teenager, brother, student, son, boyfriend. Which statuses are relevant at any one time depends on the statuses of the people we are with. For instance, when you are a student, that should be your dominant or **master status**, and I should relate to you in my then master status of tutor. When you head home, other statuses assume greater importance: you become girlfriend, car driver, and then, when you arrive home, you become daughter, sister, neighbour and so on. In each of these different social statuses, there are different ideas about how you should behave. In each of our different social statuses, to some extent, we may have to apply different social norms. So when we are a daughter we behave differently, we feel differently, we maybe think differently, to when we are a girlfriend or a student or a football fan.

Most differences in behaviour between the sexes are probably learnt. However, people very often assume that when they see general differences in behaviour between the sexes, it is because of men and women's physiological and biological differences and not because the behaviours are learnt. According to this view, for men and women to behave as they usually do is not a social but a natural thing. So people who don't behave in the expected ways are somehow unnatural.

However Margaret Mead, in her famous book of the 1930s *Sex and Temperament in Three Primitive Societies*, set out to show, by using examples from her study of three tribes on the island of New Guinea to the north of Australia, that many of the differences between the sexes often attributed to biology are in fact social in origin. One of the advantages of New Guinea as an area of investigation was that, although there were many different societies there, there had been historically relatively little mixing among them, so that within a small geographical area many different ways of doing things could be observed. Part of what she described was the socialisation of children in two very different tribes, the Arapesh and the Mundugamor.

ACTIVITY

The socialisation of an Arapesh child

The early training of the Arapesh children largely results in adults who are unaggressive and non-competitive, placid and contented, responsive and warm, docile and trusting.

During its first months the child is never far from someone's arms. When the mother walks about she carries the baby suspended from her forehead in its special small net bag, or suspended under one breast in a bark-cloth sling. If the child is fretful and irritable, it is carried in the sling, where it can be given the comforting breast as swiftly as possible. Children are held a great deal. Suckled whenever they cry, never left far distant from some woman who can give them the breast if necessary, usually in close contact with the mother's body, the child has a continuous warm sensation of security.

While the small child lies in its mother's lap, she builds up in it a trust of the world, a receptive and welcoming attitude. All of the child's relatives are repeatedly referred to in a warm, happy and positive way. And the dog that thrusts a nose under the mother's arm is gently held there, the child's skin and the dog's rubbed together, the mother quietly rocking them both.

The socialisation of a Mundugamor child

The Mundugamor child is born into a hostile world, and almost from birth the child's preparation for an unloved life is begun. Very little babies are kept in a carrying basket, which the women wear suspended from their foreheads. However, unlike the soft net bag of the Arapesh, which puts no barrier between the baby and the mother's warm body, the Mundugamor basket is harsh and stiff.

On short expeditions away mothers usually leave their babies hung up in the basket at home. When the baby cries, some nearby female resorts to the standard method of soothing restless infants. Without looking at or touching the child, she begins to scratch the basket with her finger nails, making a harsh, grating sound. If the crying continues, the child is eventually reluctantly suckled. The moment a child stops suckling, they are returned to their basket-prison. So children develop a determined attitude, holding on firmly to the nipple and sucking milk as rapidly as possible. They frequently choke from swallowing too fast. The choking angers the mother and infuriates the child. This further turns the suckling situation into one characterised by anger and struggle rather than by affection and reassurance.

(From M. Mead, 1935)

1 How does the socialisation of children in Items A and B appear to affect their personalities? Are there any aspects of their socialisation from which you feel children in our society would benefit?
2 Think about the socialisation of infants that you know. How do you think the parents' behaviour influences the child's personality?
3 Ideally, we want children in our society to feel both secure and independent. How can we bring this about through socialisation? Do you think early years socialisation can contribute to achieving these ideals?

Summary

- children who have missed out on 'normal' socialisation may not develop such abilities as walking and talking, which many assume come 'naturally'
- there are few, if any, complex behaviours which humans don't have to learn.
- different societies can 'produce' significantly different personality types by giving a very different socialisation to their children.

2

Introducing social policy

Key points

- a social policy is a statement that details how particular areas of welfare service should be organised and delivered, for example social services
- the development of social policy changes the way welfare services are funded and delivered
- the European Union is becoming increasingly influential in the decision making process in Britain

What is social policy?

There are many definitions of social policy, making it difficult to state exactly what it is. This difficulty arises because social policy covers such a large range of topics. Richard Titmuss (1974) argued that social policy was about making choices between differing political ideas. The ideas chosen could then be used to influence how society organised and delivered its welfare services.

A social policy is a statement that details how particular areas of welfare service should be organised and delivered, for example social services. It contains a course of action that in some way regulates one or all of the following:

- the way an organisation functions
- the delivery of services
- the actions of those working for the organisation

All organisations have policies that explain to their staff and users how they are going to operate. Some of these policies will be based on their legal responsibilities and some on the way they believe things ought to be. This might be called their belief system or philosophy. For instance, schools have no legal responsibility to have a policy on bullying, but most do because they believe that bullying is inappropriate behaviour. State schools do, on the other hand, have a legal responsibility to follow the **legislation** and guidelines on the **National Curriculum.** The National Curriculum forms part of society's policy for education. Social policy has historically been linked to the **welfare state.** A welfare state is one in which the government is seen as having some responsibility for the well-being of the people. The welfare state provides services that protect people from poverty and ill health. It also provides services for the public good such as education and social services. The main components of the welfare state are:

- Income Maintenance (Social Security)
- Health
- Education
- Social Services
- Housing

To simplify the administration of social policy it became focused on the areas listed above. The institutions associated with these areas were responsible for service delivery. They continue to be important in the development of social policy. However, it has become increasingly difficult to maintain this focus. The last twenty years have witnessed many changes in the way welfare services are provided with more and more private, independent and voluntary organisations becoming involved in service delivery. Many services that were once delivered by the state, have now been **privatised**.

ACTIVITY

1 Make a list of public services, for example public transport, playgroups, leisure centres.
2 On a sheet of paper draw five columns and head each with one of the main components of the welfare state. Allocate the services you identified to one of the columns.
3 Look at any you found difficult to place. Why is this?
4 What additional categories do you need?

The study of social policy

Paul Spiker (1995) describes social policy as 'the study of the social services and welfare state'. Traditionally, this field of study focused on **Social Administration**, that is the funding and delivery of services provided by the welfare state. As early as 1955, **Richard Titmuss**, a prominent writer in this field, pointed out that such a narrow focus failed to take into account other aspects of welfare provision, for example transport services or **equal opportunities**. Over time, the concentration of study on service delivery changed. The study of social policy now includes discussion about the political and social attitudes that are predominant at the time policy decisions are made.

Sociology and **Social Administration** have always played an important part in the study of social policy. Sociologists undertook research in an attempt to explain how and why societies organised themselves and functioned as they did. They were interested to see what effect social policy had on people's lives. They tried to establish the reasons why policies were developed as they were. Social Administrators monitored the effectiveness of policy and the practical concerns of service delivery. They saw their task as identifying and demonstrating areas of need in order to secure policy reform. They tried to find solutions to social problems and reduce social inequality. In effect sociologists offered a critical analysis of social policy whilst social administrators campaigned for new policies and change. The study of social policy enables us to understand the nature of society. The development of policy can reveal a great deal about the values, beliefs, politics, concerns and economic interests of that society.

Ideologies of welfare

An **ideology** is quite simply about ideas. It is defined as beliefs, opinions and attitudes which, when put together, form a set. This set of ideas, attitudes and opinions can influence social policy. The word ideology is commonly used to describe political ideals. Each political party is described as having a particular ideology. These ideologies are described in the chart '*Ideologies of welfare*' on page 11.

The type of social policy adopted by a society will have a strong influence on that society's structure, the life chances of its citizens and the way in which that society chooses to regulate and allocate its resources. Firstly a

Ideology	Core Values	View of Society	Role of Government
Anti Collective Politics: Conservative	Individualism, freedom-liberty, capitalism, efficiency and a competitive market place.	Believe that the family is of paramount importance in maintaining the balance of society. Emphasise self help and a key role for the voluntary and private sector in service delivery.	Residual and Selective models of welfare adopted. Minimal intervention. 'Safety net' principle of welfare provision.
Reluctant Collectivists Politics: New Labour and the Liberal Democrats	Individualism, self help, private enterprise and a mixed economy of welfare.	Concerned with the well-being of society and reducing inequality.	Residual and Selective model of welfare adopted with provision for state intervention to promote social change.
Collectivist (1) Politics: Socialism Old Labour	Equality, freedom, fellowship, democracy and humanitarianism	Society is seen as divided by social class (wealth and status).	Institutional model of welfare to promote purposeful action in order to modify injustice and social inequality.
Collectivist (2) Politics: Communism	Transformation of society to one where all people are equal.	Society is seen as exploited by landowners and big business due to the inequalities of status	Institutional model of welfare that redistributes wealth and resources. Government regulation of welfare services.
Collectivist (3) Politics: Feminism	Equality and a redistribution of power between men and women	Patriarchal: male dominance	Action to modify inequality and discrimination on the grounds of sex. Institutional model of welfare.
Collectivist (4) Politics: Racist Critique	Equality and a redistribution of power amongst cultures and races.	Racism: White dominance	Action to modify inequality and discrimination on the ground of race. Institutional model of welfare.

Ideologies of Welfare

society must decide what level of state intervention it finds politically, financially and socially acceptable. Secondly it will develop policy that reflects a particular model of welfare provision. Thirdly an eligibility or needs criterion is established for those who will benefit from the policy.

State intervention

This relates to the amount of government responsibility taken for the funding and delivery of services in the welfare state. Not all societies have the same level of state intervention.

The USA has limited state intervention. The government takes little responsibility for welfare services. They rely on the private and voluntary sector to provide welfare services. State welfare (welfare provided by the government) is only offered to those in extreme need.

The state in Sweden takes full responsibility for the welfare of its citizens by providing a system of social welfare that ensures equal treatment for all.

The British welfare state provides a national minimum to those in need but also funds and regulates services such as **health, education and the social services**. It has what is called a **mixed economy of welfare**. The government takes responsibility for some things but encourages the private and voluntary sectors to offer services as well.

The level of state intervention is reflected in the model of welfare adopted by that society.

Models of welfare

The concept of welfare relates to the way a society ensures the 'well-being' of its citizens. A society has to decide who should be responsible for its well-being and in what circumstances. Society has to choose which needs to meet and how it will cope with social problems. Most societies use a mixture of the models outlined below.

- the **Residual** and **Selective** models of welfare hold that the state should provide welfare if the individual, family or private sector are unable to do so. The state provides a 'safety net' based on a criterion of need. This criterion targets those most disadvantaged. Both Britain and the USA adopt this model but apply it in different ways

- the **Institutional model of welfare** holds that welfare provision is an important function of society. The institutional welfare state aims to ensure a decent standard of living for all citizens. It is based on a belief in social equality and the redistribution of resources from those with more to those with less. Similarly the **Universal** model holds that services should be available to everyone as a right. Sweden and Denmark adopt a form of this model
- the **Individual achievement** model holds that social welfare is a part of the economy, that social need should be met on merit and should reward performance, productivity and effort. Mrs Thatcher (Prime Minister 1979–1990) tended to adopt this view

Needs criteria

The concept of need is at the heart of social policy. The way in which a society defines need will influence both the level of state intervention and model of welfare adopted by that society. What people see as need is variable. We all have certain basic needs, the need for food, drink and warmth. Most would agree that life itself depends on these needs being met. In Britain the majority of people acknowledge that children, older people, the sick and the disabled have 'special' needs, some of which should be addressed by the state.

ACTIVITY

1 Make a list of what you consider to be your needs.
2 Take each need in turn and say who you think is responsible for meeting it.
3 List the needs of a child who is a wheelchair user.
4 Take each need in turn and say who you think is responsible for meeting it and why.
5 Look at the differences and similarities. What does this tell you?
6 Look at those needs you feel should be addressed by the state. Find out if existing policy is meeting these needs.

Eligibility criteria

In order to meet need, policy makers usually develop **eligibility criteria** – that is a set of statements that tells you if your needs can be addressed by the policy. In order to develop these criteria they must ask themselves these questions:

Question	Consideration
• What is the unit of need?	Individual, child, family, group or society
• What is the cause of the need?	poverty, unemployment, disability or abuse
• Who is assessing the need?	Individual, professional, expert
• What problems arise because of the need?	Poverty, homelessness, crime
• What resources are necessary to address the need?	Funding, services, specialists
• What resources are available to address the need?	Money, people, buildings
• What would happen if the need were not addressed?	Crime, violence, poverty, illhealth.
• What agency or organisation could best meet this need?	Family, education, health, housing, social services
• Whose life chances are affected and how?	Individual, group or society
• Is it in the interests of society to meet this need?	Yes, no, sometimes, never

The **Children Act 1989** contains a definition of children in need, which has to be applied before a service can be offered. This definition can be found in Chapter 6.

Developing social policy

The development of social policy reflects the ideology of welfare adopted by the society. **Banting** (1979) outlined five stages in policy making

- awareness of the problem
- importance attached to the problem
- the definition of the problem
- consideration of alternatives
- choice between alternatives

What Banting's theory suggests is that social problems and society's response to them is complex. A problem has to be recognised in the first instance: who recognises the problem will affect how the problem is defined and how important it is deemed to be. Before making a response policy makers will look at alternative actions and make a choice about the most appropriate one. For example, in 1988, a pediatrician working in Cleveland noticed that a lot of children who attended her out patients clinic showed indications of sexual abuse. Dr Marietta Higgs had become aware of a problem. Her fears required investigation and both she and the social workers involved received prominent, often negative, media coverage. An importance was attached to her discoveries. The issue was a sensitive one and many people were shocked at the levels of abuse suggested by Dr Higgs and the social workers. The public, professionals, police and politicians were so shocked that they did not want to believe abuse on this scale was possible. No one wanted to define the problem. The response was an inquiry. The Cleveland inquiry outlined the alternative strategies that could be adopted to ensure that children were protected and professionals worked together.

The outcome was the introduction of the Children Act 1989. This new legislation ensured the rights of children to protection. At the same time it changed working practices. The police and Social Services now work closely together on cases of alleged child abuse especially sexual abuse. In addition working in partnership with parents has become a priority.

Once a policy has been developed it has to be put into practice or implemented. Policies are implemented by Social Administrators. These include:

- Government Ministries or Departments
- County Councils
- Local Authorities
- Metropolitan Boroughs
- Service Providers, for example hospitals and schools

Influences on social policy

Legislation

Legislation (Law) often dictates or informs policy. The **Children Act 1989** for instance contains some **mandatory** regulations. These are regulations that a **Local Authority** must ensure are undertaken in order to meet the needs of children. All local authorities must do the same. In some cases these policies will be outlined in the act, in others guidelines are drawn up by the appropriate government ministry. Some elements of the same act are **permissive**. That is, local authorities are given a certain amount of flexibility. They are able to deliver services appropriate to local need. This explains why policies concerning the delivery of services to children vary across the country.

Politics

Social policy is influenced by politics. The ideology of the different political parties will have an impact on the policy making process, with the party in government at the time having the most influence. Individual politicians can also be very influential. They can, from time to time, present a Private Member's Bill to the House of Commons. These Bills often relate to some aspect of social life. David Alton (MP) presented a Bill in 1987. He wanted to change the law on abortion, but was unsuccessful. Local parish and county councils will influence the way a Local Authority chooses to interpret legislation and develop local policy.

Administrators

Those with a responsibility for service delivery are in a good position to influence decisions about new policy or changes to existing policy. The people that deliver the services, such as doctors, teachers and social workers, are able to monitor a policy and see if it works. They are able to report their findings to their managers at a local level. These managers or directors can pass this on to local councillors, who usually have a direct link to government via their political party. All the agencies involved in service delivery are overseen by a government ministry, for example the Department for Education and Employment (DfEE), Department of Health (DoH) and Department of Social Security (DSS). Local findings may eventually find their way back to the ministries and government through this route. Private enterprise and voluntary organisations are increasingly involved in the delivery of services for people in need, and are therefore increasingly influential in the decision making process.

The media

The way the media choose to report an issue may well put pressure on the legislators and/or administrators to review current practice. The reporting of the Rikki Neave murder in 1996 resulted in an inquiry into social work practice.

Rikki Neave was found murdered and many believed that his mother had killed him. A long court case failed to establish her guilt but did uncover some disturbing information about the family, its ability to care for Rikki and the family's relationship with social services. The press reports were very critical of social services and of Rikki's mother. Their reporting generated a lot of anger about the failure of social services to adequately protect Rikki and some Social Workers involved in the case were suspended. This resulted in an inquiry into social work practice and a recognition that many Social Services departments were over burdened with cases that involved children but did not have the staff to deal adequately with their needs.

The European Union

A directive is an instruction handed down by the **European Parliament** in Brussels to its member states. Some of these directives may conflict with established policy. If this is the case the government is usually given a period of time in which to make changes, for example cleaning up the coastline. In some cases they may 'opt out'. Britain for instance has not yet adopted all of the Social Chapter or relaxed border controls. The **European Social Fund** (ESF) provides the resources for a wide variety of projects, from road building to out of school clubs. Increasingly, this funding is being used to develop projects that at one time may have been funded by the state.

ACTIVITY

Find out about a project funded by the ESF in your local area.
1 Has the project always been ESF funded?
2 Does the project receive other funding? If so from where\whom?
3 Would the work of the project have been a state or local authority responsibility in the past? If so, why are they no longer responsible?

The general public

Everyone can exert influence on the policy making process. We can use our vote, write or talk to our MP, or become involved in a campaign group (take for example the Newbury by pass campaign by Swampy and his followers).

ACTIVITY

Devise a campaign around an issue of your choice. How would you bring your views to the attention of those influential in the decision making process?

The impact of social policy

Social policy changes as society evolves. Policies that were established at the onset of the Welfare State in the 1940s reflected the social attitudes, economic situation and political ideology of the time. These policies would not 'fit' today's society, just as the policies of the 1990s are unlikely to mean much in 2040. Social policy itself is a dynamic process which

- influences practice
- influences the delivery of services
- influences the way a society perceives need and social problems
- influences life chances
- influences social structure, beliefs and values
- influences our lifestyle
- influences future policy

Analysing social policy

In order to help us gain insight into a particular policy we need to analyse it. Analysis of social policy enables us to understand its relationship to politics, economics and other disciplines such as sociology, psychology and social work. The following questions are a useful guide. If we manage to answer them, we will have achieved a greater understanding of the policy itself and the ways in which it may have influenced or affected society, other policy and other areas of provision.

- why was the policy developed?
- what need does the policy meet?
- why do these needs arise?
- on what grounds is society meeting this need (moral, political, economic)?
- how does the policy attempt to meet the need?

- who benefits?
- how will we know if the policy has been effective?
- what do the
  administrators, general public and people using the services think of the policy?

ACTIVITY

Apply the above questions to the extract below. You may find it difficult to address some of the points and will need to do some additional research. In order to find out if the Code of Practice has been effective and how it has been received, design a questionnaire that would help you do so. In consultation with your tutor, you could ask your local schools and special needs advisory teachers to fill it in. They may even be willing for you to interview them about their views.

The Code of Practice

The Code of Practice was developed in response to a growing belief that the integration of children with special educational needs was more beneficial than segregating them in special schools. The fundamental principle that underpins the Code of Practice is that the needs of all pupils who may have special educational needs at any time during their school careers must be addressed. The Code acknowledges that these needs may be expressed in a variety of ways and require different types of provision to meet them.

> Children with special educational needs require access to a balanced education that includes all aspects of the National Curriculum. Children with special educational needs will be entitled to an assessment of their needs and, where appropriate, a statement made. The needs of pupils will be met by mainstream provision (schools) wherever possible. The knowledge, views and experience of the parents will be taken into account, with the parents, children and their schools working in partnership. There must be close co-operation between all the agencies concerned and a multi-disciplinary approach. The Code ensures that children with special educational needs are identified and assessed as soon as possible with provision made for monitoring and review.
>
> (From: HMSO (1993) Code of Practice on the Identification and Assessment of Special Educational Needs (Part III of the Education Act 1993)

Main components of the welfare state

	Education	Health	Social Services	Income Maintenance	Housing
Labour	Number one priority committed to high standards in education emphasis on basic skills and life long learning	Rebuild NHS reduce spending on administration and increase spending on patients.	Build strong families and strong communities improving community care and pensions. Adopt policies that are tough on crime particularly juvenile crime.	Provide a stable economy. Get the young unemployed and lone parents into work and off benefits.	Provide security for home owners and tenants. Tackle the problem of homelessness. Enable LA provide more housing.
Conservative	Raise standards in schools. Widen parental choice. Provide more specialist and grammar schools. Retain nursery voucher scheme.	Fund NHS economically. Enable GPs to provide a wider range of services.	Improve Citizens Charter. Crack down on crime especially juvenile crime. Provide help for carers through a Respite Care Programme.	Transform pensions and make it easier for older people to afford the cost of care in their old age. Encourage employee share ownership.	Strengthen home ownership and private rental. Introduce 'common hold'.
Liberal Democrats	Improve teaching standards. Strengthen school discipline. Improve the National Curriculum.	Invest in the NHS. Cut waiting lists. Raise standards. Restore free eye and dental checks.	New carers benefit scheme Establish national standards for community care services. Promote equality. Promote good parenting.	Help the young and long term unemployed into work. Increase tax to pay for improved welfare services.	Build more houses. Tackle homelessness. Provide security for all.

Political Roundup (Source: 1997 Election Manifestos)

Summary

- Social Policy is the study of the welfare state and social services
- the study of social policy enables us to understand the nature of society
- the level of state intervention, model of welfare and prevailing ideology adopted by a society will influence the type of social policy it develops
- the development of social policy is influenced by legislation, politics, service administrators, the general public, the media and our membership of the European Union

3

The family

Key points

- families and marriages differ greatly between societies
- dissatisfaction with the nuclear family has led to a number of experiments
- families in Britain have changed significantly, even during this century
- however, there is disagreement about whether women have achieved equality within the family
- the state increasingly looks to the family to take responsibility for helping itself
- the growing diversity of family composition and lifestyle will affect the development of social policy in the future
- the needs of children are becoming more influential in the development of social policy

What is a family?

It may seem strange, given that almost all of us have some first-hand experience of living in a family, that social scientists do not always agree on a definition of the word 'family'. For instance, according to one famous definition by the anthropologist George Murdock, a family is a social group 'which is characterised by common residence, economic cooperation and reproduction. It includes adults of both sexes, at least two of whom maintain a socially approved sexual relationship, and one or more children, own or adopted, of the sexually cohabiting adults'.

According to this definition, it seems, a homosexual couple who had adopted a child – as happened in Edinburgh in 1996 – would not constitute a family. Nor would a single parent and children.

To take into account this and other objections to Murdock's definition, some propose a simpler definition. A family is 'a social group consisting of at least one adult and child, usually cohabiting, related by blood, marriage or adoption'.

Forms of marriage and basic family structures

The structure of families depends partly on the type of marriage arrangement which is allowed in a society. In the West, only monogamy is legal. At any one time males and females are allowed only one married partner. But even monogamous marriage translates into a variety of family structures.

Monogamous marriage

The **nuclear family** consists of two parents, traditionally one of each sex, and children, either related by blood or adopted. The so-called nuclear family is assumed to be the smallest 'complete' family type, around which other parts, the **extended family**, may be added. The nuclear family can be extended, by adding a generation. In a three–generational extended family, one or more of the grandparents live either with, or within relatively easy reach of, the nuclear family. Such families have been common in the past and many still exist. Single parent families occur either because only one parent has ever lived with the children or because the nuclear family has lost a parent, through death, separation or divorce. The single parent family is now relatively commonplace, and though frequently criticised often functions very effectively. In the same way as single parent families have become a more common phenomenon, so too have **reconstituted families**, in which the adult in a single parent family marries or cohabits with a new partner.

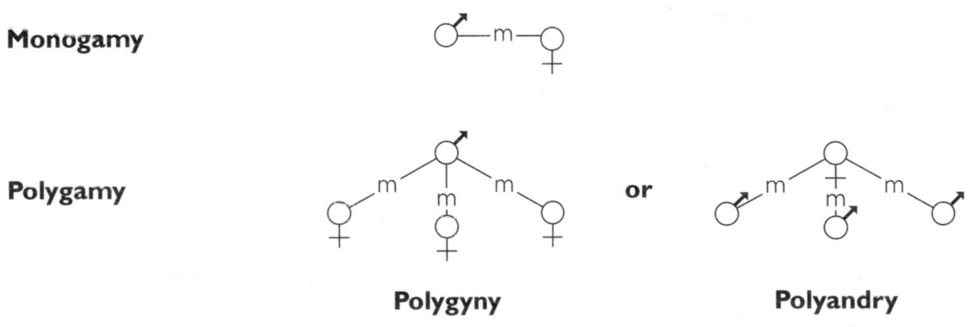

Monogamy

Polygamy **or**

Polygyny **Polyandry**

Polygamous marriage

In some societies, forms of marriage other than monogamy are allowed and so different family types emerge. **Polygamy** refers to marriages in which either a husband or a wife has more than one spouse, in a society in which that is legal or acceptable practice. Polygamy can refer to either or both **polygyny** (one husband, more than one wife; practiced in many Moslem countries) or the much less common **polyandry**, (one wife, more than one husband). If polygamy occurs in a society which only allows monogamy, it is referred to as **bigamy** and is a crime.

ACTIVITY

Marriage among the Nayar of Southern India

Before puberty every girl married a suitable man in the 'tali-ritual'. After the ritual marriage had taken place, however, the 'tali' husband did not live with his wife and was under no obligation to have any contact with her at all. The wife's sole duty to her tali husband was to attend his funeral.

When a girl approached or reached puberty, she began to take a number of visiting husbands. The men of the tribe were usually professional warriors who spent long periods of time away as mercenaries. When a visiting husband returned to the village, he was allowed to visit any number of women who had undergone the tali-ritual. With a woman's agreement, he would arrive at her home after supper, have sexual intercourse, and leave before breakfast next morning. During his visit, he placed his weapons outside the building to show the other visiting husbands he was there. If they arrived too late they were free to sleep on the verandah but could not stay the night with their wife. Men could have an unlimited number of wives, though women seem to have been limited to no more than twelve visiting husbands.

Knowing children's biological father was not important, because husbands were not expected to maintain or socialise children. Indeed, it was frowned on if they tried to. Instead, they were brought up in a unit which consisted of adult brothers and their sisters, their sisters' children and their daughters' children, with each 'family' group headed by the oldest male.

(From: K. Gough, 1959).

1 What do you think were the advantages of their system of marriage for the Nayar people?
2 Do you think that the children would be well-adjusted, being brought up in such an arrangement? Given their marriage arrangements and way of life, would there have been any alternative and how would that have been preferable?

Conscious alternatives to the nuclear family

Most types of family living arrangements, such as those described above, seem to have evolved over time, often in response to the economic and other circumstances of the society, and without conscious planning. However, there have been some cases in which groups of people have consciously chosen to construct their own type of family. In societies where the nuclear family has been the cultural ideal, some groups have devised non-nuclear alternatives. Many of those who have consciously experimented with unconventional family structures have been motivated by religious or political beliefs. For instance, the Oneida Community of North America was a Christian-inspired religious community. The Israeli kibbutzim movement was largely inspired by political beliefs. Both imply serious criticisms of, and dissatisfaction with, the conventional nuclear family.

The criticisms of the conventional nuclear family are typically that nuclear family life tends to encourage undesirable attitudes, such as possessiveness in human relationships, competitiveness between individuals and between families, and personal greed. Conventional family life is also said to subjugate women and to leave children too much at the mercy of inadequate or mentally ill parents.

ACTIVITY

The Oneida community

The Oneida Community was founded in 1848 at Oneida Creek in New York State by John Humphrey Noyes, a Christian preacher seeking to create the Kingdom of God on Earth. The community, of several hundred members, believed in spiritual, economic and sexual equality. They tried to achieve economic equality by sharing their wealth and income with each other. They tried to achieve sexual equality by practicing a very unusual form of group marriage with each male married to each female.

Oneida's system of marriage was based on the belief that members should all love each other. Members did not live as couples. A man wanting sexual relations with a particular female member would make his approaches through an older, respected member of the community. That person approached the woman, who could then accept or decline the approach.

It's not known whether the women could make such advances to men. What is clear is that, however unusual this system of sexual relations, Oneida remained a very moral community. Coarse and suggestive behaviour were not allowed.

The entire community were housed in one large building, although each adult had his or her own room. All the activities at Oneida were designed to emphasise the 'we' rather than individual desires. Dancing and card playing were allowed because they brought people together, but the use of alcohol, tea, coffee and tobacco was resisted because this was seen as too individualistic. Any member who caused problems was brought before a committee of peers for a frank discussion. This system of mutual criticism seems to have been well accepted, with members testifying to a remarkably stable and happy community.

Children were looked after by their mother for the first 15 months of their life. They were then moved into the children's section of the community house. Oneida made a conscious effort to play down any feelings of affection between individual parents and children. All the adults in the community were expected to treat all children as if they were their own.

The community grew to several hundred members, but pressure from the authorities and the local churches led to its collapse. The members were accused of irregular sexual activity, Noyes fled to Canada, and the community broke up in 1880 (from A. Wilson, 1985).

The Israeli kibbutz

The establishment of a system of **kibbutz** settlements (plural=kibbutzim) in Israel, after that country's independence in 1948, was a deliberate attempt to offer women a new, free life of equality with men by transforming women's traditional roles. In the pre-independence European ghettos, the woman had been the mainly stay-at-home child rearer and all-providing mother. The male was unquestioned head of the family and, in gratitude for his lot, thanked God for not having created him female.

In the kibbutz a close mother-child bond was deliberately discouraged from birth. The mother kept her baby with her for just four days. On the fifth day it went with the parents' agreement to the children's house and was placed in the charge of a *metapelet* (which, in Hebrew, means 'to take care').

The mother was then free to continue working in the fields or elsewhere and stay in the community. Breastfeeding by the mother was encouraged, but not allowed beyond six months. In some kibbutzim parents didn't put their babies to bed in the evening.

The main aim of the kibbutz was to make each woman as free as a man, to allow her to play her full part as a working community member. Her first loyalty was to the community.

A second major aim was to protect children from possessive mothering. Parents could spend up to two hours each evening with their children, but the rest of the time the children were cared for by the *metapalet*, who tried to treat each child much the same as any other. All accepted that the child's proper place was with their peers and not in the family.

1 Do you think the Oneida Community was a family? Explain your answer.
2 What do you see as the advantages and disadvantages of the child care system in a kibbutz?

How has the family changed over time?

The industrial revolution

Before we can talk about how the family in Britain has changed in the last few centuries, we need to say something about the **industrial revolution**. A revolution means that the social order is turned upside down, and the industrial revolution did indeed transform the world. England was the first country in the world to undergo industrialisation. It started around the 1740s, and in Britain it lasted until the late nineteenth century. Some countries, such as India, are just experiencing it now.

Although industrialisation is a highly complex process, some of its key features can be identified. First, it involves the building of factories. Although factories had existed for hundreds of years, the machinery in them had been worked and powered by people. However, in the industrial revolution, machines were created which were powered first by water, then by steam, later by oil and later again by electricity. These technological changes helped shape the British family.

The social classes

In these new factories of the eighteenth and nineteenth centuries, it is possible to see three main groupings of people, each playing a different part. Some of the people who raised the money to build the factories, the mines, the warehouses, the canals and so on were successful and became rich. They became, in time, part of an **upper-class**, previously dominated by the landed gentry. The men, (and in the early days of industrialisation, the women and children), who worked on the factory machines or down the mines, were mainly illiterate, and worked with hand (manual) skills and bodily strength. Those handworkers became part of a so-called **working-class**. The male clerks who worked in the offices, away from the machinery, were literate and **middle-class**, regularly changing the white collar they fastened to their shirts (hence, also, 'white-collar workers').

Until quite recently, most people in Britain were doing (manual) working-class jobs. So the discussion below, about how the British working-class family has changed, applies to the majority of the people for most of that period. (For more on social class, see Chapter 4.)

According to sociologists Peter Willmott and Michael Young, the working-class family in Britain has evolved through three stages, beginning with the type of family which existed before the industrial revolution – the pre-industrial working-class family.

The pre-industrial working-class family

Before the industrial revolution most working-class families lived in rural areas. Most people today probably imagine them as large, three generational extended families, with many children, and grandparents, aunts and uncles living near to the parents and their children.

However, according to the historian Peter Laslett, most ordinary people probably lived in nuclear, not extended, families, and for two main reasons. First, people married and had children relatively late – many women would marry in their late twenties. This was partly because they needed to save money and items in order to set up house. Secondly, life expectancy was less and many people didn't live long enough to become grandparents. For example, if a woman had her first child at 28, and that child (a daughter) also gave birth aged 28, the grandmother would have to live to 56 to see her grandchild. Many didn't.

These nuclear families survived by cultivating a bit of land, keeping one or two animals and, in some parts of the country, producing fabric woven out of wool or cotton. The wife would do the spinning and the husband would do the weaving. Ann Oakley (1981) argues that male and female regarded themselves as roughly equal. Children would be largely looked after and raised by the eldest brother or sister.

The early industrial family

In the mid-eighteenth century, the invention of powered weaving looms signalled the end of these cottage-based industries. Installed into newly built factories, the powered looms produced so much more cloth than the hand-powered looms of the cottages that the cottagers could not compete. In order to survive, many moved to the growing towns to get factory work and subsequently settled there.

Living in densely populated areas, with perhaps up to twenty sharing a small terraced house, children grew up, met and married, usually hoping to live locally. When the rent man came to collect the rent, a mother whose daughter was wanting accommodation for herself and her husband (actual or prospective) would ask him about any known or expected vacancies. The result was that married daughters often ended up living within easy reach of their mothers.

This relationship, between 'Mam' and her married daughters, was the central relationship in this extended family. The males, by comparison, were fairly uninvolved, spending time out of the house, including at the pub, with male relatives and workmates and spending little time with their wives. **Conjugal**

roles were segregated, with husband and wife having largely separate tasks and responsibilities in and around the home.

This basic family structure, which first emerged in the mid-eighteenth century, was remarkably common throughout the country for some 200 years (until the 1950s and 1960s) and can still be found today. In the following sections, we focus on this working class-family and its community, particularly as it was during the first half of the twentieth century. We look too at why it eventually declined.

Home and family life

In general, working-class parents up to the Second World War (1939) had relatively little time for their children. Many men were not back from work before their children's bedtime. For women, with few labour saving gadgets, housework and childcare involved long hours and heavy work. Life was hard, with little leisure and less luxury. The family life of the better off middle-classes was generally more private and home based, with children's play being more closely supervised by the mother.

In thinking over what she had observed as a working-class child growing up in the Lancashire cotton town of Bury, the sociologist Bernice Martin concluded that many of the working-class attitudes and behaviours reflected people's need 'to create order and meaning in conditions of scarcity'. One way in which people created a sense of meaning and order for themselves was by establishing boundaries, for instance by drawing a distinction between the 'respectable' and 'rough' working-classes. For people living around the poverty line, trying to hang on to a reputation for respectability was one way of providing meaning, purpose and motivation. In trying to maintain respectability, Martin notes, people attempted to present a certain 'public face', in which their respectability is partly demonstrated by an emphasis on order and symmetry.

Talking of the traditional working-class terraced house, Martin quotes the anthropologist Mary Douglas:

> The first thing that is striking about the English working-class home is the attempt to provide privacy in spite of difficulties of layout. The back of the house is allocated to cooking, washing and lavatorial functions. The front parlour is functionless except for public, social representation. This space is by no means wasted, however: it is the front of the house which speaks composedly and smiles for the rest of the body.

In the traditional working-class terraced house the front of the house, the family's public face, wears its curtains with the pattern facing the street and not the inside of the room. The important rule is that the curtains at all the windows should match each other and the colour scheme of the external paintwork, rather than the interior decoration and furnishing of each room.

A symmetrical 'public face' is associated with order and respectability. Quoting a study of inter-war Salford, Martin also notes how families falling on hard times would pawn important objects such as beds and tables rather than part with ornaments which were on show through the half-open front door. Symmetry was also maintained in the window displays which adorned the downstairs sills.

The need to show a good 'public face' also led to housewives washing and scrubbing the front step and pavement down to the kerb. Many housewives felt such an urge to protect the public face of the front of the house that they would never go out of their front doors wearing less than their Sunday-best clothes. They would always nip out to the shops from their back door. In fact, rather than clean her front step by popping out of the front door, an aunt of Martin's always insisted on going out of her back door and walking half way round the block instead!

Trying to secure privacy in a crowded house led to careful rota systems being organised, with someone watching the door for the Friday night bath in a tin tub in front of the living room fire. Such activities were structured by ritual and hierarchy, with adults having preference. Attempts to secure some personal space were seen in certain members, especially the parents, having particular chairs 'belonging' to them. Even through the 1930s in some areas, only adults would have chairs and plates for eating. Father would eat and hand out scraps and titbits to the children according to their age and sex.

Martin argues that, in this culture of order and control, ritual and repetition ran through every aspect of living. The dietary pattern followed an unchanging weekly cycle. So too did household chores, with Mondays devoted to washing, Tuesday to ironing, Wednesdays and Fridays baking, and shopping on Saturdays. To show how the chore rituals were moralised, she quotes part of a street rhyme:

Them as wash on Thursday are folk that wash for shame. Them as wash on Friday more likely to wash in need. But them as wash on Saturday – they are sluts indeed.

In her overall assessment of respectable working-class culture, Martin concluded that it was one which highly valued boundaries – whether between classes, sexes or races – and was uncomfortable with, or actively disliked, mixed categories of all kinds.

ACTIVITY

Traditional conjugal roles

> In those days,' says Gladys Smith who was a young woman in the 1920s, 'you knew what was expected of you when you got married. Your husband was the breadwinner and you gave up your job to look after him and the house. That was the bargain. As for asking your husband to help with the housework, it wouldn't have crossed your mind. You were considered to have a gem if he helped drying-up. My Jack was wonderful. He'd dry up, wash vegetables and he'd never let me turn a mattress on my own. But he was the exception.
>
> (*TV Quick*, June 1991)

To the modern ear her life as a housewife sounds like a catalogue of work. But life wasn't as complicated as it is now. Roles were clearly defined and everyone knew where they stood. 'You didn't mind because you knew no different,' says Gladys.

Traditional working-class communities

Although changes to working class communities were already beginning to occur from the 1920s, in many parts of the country working-class life stayed strongly communal even through much of the 1950s. Contact with neighbours and relatives living nearby was frequent. Traffic in most working-class communities was minimal throughout the 1920s, allowing children to play marbles, football, skipping or hop-scotch in the street, with mothers relatively unconcerned. The street was a communal space, with adults often standing or even sitting on chairs brought out from the house, chatting and informally supervising the children's play. There were many ritual street events, such as 'Bonfire Night', when the celebration would include a party involving the whole street.

At weekends, in the towns and cities, many working-class sons and fathers went together to support the local football team. They would come across the same people standing in the same spot at every home match. Many children went to the cinema on Saturdays, where they would meet others from their neighbourhood.

For holidays, in the 1920s and 30s, in parts of Lancashire, the local factories shut down for the 'Wakes Weeks' holiday fortnight. Many from the working-class communities would then take their annual week's holiday in Blackpool. Because so many were taking their holidays at the same time and in the same resort, it was almost as if their community was being temporarily transplanted, with neighbours meeting up.

Meanwhile, in the South East, some working-class Londoners, on the other hand, spent their summer 'holidays' hop-picking in Kent. That too had some of the advantages and attractions of community life, as they worked and their children played together, and communal cooking was often accompanied by communal singsongs.

Socially, people 'knew their place' and sought to keep to it, even within the working-class. Like everything else, courting went in status categories. In Bury, groups of unmarried males and females strolled, met and chatted on the streets, but they knew which part of town was the appropriate part for them. Going 'Up to t' top o' t' Street' (by the parish church in the town centre) was for the 'toffs', the skilled working-class elite. The middle of the respectable working class had Union Square, while those frequenting Princess Street were 'really quite low'.

1 What term would sociologists use to describe the division of labour of Gladys and Jack in the 1920s? What other characteristics would you associate with that sort of family?
2 What do you think were the advantages and disadvantages of living in a traditional working-class community?
3 How do you think living in such a community may affect family relationships and family life?
4 How does the traditional working-class community described above resemble or differ from the community in which you live now?

The decline of the working-class extended family

By the 1930s, a number of social changes meant that in many areas, working-class, communal-type living was beginning to imitate the home-based life-style of the middle-classes. First, from the 1920s, the provision of council houses with gardens of their own allowed children to play at home. Secondly, the wireless became a popular reason for staying at home. Thirdly, in the 1930s, driving into the country in one's motor car started to become popular, including among some working-class families. In the towns and cities, this increase in traffic meant that for the first time the streets became dangerous for children.

After the Second World War, the pace of change quickened. The creation of more jobs, and a greater variety of jobs, and the creation of better educational opportunities meant greater geographical and social mobility. The establishment in the 1940s of the Welfare State and, from the early 1950s, a gradual increase in prosperity, meant that the nuclear family was less likely to have to rely on relatives for support services such as child minding, nursing, and for advice on child rearing and health.

From the 1950s, the extended family was further challenged by the spread of 'slum clearance' (the knocking down of poor and inadequate housing) and rehousing schemes. In many cases, such as those reported by Willmott and Young in Bethnal Green, East London, the young nuclear family was rehoused some distance away from their parents, and face-to-face contact between the ageing parents and married children diminished. However, this was found to be at least partly compensated for by the spread of telephone and car ownership, and improved public transport, which meant that in many cases fairly regular contact could be maintained despite the distances.

The privatised, symmetrical family

How has the family changed in the last few decades? One major suggestion is that the family has become 'symmetrical'. A different claim is that the modern family has become increasingly 'privatised'. We'll discuss the idea of the 'symmetrical' family first.

The symmetrical family

According to Willmott and Young, especially since the 1950s, working-class families have become more like those of the middle-class. They claim that the family today is generally nuclear and small (usually between one and three children), with husband and wife having **integrated conjugal roles**. In other words, they share the domestic tasks. They have largely abandoned the rigid, traditional division of domestic labour into 'man's work' and 'woman's work'.

Willmott and Young describe this family type as **symmetrical**. This is because they share their roles more. For instance, the male is more involved in housework and child care, and the female is more involved in traditionally male activities like going out to work and decorating. Also, the couple have a more equal partnership and take more important decisions jointly. According to Willmott and Young, this 'symmetrical' family is a more equal partnership partly because it is typically a dual-worker family (with both partners working outside the home). Also, marriage is now perceived to provide companionship as well as economic, sexual and other benefits.

The privatised family

Other sociologists, such as David Lockwood and John Goldthorpe, have emphasised the '**privatised**' nature of the modern family. In other words, this modern nuclear family is more private and inward-looking than the family used to be.

The modern family is seen as relatively privatised because of its home-centred orientation and because of its reduced contact with relatives, neighbours, and other members of the community. Family members spend much of their leisure time at home or with the family, pursuing solitary or family activities, such as gardening, watching TV, shopping and DIY, rather than in more communal activities such as churchgoing, attending political or trades union meetings, going to their 'local' pub or just sitting outside their house on the street watching and socialising. Such social contacts as people do have are often spent in the company of a few friends, perhaps eating out, or with take-away meals and alcoholic drinks without even leaving home.

ACTIVITY

Participation in leisure activities away from the home: by gender, 1994–95, Great Britain

		Percentages*	
	Males	**Females**	**All persons**
Visit a public house	70	68	64
Meal in a restaurant (not fastfood)	60	64	62
Meal in a fastfood restaurant	45	40	42
Cinema	35	32	34
Theatre	19	22	21
Disco or nightclub	29	22	25
Historic building	27	24	25
Spectator sports event	31	13	22
Drive for pleasure	47	47	47
Short break holiday	32	28	30

(from *Social Trends 26*, 1996)

*Percentage of the population aged 16 years and over participating in each activity in the 3 months prior to interview

1 Looking at how people spend their time, is the claim that the modern family has become privatised on the whole supported or refuted? Explain your answer.

Is the modern family really 'symmetrical'?

The trends which Willmott and Young identify – the decline in the extended family, and the movement to fewer children and towards greater sexual equality in the home – seem valid and important. However, their claim that the modern working-class family is 'symmetrical' – implying that the sexes have achieved, or come close to achieving, domestic equality – has been much criticised.

Some of the major charges are made by feminist critics. First, they reject the claim that the division of domestic labour is equal. In many working-class families especially, male participation in housework and child care is highly selective, and the least desirable tasks are left to the female. At best, it is claimed, many men see themselves as 'helping', clearly implying that the real responsibility remains the woman's. Many men still need to be thanked for their efforts!

Secondly, feminists claim, Willmott and Young's analysis of the family, with its implications of equal status for male and female, ignores the often high levels of dissatisfaction among women, both in and out of the home. Although most women now have paid employment out of the home, much of it is part-time (which suits many but not all), often relatively poorly paid, and may be short-term or otherwise insecure. As suggested above, even when women are in paid employment, the bulk of housework and child care still falls on them.

In the home, the roles of housewife and child care are often sources of stress and dissatisfaction rather than of positive experience and self-esteem. For instance, in her studies of middle and working-class housewives, Ann Oakley found that rates of frustration and dissatisfaction with housework were high, with 75 per cent claiming to be either 'dissatisfied' or 'very dissatisfied'. The main reasons were that, while housework is hard work, with long hours (on average, in her sample, 77 hours a week and in some cases as high as 105), at the same time it has low status and is often not considered work at all. It is also experienced as fragmented – as a series of unconnected tasks, none of which requires the person's full attention. Frequent time limits are another big problem. As Oakley notes, 'Cooking, for instance, recognised as a potentially creative activity by the majority of housewives, often is not because husbands and children demand certain sorts of meals at particular times during the day, and the housewife also has to meet a mass of other demands on her time'. For many, too, with limited contact with relatives or neighbours, isolation is another problem.

Part of the problem, Oakley concludes, is to do with the lack of involvement of many males. When she studied their husbands' participation in housework and child care, Oakley drew three main conclusions. First, participation by the husbands varies according to social class, with working-class husbands less involved in both housework and child care. Secondly, both middle and working-class males are more likely to participate in child-care than in housework. Thirdly, as a consequence, the evidence does not support the claim that the sexes are equal in modern marriage.

A third important criticism of Willmott and Young's picture of the family as 'symmetrical' is that it ignores evidence that the benefits of marriage tend to favour the male, and that for females marriage is often a much less attractive 'deal'. Their optimistic picture seems to overlook a variety of evidence: for instance, that females are more likely than males to seek psychiatric help, that it is females much more than males who initiate proceedings to divorce, and that male violence against their partners is not uncommon.

In some interesting research in which she compared married and unmarried men and women, Jessie Bernard concluded that married, more than unmarried, men were likely to have successful careers, good mental and physical health, and to live longer. Among women, however, it was the married who were more likely to suffer depression, neuroses and other psychological ailments and experience poor physical health. When she compared married men and women, she found it was the women who were the more likely to express frustration and dissatisfaction, to initiate divorce, and to suffer stress, anxiety and depression. Unmarried women, she concluded, are often the 'cream', whereas unmarried men are often the 'pits'. She explained the greater distress of married women compared to married men by saying that in marriage women have to adjust and adapt their personalities much more than do men. A common consequence for women is a deterioration of their self-image and a tendency to become more passive and dependent, all of which commonly results in feelings of dissatisfaction, anxiety or depression.

ACTIVITY

1 Use the chart below to analyse who does what in a family you know. Add some more household or childcare tasks. Tick under the appropriate headings.

Household/ Childcare Task	**Male**	**Female**	**Either**
	Sometimes Usually Always	**Sometimes Usually Always**	**Sometimes Usually Always**
ironing washing deciding dinner cleaning toilet small repairs			

2 Looking at the evidence you have collected, which activities are the most gender-linked?
3 Why is this? Test yourself by identifying what you expect, hope for or experience in a male-female partnership.

4 Has there been a change between your parents' experience and your own hopes or reality?

Marital breakdown and divorce

Concern about the health of modern marriage is prevalent. Among the many concerns expressed, the most fundamental is that marriage as an institution may be doomed.

Similar concerns are expressed in many other Western countries and there are a number of reasons for such pessimism. First, the substantial, and sometimes dramatic, rise in the divorce rate. (The divorce rate can be defined as the number of couples divorcing per 1000 married couples in a given year.) Secondly, the apparent fall in the numbers choosing to get married. Thirdly, cohabitation without marriage has become more popular. So have other alternatives to marriage, such as opting to live alone and choosing to have a child and raise it outside of marriage. Taken together, these trends have encouraged fears that the death of marriage is nigh.

The divorce statistics, on the face of it, appear awesome. In England and Wales, in 1911, fewer than 1 in 10 000 marriages ended in divorce. Right up to the outbreak of the Second World War in 1939, fewer than 1 in 1000 marriages ended in divorce. By the late 1950s, about 1 out of 500 marriages ended in divorce. But by 1995, the likelihood of a marriage ending in divorce had escalated to an estimated 1 in 3: from 1 in 10 000 to 1 in 3 in less than a century!

However, it is worth distinguishing between divorce – the legal termination of a marriage – and marriages in which at least one partner feels it to have failed or been unhappy. Not all such 'failed' marriages end in divorce. The higher divorce rate today doesn't necessarily prove that more marriages fail than in the past. It is at least possible that more marriages failed in the past but that marriages were more frequently terminated by the desertion of one or other partner, or by the couple's unofficial separation, or by a premature death. Many more may merely have endured an unsatisfactory relationship and stayed together in an 'empty-shell' marriage. We have no real way of knowing.

Nevertheless, despite the uncertainty, many observers tentatively agree the following. First, that more marriages probably are felt by the couple to have failed or broken down than in the past. Second, that a higher proportion of people in these failed marriages are now legally and officially ending them through divorce.

ACTIVITY

Women's domestic burden

Increased opportunities to end unhappy marriages have provided an escape route for many wives 'trapped' in marriages they have come to regard as stifling. It is not marriage itself which women seem increasingly to resent, as most divorcees will 'try again'. In most cases, it is a certain type of marriage which women seek to leave.

Despite all the so-called advances of recent years, women still take primary responsibility for domestic affairs and the care of any children. They take the major burden of housework, regardless of whether they have paid employment or not. It is this belief – that women should be responsible for the housework and for childcare just because they are female – which is the basis of women's unhappiness with their marriages – no more, no less.

(From AEB 'A' Level Sociology Exam Paper 1, 1991)

1 Why does the undoubted rise in the number of divorces not prove that a higher proportion of marriages 'fail' now than in the past?

2 'Despite all the so-called advances of recent years, women still take primary responsibility for domestic affairs and the care of any children. Women take the major burden of housework, regardless of whether they have paid employment or not.'

Do you believe that dissatisfaction with these traditional domestic responsibilities is the main reason for the increase in divorce this century?

Working in pairs, make a mind map/spidergram of as many reasons as you can think of for why the divorce rate has increased so substantially this century.

3 Do you think that women's attitudes to taking almost total domestic responsibility have changed over time? Why do you think this may be?

Why has the divorce rate increased?

Here, we are concerned not so much with why people get divorced or why marriages break down, but with why a *higher proportion* of couples are now getting divorced than in the past. Attempts to explain the rise in divorce throughout the century can be grouped under two main questions: are more marriages failing; if so, why are more ending in divorce?

Why may more marriages be failing?

One explanation is that people's expectations of marriage today are higher than they were. People require their partner to be sexually and emotionally compatible, while also being 'best friends' and companions over many years, and spending much of their leisure time together. Financial and lifestyle expectations are also probably higher for most people, and women are less inclined to put up with male domestic violence.

Greater equality between the sexes has also probably increased the potential for conflict. Women, now better educated, more employable and potentially more financially independent than before, are more likely to want to be involved in important decision making.

As more women are now in paid employment, males and females are now in greater sustained contact out of the home. Moreover, with a higher proportion of the population living in cities, it is easier to achieve anonymity and to escape from the informal social control previously provided by relatives and neighbours. It is now easier for both men and women to have a relationship outside the marriage.

People are also living longer than they did. Moreover, for much of this century until the last decade or so, people were on average marrying younger. The consequence, as Ronald Fletcher memorably put it, is that marriage today for most is 'a longer sentence' than previously. At the beginning of the century, the likelihood of a marriage ending in the death of one of the partners in their 40s or 50s – having perhaps been married only 15 or 20 years – was much greater. Today, with average life expectancy in the 70s, many people can expect an undissolved marriage to last 50 or more years. Younger marriages are particularly prone to divorce, with divorce rates for women marrying at 20 years or less twice as high as for those who marry between 20 and 24 years. Younger women are more likely to be marrying partly to legitimise a child. Consequently, the trend to earlier marriages for much of this century has been accompanied by a rise in divorce rate.

Why are more failed marriages being formally ended by divorce?

One important factor in helping explain the substantial rise in the divorce rate this century is changes in the law which have made securing a divorce easier. Before 1937, the only grounds for divorce were adultery. Changes in the law in 1937 added desertion, cruelty and incurable insanity. In 1969, the Divorce Law Reform Act allowed couples to agree to seek a divorce on the grounds that they felt their marriage had broken down 'irretrievably'. In 1949, the Legal Aid Act allowed less well off people to afford the legal costs of divorce.

Changes in attitude to divorce and to divorced people, and a lessening of the shame associated with it, have also been important. In part, this reflects the decline in the influence of religion, because many churches traditionally emphasised marriage as a life-long contract entered into before God and only dissolved by death. Also, some of the churches, particularly Protestant denominations such as the Methodists, Baptists and United Reformed Churches but also to a lesser extent the Church of England, have become less hostile to divorce over time and more prepared to remarry divorcees in church. The lessening of social hostility to divorce may also reflect our greater geographical mobility; divorcing has perhaps become easier when at a greater distance from parents, relatives or old friends who might disapprove.

It is also probably more feasible for couples to live apart and survive financially. Significantly, given that some 70 per cent of divorces are initiated by women, it is easier nowadays for women to support themselves financially without having to depend on voluntary help from a former spouse. This is both because there is more financial support from the state and because, with better qualifications and better employment prospects, women are better able to support themselves, and because of generally improved divorce settlements made by the courts.

Finally, returning briefly to the question of whether the dramatic rise in the divorce rate means that the future of marriage is in jeopardy, it is also worth noting that a high proportion of divorcees remarry. This suggests that divorce is usually not so much a rejection of marriage itself as the rejection of a particular marriage. Having said that, the divorce rate for second marriages is higher than for first.

The consequences of divorce for children

Because of the significant rise in divorce, separation and unmarried cohabitation since the 1960s, only about half of all children in Britain are likely to spend their entire childhood living with their married, natural parents.

Unsurprisingly, perhaps, children whose parents are undergoing serious marital difficulties are themselves likely to experience emotional and behavioural problems. Research suggests that children whose parents divorce have often shown behavioural problems some time prior to the separation.

The consequences of their parents' separation on children seem often to be long-lasting. Although many separating and divorcing couples do work together harmoniously and conscientiously to minimise the negative effects on their children, some 30 to 40 percent of fathers seem to lose touch with their children within 5 years of divorce and for some children the experience of their parents' divorce seems to be even more damaging than the death of a parent.

According to the National Child Development Study (NCDS), children whose parents stay together are less likely than children living with a divorced mother to leave school at 16, leave home due to friction, marry in their teens, and divorce later. However, according to the findings of the NCDS, these patterns of behavior seem to be even more likely among children whose parents remarry than among those whose divorced mothers remain single.

A second important consequence of marital breakdown and parental separation which has an impact on children is the likelihood of a sudden drop in living standards, and a plunge into poverty. This is particularly likely when the lone parent is the mother, as in about 90 per cent of cases. Lone mothers are about as likely to work full-time (that is 16 hours a week or more) as are married mothers. However, wages are often low and, without the support of a second wage, many more lone mothers require financial support from the state. Many others cannot take up full-time work either because it is not available or because they cannot find affordable child care. Some take up part-time employment. However, the proportion of lone mothers working part-time is smaller, largely because, while state benefits (Family Credit) are paid to full-time workers on low wages, part-time workers lose benefits once they earn above a certain (very low) level. Consequently, some 70 per cent of all lone mothers still need financial support from the state, and such benefits do not allow a high standard of living.

Indeed, it is a much argued point whether the negative effects on children of parental separation are to do primarily with the separation or whether they are at least as much to do with other factors, such as the likelihood of mother's unemployment, low income, poor living conditions and totally inadequate, and impossibly expensive, childcare options.

ACTIVITY

1 Do you feel that parents separating inevitably damages their children? How can any damage be minimised?
2 Should single parents be provided with cheaper, more accessible childcare and more generous financial support, to enable them to 'stand on their own two feet' and support their children? Or would that merely encourage more illegitimate births and higher separation rates?

The variety of living arrangements

Although many people in our society live in families – that is, two (or more) generational groups of people related through blood, marriage or adoption – it is important to remember that many don't. For instance, some 25 per cent of all households now consist of people living alone, such as widows or widowers, and they are an increasing number. Others, about 27 per cent of British households, consist of married couples living together without children, either because they do not (yet?) want children, because they are unable to have them or because the young have grown up and 'left the nest'. Some others who live and perhaps eat together in a household are unrelated, as for example students or workers sharing a house.

Then there are those who live in families. Many live in nuclear families, and many still live in the three generational extended family type which emerged during the Industrial Revolution. Additionally, there are some other family types which have become commonplace.

The lone parent family

One of the more common types of family today is the **lone parent family**, where one parent, (in 90 per cent of cases the mother) lives with her dependent children. The increase in this sort of family reflects the higher incidence of separation and divorce, but also that more women are having children outside of marriage.

The number of children living in lone parent families in Britain more than doubled between 1971 and 1991, representing, in 1991, almost 1 in 5 of all dependent children living in familes. Only 10 per cent of those lone parent families were headed by the father.

On average, lone mothers get married within five years of having a child, though never-married women are likely to marry a little more quickly than those previously married. Of previously-married women, the least likely to remarry are older women, those with large families and those in paid work.

The cohabiting family

Just as the numbers of people marrying has declined, so there has been an increase in the number of couples who are cohabiting. In fact, the increase in cohabitation has been striking. The peak age for women cohabiting is 20 to 24 (about two years older for men). For this age group of women, cohabitation rates increased between 1981 and 1990 from 6 per cent to 16 per cent. About 10 per cent of women between the ages of 20 to 29 are now cohabiting at any one time. However, many – especially older – women who are cohabiting are simply in the process of transferring from one marriage to another.

Because many of the officially 'single' (that is never-married) women giving birth are cohabiting, they are not really lone parents. For instance, nearly three-quarters of babies born to never-married women in England and Wales were registered in the names of both parents, about half of whom were thought to be cohabiting.

The reconstituted family

The rise in divorce has not only added to the number of lone parent families. It has also led to a large increase in the number of **reconstituted families**. These are families in which one or both partners has children from a previous relationship. The family which results commonly includes children from two previous marriages. Over one-third of all marriages now involve at least one partner who was previously married.

Ethnic minority families

Ethnic minorities are, of course, diverse in their family arrangements. However, to oversimplify, Afro-Caribbean families have a relatively high incidence of female-headed lone parent families. People with Indian, Pakistani, Bangladeshi and Chinese backgrounds are more likely than the white community to live in three-generational extended families, which are often well integrated into an ethnic sub-cultural community.

ACTIVITY

1 Cohabitation among never-marrieds is more widespread nowadays. Why? Is marriage no longer valued? Are people disillusioned with marriage? Are they unwilling to commit themselves? What other factors could explain this change?
2 Should couples be encouraged to marry rather than cohabit, and how can they be persuaded? (for example by tax benefits?)
3 What do you think are some of the difficulties which can result from reconstituted families? What can be some of the benefits and positive gains?

Social policy and the family

Policies that reflect the needs of the family are based on the traditional **nuclear family** unit. Social policy has often made assumptions about marriage patterns, parental responsibility and bringing up children. Policies that directly affect families cover a wide ranging field of service provision and delivery, for example **health**, **education**, **social security**, **housing** and **social services**. Britain has traditionally had no one body or person responsible for the family unlike some other European counties, such as

Sweden. This means that policy is developed by different groups each of which has its own priorities. This can lead to difficulties in co-operation between services, resulting in overlap and gaps in provision.

ACTIVITY

1 Make a chart with five columns headed: health, education, social security, social services and housing.
2 Under each heading list the services they provide for children and their families.
3 Draw a red line between the services in each column that you think have something in common.
4 What problems might result if the services were working with the same family and did not work together?

Working together

A number of agencies are involved in the delivery of services for children. An agency is an office or business that has overall responsibility for service delivery. Sometimes the word sector is used instead of agency. There are three main types of agency involved with children and their families.

STATUTORY AGENCY

These are agencies that have a legal responsibility to provide care, protection and services for children and their families. Statutory agencies include the **police**, **social services**, **health and education** departments. Unusually the **NSPCC**, which is a voluntary agency, has been given statutory responsibility because of its role in the care and protection of children.

VOLUNTARY AGENCY

These are agencies that are organised by **charities** or non-profit making organisations. They often provide services on the basis of **need**, for example Childline or where the statutory agencies are unable to help (with grants for education and funding for research and so on).

PRIVATE INDEPENDENT AGENCY

These are agencies that are run like a business and provide services at a cost.

Some secure accommodation or specialist therapeutic centres for children are run in this way. If **social services** or **education** departments wish to place a child in their care they have to pay for their services.

The **Children Act 1989** recognised the need for inter-agency co-operation. 'Working Together Under the Children Act 1989' produced by the Home Office (1991), encourages and in some cases insists that all professionals involved in the care and protection of children co-operate with each other.

'It is well established that good child protection work requires inter-agency co-operation . . . It is therefore essential that **Area Child Protection Committee** (ACPC) procedures provide a mechanism whereby, wherever one agency becomes concerned that a child may be at risk, it shares its information with other agencies. This applies to the **police**, **social services**, **health service** and **education** (HMSO, 1991, Working Together, Under the Children Act 1989).

ACTIVITY

1 Find out about your local ACPC, where it is, who belongs to it and what are its responsibilities.
2 Consider the needs of children outside the **child protection** arena. For instance children with special needs. Do you think co-operation would improve service delivery for these families?

The changing family

The state prefers to keep a low profile in family matters. The family is considered to be a 'private' institution. The state only becomes involved if the family has been defined as 'in need' or proves to be a danger to its members or other members of society. The state supports family life by developing policies and legislation that encourage certain practices, for example marriage, and discourage others such as lone parenting. The changing nature of the family has made policy makers increasingly concerned with

- the rising **divorce** rate
- growth in **lone parenting**
- increase in **co-habitation**
- the need for women to go to work
- fears of moral degeneration and delinquency amongst children

For these and other reasons, policy makers have attempted to develop policy that strengthens the family. The phrase 'back to basics' was coined by the **Conservative party** in the early 1990s. They believed that the family provided a stable, secure and safe passage to adulthood. The family was seen as the best place for children to learn the values of society and standards of good behaviour.

What is clear is that there is increasing diversity in **family composition** and lifestyle. All families are different, some children live with both parents, some with one parent, some with step-parents and some with carers. This is making it more difficult for policy makers to 'fit' policies to families.

ACTIVITY

1 Collect a number of magazines and cut out all the pictures of families and stick them onto a sheet of paper. Look at them carefully and write down the main features, for example gender, age, race, number and lifestyle image.
2 Think of four friends or children you know. Cut out magazine pictures to represent their families and stick them on a sheet of paper. Compare these images to your first picture. Do the families look the same or different? Make a list of the differences. What does this tell you about family composition?

Parental responsibility

The Poor Law of 1601 made it the responsibility of the **family** to care for its members including children and older people. Throughout the eighteenth and nineteenth centuries the state provided few **welfare** services and rarely interfered in family life. What care and protection existed for children was usually provided by the **church** or **charitable organisations**. Children were seen as the responsibility of their family.

The concept of **parental responsibility** was introduced in the **Children Act 1989**. This was the first time that the law had made it clear that parents were responsible for their children. A person(s) with parental responsibility has to ensure that the child is safe, healthy, educated and cared for. Both the mother and the father automatically have parental responsibility, if they are married at the time the child is born or get married after the child is born. Otherwise only the mother has parental responsibility. An unmarried father does not have parental responsibility but in some cases can be given it by the court. Unmarried fathers do have a financial responsibility for their children.

ACTIVITY

Research the Children Act 1989.

1 Find out how an unmarried father can be given (acquire) parental responsibility.

2 Find out who else can be given parental responsibility and in what circumstances.

3 In what circumstances can the birth parents lose parental responsibility?

In most cases, parents/carers are able to meet the needs of the children in their care. The National Children's Bureau believe that 'parents are primarily responsible for nurturing and supporting their children and that this role should be more highly valued by society'. In addition they emphasise the need for service providers and parents to work in partnership. ('A Policy for Young Children: A Framework for Action', 1990). The same report argues that policy should:

- provide parent education
- support fathers to take more responsibility for child care
- provide parents with access to information about appropriate services
- enable parents to be consulted about the running of services
- enable parents to choose the form of child care they prefer, from a range of options
- provide training and support to parents who wish to become involved in the running of pre-school centres
- enable parents who support children with **special needs** to have access to a range of support services

- enable parents to stay with their children in hospital
- provide realistic **child benefit** and benefits to support child care
- provide for maternity leave
- provide for paternity (fathers') leave and leave for family reasons
- enable flexible working hours

The report talks exclusively of parents, however some children are cared for by substitute parents, such as foster parents, grandparents or other family members.

Some of these issues have been addressed in the policy of the 1990s, however there are still areas where little choice or flexibility exists, for example in paternity leave, family leave and pre-school provision. The parent\carers' 'right to be consulted' and 'right to make decisions and choices' on behalf of their children has been promoted in a number of ways:

- The Children Act 1989
- The Education Reform Act 1988
- The Parents Charter 1991 (Education)
- The Code of Practice for Children with Special Needs 1993
- Health Service and Community Care Act 1990

Community care

Services provided by the state amount to only a fraction of the total care provided to people in need. A great deal of care is provided by informal networks such as families, friends and neighbours. Fiona Williams (1994) argues that the majority of informal carers are women, who care for members of their own or extended family. In 1984-5 **The House of Commons Social Services Committee** on Community Care presented a report that recommended that **mentally ill** and **mentally handicapped** people should as far as possible be cared for in the community. In December 1986 the **Audit Commission** report, 'Making a Reality of Community Care', emphasised the need to provide services that enabled people to remain in the their own homes. Sir Roy Griffiths was asked to advise the government on future policy. In 'Community Care: Agenda For Action' (1988) he proposed that local social services

- in co-operation with the health service, assess the community care needs of their locality and develop local plans that involve the statutory, voluntary and private agencies
- identify and assess the needs of individuals and design packages of care best suited to enabling the person to 'live as normal a life as possible'
- arrange delivery of **packages of care**, using informal carers and neighbourhood support. If necessary domiciliary (Home Care) services and day care services could be used in place of, or to support, informal care. Residential care to be offered only if necessary

Community care was not a popular policy and so its introduction was delayed. Howard Glennerster (1995) suggests that community care was just another way of cutting costs. **The National Health Service and Community Care Act of 1990** nevertheless saw the biggest change to the structure of the Health Service and delivery of services since 1946. In 1996, legislation was introduced to provide support for those that cared for people in their own home or the home of the carer.

Children and social policy

Historically children in need have been seen as 'sad, bad or mad'. That is, they are at risk and need protection; they are delinquent and society needs protection from them, or they have special needs. During the mid-nineteenth century, children's societies like Barnardos set out to protect children from cruelty and **neglect**. At the same time child **crime** was seen as a problem. Many children were **homeless** and resorted to crime in order to survive. Industrial schools and reformatories provided a harsh regime of correction and punishment. **Religion** played an important role in providing services for children and continues to do so. Some religious groups separated children from what they saw as **poverty**, squalor and bad parents in order to 'save' them. The growing poverty of children forced the **Poor Law Commission** to provide services for them. These included separate workhouses, schools and foster homes. It was here that children were prepared for employment. Girls often went into domestic service and boys to the armed services. The first legislation that attempted to protect children from the cruelty and neglect was in 1889. This allowed the removal of children from their parents for the first time. In 1919, the **women's**

movement began to highlight the plight of children. This resulted in a general improvement in the conditions of children.

The Curtis Committee in 1944 recommended the establishment of separate children's departments in local authorities. It also called for 'specialist' staff to work with children and their families.

The 1948 Children Act became known as the '**children's charter**'. The act represented a step forward. It focused on providing care for children away from home. This meant many children did not benefit.

The Children and Young Persons Act (1963) made it possible to provide services to prevent abuse and neglect.

The Seebolm Committee (1968) was appointed to review the structure of social services. Their report recommended that the children's departments become part of social services departments.

The Children and Young Persons Act (1969) came about when the Labour party came to power in 1964 and wanted to provide a 'family service'. The Act addressed not only children in need of protection but also the needs of young offenders.

The Social Services Act of 1970 put Seebolm's recommendations in place. Social workers worked on generic (general) caseloads rather than specialise in child care. A number of child care scandals and tragedies, such as Maria Colwell (1974) and Jasmine Beckford (1985), led to change. Both cases involved extreme forms of neglect and both girls died as a result. Their deaths in part were blamed on a lack of specialist experience on the part of the social workers involved. The lack of communication between both social services departments and other agencies such as the NSPCC was also criticised. In the 1980s specialist child care social workers were introduced again.

The 1975 Children Act made adoption easier and the term 'permanency planning' became important when making decisions about the future of children in long term care. It was felt that children needed stability and not to be moved from one place to another. Research highlighted cases of children having many foster placements with little continuity of care.

The House of Commons Social Services Committee (1984) reported concerns about the standard of services offered to children and their families.

This led to a review of child care law and the introduction of a **Children's Bill** that was seen as revolutionary.

The Cleveland inquiry (1988) highlighted many concerns about child protection services and the lack of co-operation between the various agencies involved in child protection cases.

The Children Act (1989) was influenced by the Children's Bill and Cleveland inquiry. It drew together all legislation concerned with child care and protection except adoption.

The Child Support Act (1991) gave powers to the DSS. This enabled them to ensure that parents continue to financially support their children, when they are not living in the child's home (from the work of D. Gladstone (1995) and H. Glennerster (1995)). It was hoped that this would enable greater liaison between the various agencies responsible for children, and a pooling of specialist knowledge.

The Children Act 1989

The Children Act attempted to achieve a balance between child protection and family support. It drew together a mass of complicated legislation and replaced it with a law that seeks to address most circumstances concerning children and young people. The act deals with

- family proceedings (separation and divorce)
- Local Authority support for children and their families (children in need)
- child protection
- the registration of residential and day-care services

ACTIVITY

Using the library

Research the Children Act 1989. Most libraries have a copy of An Introduction to the Children Act, published by HMSO. In it you will find the answers to the following:

1 What are the main principles of the act?
2 How are children defined as 'in need' under section 17 of the act?
3 What are section 8 orders and to whom do they apply?
4 Which child care facilities must register with social services?

The Children Act 1989 has changed the way that services are provided to children. The **paramouncy principle** views the child as central. The rights of the child are seen as important with any decisions made about them having to be in their best interest.

Children's Services Plans

The local authority are required by law to publish a Children's Services Plan for their area. They are required to

- assess what services need to be provided for **children in need**
- consult with other agencies and organisations and plan how these needs will be met
- publish the results

The guidelines issued to local authorities state that services should be provided for:

- children with disabilities
- children and young people with mental health problems
- children under eight
- children looked after by the Local Authority
- young runaways
- adoption services
- children and young people leaving care
- family support for children in need and child protection
- children in conflict with the law

ACTIVITY

Find out about the Children's Services Plan for your area. These are available from Social Services or your local library. How does it plan to meet the needs of children in the above categories?

Summary

- the idea of the nuclear family remains popular, but may produce over-possessive parents, vulnerable children, and dependent women
- such concerns have encouraged various experimental alternatives
- this century extended families have declined and nuclear families increased
- despite some movement towards equality in the home, it has not yet been achieved
- concerns about modern marriage focus on the fall in numbers marrying, and the rise in cohabitation, single parenthood and divorce
- higher divorce rates reflect changes in the law, in women's opportunities, in expectations of marriage, in religious influence, and greater life expectancy
- divorce can have long-term negative consequences for children, but they may be due to factors such as the decline in living standards, isolation, or extra stress
- today many previously 'unconventional' living arrangements exist, such as lone-parent, cohabiting, homosexual and reconstituted families
- the needs of children have increasing influence in the development of social policy
- the Children Act (1989) was seen as revolutionary and has had a major impact on service delivery

4

Social class

Key points

- social class influences all areas of our life
- the major inequalities are of wealth and of income
- in addition to the upper, middle and working-classes, an underclass may have developed among the poor
- recent changes in work have affected levels of unemployment and social mobility
- in a number of respects, Britain still does not seem to adequately reward effort and ability

Introduction

When sociologists use the term 'social class' (or 'class'), they are using it neutrally. There is no implication that middle-class people are 'better' than working-class people, or that upper-class people are 'better' than both. But, by using the term 'class', sociologists are recognising that it is important. It is probably as important in Britain – especially in England – as anywhere else in the world.

The importance of class

We can distinguish between the class into which one is born (**class of origin**) and the class one ends up in (**class of destination**). For many they are the same. Others, however, through **social mobility**, move up or down the social class scale.

Our class of origin is important because it significantly *influences* all our lives. However, while class influences, for instance, our educational achievements, it does not *determine* them. This is because, to a varying extent, individuals (and their families) can also influence their own lives.

Our social class influences our chance of:

- being born alive
- surviving the first year of life
- reaching adulthood
- going to university
- being unemployed
- divorcing
- reading certain newspapers
- living in certain neighbourhoods
- holidaying – if at all – at certain places
- voting in a certain way
- and more

In the listing above, some factors are influenced by one's class of origin and others more by one's class of destination. Also, some factors are **life chances** (that is statistical likelihoods of something happening – for example likelihood of being born dead) and others are more personally selected matters of **life style** (for example the newspaper one reads). However, thinking about life style questions (perhaps how one votes) does help us recognise that people often change their behaviour if and when they have changed their class.

ACTIVITY

1 What other life chances and opportunities or life style factors and behaviours do you think are influenced by social class?
2 Look at the list above, and/or your additional suggestions. Which do you feel are more influenced by a person's class of origin and which more by their class of destination? Explain why.

Inequalities of wealth and income

Although a lot of people in Britain don't like talking about social class, it seems self-deluding to pretend that inequalities based on class don't exist.

The substantial differences in life chances and life styles themselves reflect what are, perhaps, the major inequalities between classes, in:

- wealth
- earned income

ACTIVITY

Inequality of wealth, United Kingdom, 1989

The wealthiest (% of pop.)	Own (% of all private wealth)
1	18
5	38
11	53
25	75
50	94

Inequality of income

If we could organise an hour-long parade of everyone in Britain who receives an earned income, and could construct people in proportion to their income, the average male would be about 5 ft 9 ins tall.

For the first few seconds the people passing by would be no bigger than matchsticks: paperboys and girls earning pocket money, wives earning a bit to supplement the income. But soon they would be followed by people 3 ft high: people living on state benefits, low paid workers, shopkeepers with low profits. Some would be students and artists. Fifteen minutes later there would be 4 ft tall unskilled manual workers and shop assistants. So far, a lot of the people passing will have been women and a lot black.

Another 10 minutes and the people passing would reach the shoulder of the average man: mainly skilled manual and white collar workers in routine jobs. What would surprise us is that these less than average height people would keep on coming. Indeed, it would take 45 minutes after the parade had begun – three-quarters of the way through – before people of average height began to pass. These, when they came, would be teachers, some well paid manual workers, insurance agents, jobbing builders, and so on. From this point on, however, the size of people in the parade would increase rapidly, for it would now be the highest paid 10 per cent of the population who would be passing.

At about 6 ft 6 ins we would still be seeing people in fairly modest jobs: headteachers, college principals. In the last few minutes of the parade, giants loom into view: a lawyer 18 ft tall, a colonel about the same size. We would see doctors and accountants, university professors, senior officials in large companies between 20 and 30 ft tall. At 40 ft, High Court Judges, and at 60 ft eye surgeons, more accountants and Chairpersons of national companies.

In the last few seconds, we would see colossal forms, as tall as tower blocks. Most will be businessmen, but there will be some pop stars and members of the Royal Family. Prince Philip, for instance, at 180 ft high. As the parade nears its end, we'd be measuring people in miles, not feet. Pop star Tom Jones at about one mile, the owner of the Financial Times and Penguin Books at 8 or 9 miles. If we'd invited some American guests such as a Rockefeller, we'd see people up to 100 miles tall. The instep of one of these giants would tower miles above that of the average income earner.

(source unknown)

1 According to the first item, how much wealth is owned by a) the richer 50 per cent of the population, and b) the poorer 50 per cent?
2 In the second item, how is it possible that people of average size would not appear until the parade was three-quarters over?
3 Divide into two groups. One group should try to think of arguments which support an unequal distribution of wealth and income, the other group arguing against.

Who are the social classes?

One way of looking at social classes is to think of our society as divided into three or four main classes, each of which contain a number of quite different groups. These social classes are the upper, middle and working-classes. Some people argue that there is also now a fourth – an underclass – of people cut off from much of the rest of society through poverty and their own attitudes and behaviours. However, though many people do live in poverty, many sociologists dispute the idea of an underclass.

How do the classes differ?

A traditional way of identifying the social classes divides people into an upper class of very wealthy people, a middle-class of non-manual workers and a working-class of manual workers. (Manual refers to working with one's hands, though a few middle-class jobs, such as surgeon, involve skilled handwork. All jobs, of course, require use of the brain). Each class is divided in turn into sub-groups. We begin with the upper class.

The upper-class

In simple terms, membership is primarily to do with being very wealthy. The upper-class are generally sufficiently wealthy that neither they, nor their dependents, would have to work – though many choose to (getting paid, in the main, a high income for doing so).

According to the sociologist Anthony Giddens, the upper-class now consists of three main groups, whose original wealth came in different ways: the aristocracy; industrialists and financiers; and the 'glitterati'. (In the examples given below, the figures, in millions of £s, are estimates of their wealth made by the *Sunday Times* in their 1997 annual 'Rich List'.)

Upper class	Aristocrats, landed gentry: includes all hereditary lords & families Industrialists, financiers, merchants, retailers 'Glitterati': music, sport & screen stars	**Key criterion:** Wealth/property ownership

THE ARISTOCRACY

Examples here could be the Duke of Westminster (£1700 m) and Viscount Chelsea (£500 m). This group include some whose origins are medieval and whose family wealth came from owning large and valuable tracts of land. Among the older families, the land may have been given to their ancestors by the monarch of the day. The Queen (£250 m) is at the pinnacle of the aristocracy, though not necessarily its richest member. However, some members of the aristocracy now find themselves owning and responsible for large houses and estates which they claim, with their tax bills, they cannot afford to maintain (for example the Duke of Devonshire, worth £375 m).

CAPITALISTS, FINANCIERS AND MERCHANTS

This group have gained or inherited their wealth through their ownership of industries, for example Richard Branson with music and an airline (£1700 m), financial companies such as banks (the Schroder family – £1050 m), or through their activities in commerce, trade or in retailing for example Sri & Gopi Hinduja in oil trading and a theme park (£1100 m) and David Sainsbury with supermarkets (£2500 m). Many derive their wealth from a number of sectors.

THE 'GLITTERATI'

They are the relatively new, jet-set wealthy who have gained their wealth working in the entertainment industries of music, film or sport, such as Paul McCartney (£420 m), Sean Connory (£50 m) and the golfer Nick Faldo (£50 m).

Although the wealth of the aristocratic landowner, the capitalist industrialist and the glitterati pop or sports star are derived differently, once wealthy, people tend to spread into different spheres. So aristocratic landowners are likely to be industrial shareholders as well; successful pop or sports stars establish businesses, and wealthy capitalists buy farms and football clubs.

Together, the upper-class number a few thousand in Britain and most people can expect over a lifetime to have little or no direct contact with any of them. They generally live in their own neighbourhoods, send their children to exclusive, fee-paying schools, visit different doctors, stay in different hospitals or wards, and holiday at different resorts. However, as they often employ staff, including nannies, au pairs or other child care support, people doing such jobs may sometimes come into contact with them in this role.

The middle and working-classes

Although the large majority of people who are not members of the upper-class vary in how much wealth they have, most people have either to take paid work, or depend upon state benefits, to support themselves and their dependents financially. Those who work are usually divided into the middle and working-classes. As a rule of thumb, middle-class people do non-manual jobs and working-class people do manual jobs.

When the Registrar-General and colleagues conduct the national census near the start of every decade, they divide the population according to the occupation of the 'head of the household'. Occupations are then grouped into six '**socio-economic groups**'. Each socio-economic group is made up of occupations which are similar to each other in terms of their prestige, the level of education required, and the general level of pay and working conditions. Occupation is a useful thing to know about people because it is quite a good indicator of other characteristics.

As shown in the chart below, what is usually called the middle-class traditionally includes three socio-economic groups, which we can call the upper-middle, middle-middle and lower-middle class. People in the working-class have traditionally been divided into three more groups, of skilled, semi- or part-skilled and unskilled manual workers, and their respective families.

Middle-class	Upper-middle class: 'higher' professions, senior management (for example lawyer, doctor) Middle-middle class: 'lower professions, middle management (for example teacher, social worker) Lower-middle class: (clerical, routine 'white-collar')	**Key criterion:** Non-manual ('white-collar') employment
Working-class	Skilled manual: (for example trained electricians, carpenters, plumbers) Semi- or part-skilled manual. (for example postal worker, cashier) Unskilled manual: (for example labourer, cleaner)	**Key criterion:** Manual ('blue-collar') employment

Within both the middle and working-classes there is a very substantial range of incomes and job conditions. In the middle-class, for instance, there are big differences in opportunities and life style between the upper-middle class corporation lawyer earning £80 000 a year, the middle-middle-class teacher on £17 000 a year and the lower-middle class clerk selling you your train ticket and earning £12 000 a year.

Within the working-class, highly skilled workers are likely to be in a very different position to an unskilled worker with no qualifications.

However, there is a big debate about whether there are any longer any significant differences between the status and income of people at the lower end of the middle-class and the top end of the working-class. Should such routine white-collar workers as clerical workers and secretaries still be regarded as middle-class and distinct from skilled manual workers? For, although until well into this century such workers took a pride in their superior status and working conditions to the working-class, their social and economic superiority is nowadays much less clear.

According to one point of view, their jobs are now so similar to those at the top end of the working-class in terms of their pay and conditions, fringe benefits and vulnerability to unemployment, that it makes more sense to see them as working-class rather than middle-class.

Others argue, however, that there are still a number of important differences which give clerical workers a superior position to manual workers, and a legitimate sense of superiority. These differences would include the level and nature of the qualifications required, their superior working conditions (including relative absence of noise and dirt), the relative prestige of their 'brain work' and their regular interaction with, and closeness to, management.

ACTIVITY

1 Pick any *two* of the three social classes discussed above (the upper, middle and working-classes). How would you describe the main differences between them?
2 Within the middle and working-classes are subgroups which differ from each other. Choose any *two* socio-economic groups from the same social class and compare the sort of life style and life opportunities you think they have. Compare impressions with your colleagues.
3 It is suggested that a person's occupation is useful to know because it is quite a good predictor of other characteristics. What else do you think you might be able to predict about people if you know their occupation?

The poor and the 'underclass'

Most of the people living in poverty are either themselves in, or depend on people in, one or more of the following categories:

- unemployed
- elderly

- single parents
- people with a disability or long-term sickness
- people doing low paid work

They are mainly poor because of their relationship to the labour market (see Chapter 7). Many in all categories are outside it altogether, for example the long-term unemployed. Some others are on the bottom edge of it, for example single parents doing unreliable, low paid home-work. Others, such as the blind, or others with special needs, may be in a weak position competing for jobs in the labour market.

Since the early 1970s, the concept of a so-called '**underclass**' has become quite commonly used, both in Britain and the USA. Unfortunately, there is no agreement about who is included in the concept. Most writers probably do not include elderly pensioners (who have worked), or pupils or students (who may work in the future) or people with special needs (who would want to work). The term tends, therefore, to be mainly limited to the long-term unemployed, single parents, the low waged and, because some ethnic minorities are over-represented in those categories, the underclass is often perceived as having a high ethnic minority content.

For many, the underclass is perceived as a grouping which has almost split away from the bottom end of the working-class, and from others on low incomes. But there is much disagreement about why such a grouping may have emerged, and how members of the underclass differ, if they do at all, from others in the working-class, or even from others in poverty who are not part of an underclass.

For many, such as the American theorist Charles Murray, the key to the underclass is their *behaviour*. In Murray's view, they produce illegitimate, violent children, are violent themselves, commit often violent crime, take drugs and avoid work. They are 'welfare dependent'. With a steady, if low, income provided by the state, they feel no need or wish to work, nor to marry or behave responsibly towards their offspring. It is not their poverty which characterises the underclass, according to Murray (for other poor people, including many pensioners, do not share the values or behaviours of the underclass). It is their 'deplorable behaviour in response to that condition' (Murray, 1990).

Others are critical of this sort of analysis. Some claim that there is not much empirical support for the idea that large numbers reject conventional beliefs and hopes about work, children and family life. Among the poor of working age, most want to work; among the unmarried poor, most want to marry.

Critics of analyses which emphasise the underclass's allegedly deviant culture claim that, even if such a subculture exists, such analyses cannot explain its origin. Where does the deviant subculture come from? What produces or encourages it? Analyses of the underclass which focus only on its supposedly distinctive culture may explain how it survives over time – through socialisation of the next generation – but not why it emerges.

According to critics of the cultural view, the key to the underclass is their *restricted opportunities*, rather than their attitudes or beliefs. If people have low aspirations and don't plan for the future, this isn't because they are less conscientious or ambitious. Most unemployed people *would* like to work to earn a decent income. It is because they have seriously restricted opportunities, and they know it.

In this view, the creation of a welfare-dependent section of the population is blamed on

- long-term unemployment
- lack of affordable child care
- an almost 20 year squeeze on welfare benefits
- the infamous 'poverty trap' whereby people are penalised when they earn anything more than a low minimum

Long-term unemployment has come about primarily because of the disappearance for good of many working class jobs and the automation of others, for example in mining, car making and so on. Although the most directly affected are men in middle age, many younger men, and women, unless they possess special skills, are also 'thrown onto the scrapheap' or face the possibility of permanent unemployment. This, in many cases, is without their ever having made it onto even the lowest rung of the occupational ladder.

Long-term unemployment is now, clearly, a feature of many Western countries. As much as anything it is this, and the failure of adequate political action, which has impoverished and demoralised many of the more marginal members of the working class. Their sometimes 'deplorable behaviour', and lowered expectations and ambitions, are a not-necessarily conscious response to their circumstances.

Social mobility

Social mobility refers to movement either up or down the social class ladder. Traditionally, there have been two main ways of measuring the amount of social mobility in a society. It has been measured by

- inter-generational social mobility: comparing parents' occupations with those achieved by their children, or
- intra–generational social mobility: measuring the movement up or down the class scale which individuals achieve in their lifetime.

How much upward mobility is possible depends on three main factors:

- the number of jobs to be filled: for instance, if more professional and managerial jobs are created, that allows more upward mobility for those from below
- the extent to which the higher socio-economic groups reproduce themselves: if they have few children, there will be 'vacancies' for other children to fill
- adequate education, training and qualifications: without sufficient people having these, jobs could remain unfilled

How much mobility has there been?

In a number of studies conducted in the 1970s and 1980s, it seems that, while there was some downward mobility, there was much more upward movement. This was largely because of the increase in white-collar, middle-class jobs and insufficient middle-class children to fill them. About one-third of people in professional and managerial jobs were from working-class backgrounds. However, upward mobility was much more difficult to achieve for women and members of ethnic minorities.

Recent developments

The world of work has changed substantially in the last two decades. It has affected the number and types of jobs available, and therefore the prospects for mobility.

Changes in the work available

- There is now a higher proportion of managerial and professional jobs (although the number of people competing for them has also increased, especially with more women entering the labour market at these levels).

Many traditional, working-class jobs have disappeared, in manufacturing (for instance car production) and in extractive industries (for instance mining and fishing). This has resulted in significant numbers of '**structurally unemployed**' – people whose jobs have gone forever, many of whom are now in long-term unemployment.

Changes in the conditions of work

There has been a growing 'polarisation' of the labour market. Jobs have tended to divide into two, very different, types:

- the mainly non-manual, middle-class jobs which employ a core of secure, well paid workers, with good occupational rights, such as pensions and holiday pay: such work seems increasingly stressful and people seem increasingly likely to leave it, or accept demotion, as they get into their late 40s or 50s
- the insecure, often part-time or casual, low paid, low skill jobs, in mainly manual or routine white collar work. Often these jobs have few occupational rights (for example there may be no holiday or sickness rights and no occupational pension)

However, although this latter type of work primarily applies to manual or routine white collar jobs, it has also entered more professional areas such as teaching, where a growing number are being employed on those terms. How, then, may different groups be affected?

THE LONG-TERM UNEMPLOYED

They and their children are in many cases unlikely to work unless they can acquire an education and skills necessary for the sort of work anticipated: non-manual, and knowledge- and information-based.

QUALIFIED AND SKILLED WORKING-CLASS CHILDREN

It seems likely that there will continue to be insufficient middle-class children to fill the non-manual jobs available (especially if one adds the vacancies which will occur if many middle aged professional and managerial workers continue their early departure). Consequently, there should still be opportunities for children from working-class backgrounds to get non-manual work, assuming they gain appropriate skills and qualifications.

MIDDLE-CLASS CHILDREN

Their chances of getting non-manual jobs are still better than those of working-class children. However, the type of work available has changed, with the erosion of jobs offering a secure, life-long position.

GENERAL TRENDS

For both middle and working-class people, the possibility of downward mobility seems to be increasing.

The loss of full-time jobs means that the numbers of unemployed (from both middle and working-class jobs) have grown.

More middle-class employees will accept downward mobility towards the end of their career, either in the form of redundancy or demotion (though better pensions should provide some protection financially).

ACTIVITY

Downward mobility for middle-class workers

> The next generation of full-time workers in all classes will start their full-time careers later and leave them earlier. More will leave full-time work in their late 40s or early 50s, partly because they don't want the growing pressure of such work, but mainly because there will be younger, more qualified and more energetic people available. People will not stop working after 50 but it won't be the same sort of work.
>
> (from C. Handy *The Age of Unreason*)

The extract above gives one, not-very-obvious, way in which some people nowadays may experience 'downward mobility'. What do you understand by downward mobility? What are the main causes of it?

Is Britain a meritocracy?

A **meritocracy** is a society in which the most rewarded, most prestigious jobs go to those who merit (deserve) them by virtue of their ability and effort. No completely meritocratic society seems to exist, but some societies are more meritocratic than others.

In our society, and probably even more so in the USA, many people believe that individuals can succeed if they have ability, work hard and have, perhaps, 'a bit of luck'. As there seems to be no convincing evidence that children are born more intelligent the higher their social class, in a meritocratic society children from a working-class background should be about as well represented in top jobs as people from other classes. But what is the evidence?

- most people end up in their class of origin
- what upward (and downward) mobility does occur is generally short-range, that is from one level to an adjacent, or nearby, one – for example son of plumber (skilled manual) to clerk (routine white collar) or teacher (lower professional); daughter of teacher (lower professional) to doctor (higher professional). There is relatively little long-range mobility, for instance from the working-class to the upper class
- very few get to the 'top' jobs: this is partly because, of course, there are not that many top jobs to get to. But those that do are most likely to have had a father who was himself in the higher classes

Why isn't Britain more meritocratic?

Those in positions of wealth and influence can pass on many of their advantages to their children.

Wealth

Among the very wealthy (£15 m+), the proportion who inherited substantial wealth seems to be declining (from about 57 per cent in 1989 to 31 per cent in 1997). Neverthless, even if they don't come from the 'super-rich', most of those in the upper-class came from pretty prosperous families.

A PRESTIGIOUS EDUCATION

Other advantages are passed on or reinforced by attending a prestigious public school. The quality of the education or academic qualifications gained are, of course, important, but there are other advantages. Children also acquire life-long social contacts, high social prestige and learn the 'appropriate' styles, manner and bearing of those who expect to lead, all of which later prove helpful in gaining success. Consequently, a high proportion of former public schoolboys are still recruited into the most prestigious and best paid jobs. Most people outside the upper-class can't afford to send their children to such schools.

For the remainder – the large majority of the population – middle-class children are still more likely than working class children to be successful in education (see Chapter 8). This is so even when the children are of the same measured IQ. Inqualities of income and wealth between the classes are important factors in this, but so are attitudes.

Women continue to face disadvantages which hinder their upward mobility. Primary responsibility for children and housecare, and the shortage of affordable childcare are two factors limiting mobility.

Some ethnic minority groups are seriously disadvantaged by racism: in housing, education and employment. Afro-Caribbean and Bangladeshi people seem particularly disadvantaged in these regards, perhaps partly reflecting their social class origins compared to those of other ethnic groups.

Summary

- class affects people's life chances (for example of survival) and life styles (for example their newspaper readership)
- the upper-class owe their position to the ownership of wealth: the richest 5 per cent own almost 40 per cent of all private wealth
- the middle and working-classes are differentiated by the type of work they do: either non-manual or manual jobs
- in general, middle-class people are wealthier and healthier than working-class people
- some routine white-collar and skilled manual jobs are now so similar in status, pay and working conditions that it is uncertain whether to see them as of the same or different classes

- the idea of an underclass is also controversial. If some of the unemployed do seem insufficiently motivated, is that why they are unemployed? Or are such attitudes a realistic response to widespread, long-term structural unemployment?
- upward social mobility has increased because there are more higher level white collar jobs to be filled
- however, unemployment has increased in both middle and working-classes. Also, demotion at work and poorer working conditions have become more likely for some middle-class employees
- Britain remains unmeritocratic because the rich still confer many advantages on their children. Also because able working class, female and ethnic minority children still find upward mobility difficult to achieve

5

Demography

Key points

- the United Kingdom's population has grown in four main stages
- its structure (or composition) has also changed: it has aged and become more ethnically diverse
- despite some differences in relationships in cities and villages, close-knit communities can also be found in cities

What causes changes in the population?

Populations grow or become smaller because of changes in one or more of three factors: the birth rate, the death rate, or the numbers leaving or coming into the country (emigrating or immigrating).

A country's **birth rate** is the number of live births, for every 1000 of its population, in a given year. A country's **death rate** is the number of deaths, for every 1000 of its population, in a particular year.

Migration refers to any movement of significant numbers of people. Migration can be international (between countries) or internal (within a country). In the United Kingdom, **emigration** officially refers to those people who leave a country for at least one year, and **immigration** to those who enter the country for at least one year. **Net migration** is the difference in numbers between the two.

A country's population will *increase* if

- the birth rate is higher than the death rate, or
- more people enter the country (immigrate) than leave it (emigrate).

It is important for governments and others to know what these changes are in order to plan the necessary services such as health care, schools, and social security.

How Britain's population has changed in size

The changes in Britain's population over the last few centuries have happened in four stages, beginning with a pre-industrial phase.

1 **Pre-1740s:** before the Industrial Revolution, Britain's population *growth* was *slow*: a *high birth rate* was mainly cancelled out by the *high death rate.*
2 **1740s to 1880s:** the population '*exploded*'. *Birth rate remained high* but *death rate fell.*
3 **1880s to 1920s** *Death rate continued to fall* but there was now a sharp *decline in the birth rate.* Population *growth slowed*, though births still higher than deaths.
4 **From 1920s to present** *Birth and death rates* stay relatively *low* and population *grows* only *slowly*. There are, however, fluctuations partly because of the 'baby boom' when service people returned home after the Second World War.

Why did the death rate fall?

The death rate began to fall primarily because of changes associated with the agrarian and industrial revolutions, from about the early 1700s:

- agricultural technique improved food production and improved transportation and distribution of food meant people had an improved diet and the threat of famine and malnutrition declined
- people's clothing also improved, thanks partly to large scale, machine production of woven cloth
- public health measures – the introduction of piped, cleaner water, more effective sewage disposal, flush toilets, shared only by family

Why did the birth rate fall?

The fall in birth rate began around the 1880s, and happened first among the middle-class, and for mainly economic and social reasons.

- improvements in the child mortality rates meant that more children were surviving to adulthood: parents began to feel more confident that they would be supported in old age without needing to produce large numbers of children
- although people had become financially better off, many were concerned about growing inflation, with costs rising for many necessary middle-class items, such as servants and horses, as well as food and other necessities
- children became more expensive: middle-class professions increasingly required qualifications, so middle and upper-class parents increasingly had to pay for an extended education for their (male) children. With compulsory basic education introduced for all in 1880, working-class children – no longer as able to earn – also became more expensive
- from 1908 old age pensions were introduced, which lessened people's dependence on children in old age

Some consequences of population changes in the West

In this section, we look at four important changes occurring in Western populations such as ours:

- it is ageing
- it contains large, financially-dependent age groups
- it has more women than men
- it is multi-ethnic

1 An ageing population

Like most other Western countries, the British population is often described as ageing. That is because

- people are generally living longer
- elderly people have become a larger proportion of the population

Life expectancy has increased for both males and females over the last 100 or so years. The number of elderly is increasing while the number of those under 16 has been falling. So the elderly are both growing in numbers and in proportion to the young. In 1971, those aged 65 or more were 13 per cent of the UK population. By 2051 they are expected to be about 24 per cent of the total. Because women live on average longer than men, the proportion of females in the population increases with age.

Problems for the elderly

In small-scale societies where the pace of social change is slow, the elderly typically have high status partly because, having lived longest in a society where things change very little, they have acquired the most knowledge. In such slow-changing societies knowledge acquired over a lifetime is still valid, and is seen by those younger as 'wisdom'.

In our sort of society, however, change is rapid: ideas, technologies, knowledge, fashions and social norms are in a state of constant change. So, the ideas and techniques the elderly acquired when younger can become out of date and inappropriate, and the advantage shifts towards the young.

In other ways, too, growing old in western societies can be a difficult experience. Some common experiences associated with growing old in the West are:

- a drop in status, and threat to one's sense of identity: retirement particularly can undermine people's sense of themselves, sense of purpose and self-respect
- isolation: with the decline of the extended family, and of community activities and involvement, the elderly may become isolated and lonely and again, retirement may well increase the sense of isolation
- financial difficulties: retirement and old age have typically been accompanied by a sharp fall in income, which can lead to physical hardship as people try to economise – for instance, on food, heating, or their social life

ACTIVITY

Life expectancy and population under 20

Life expectancy (years)		Year	Population under 20 (%)	
Males	***Females***	–	***Males***	***Females***
41.2	43.3	1841	47.1	45.1
39.2	41.2	1851	46.3	44.2
39.8	42.2	1861	46.5	44.1
40.2	43.2	1871	47.0	44.5
42.1	45.3	1881	47.4	45.1
43.7	47.2	1891	46.5	44.0
45.3	49.2	1901	43.7	41.2
50.6	54.2	1911	41.2	38.8
56.1	60.0	1921	38.9	35.4
58.0	62.0	1931	34.1	30.9
59.4	64.5	1941	33.5	27.1
65.8	70.7	1951	30.0	26.9
68.0	73.9	1961	31.6	28.4
69.3	75.5	1971	32.2	28.9
71.1	77.1	1981	30.2	27.2
73.4	78.9	1991	26.7	24.2

(from The Health of Our Children, p.2)

Briefly summarise the trends shown by the table above.

2 Large, dependent age groups

The population can be divided into three age groups: the young, the working age group, and the elderly. The first and last groups are regarded as dependent age groups because they must be, to some extent, kept by those in work. Combining the two, the total who are financially dependent has grown over this century in all Western societies.

First, there is a large and growing number of elderly people, as well as a growing number who are now retiring before the traditional age (for men) of 65.

At the other end of the age scale, although the number and proportion of young people has been falling, they have become financially dependent for longer. Growing numbers have been continuing in education or training, because the school leaving age has been raised over the years, there are fewer job opportunities and more are continuing to higher education. Add the increased numbers of working-aged unemployed, or on other state benefits, and it is clear that the proportion of people creating the bulk of the nation's wealth and working – especially full-time – has been falling.

3 More women than men

Although females in Britain report more illness than males, on average they live longer and, at every age, are less likely to die than males. However, this has not always been the case. In the mid-nineteenth century, females from their early teens to their 40s were more likely to die than males, mainly as a result of childbirth and related diseases, or of tuberculosis which killed more women than men. Although the death rate has declined for both sexes, since the mid-nineteenth century it has fallen more for females, as women have fewer children, ante-natal and post-natal care have improved, and the threat from tuberculosis has been reduced.

Although biological differences may well play an important role in explaining why men die younger, social and behavioural factors also seem to contribute to the differences. Two common explanations why males, on average, die younger focus on:

The type of work men have typically done

- the jobs with the highest accident and death risks are typically male
- the loss of work, with unemployment or retirement, can be health-damaging. Many men die within two years of retirement

Men's health-damaging ideas about 'masculinity' and 'appropriate' male role behaviour:

- it has been more acceptable for men than for females to smoke and drink
- men are less likely than females to look after their health adequately, (they report illness less, consult doctors less, and are taught to 'shrug off' illness)
- they have a higher incidence of road accidents: more drive cars and ride motor bikes and they are more aggressive and take greater risks
- the masculine taboo on emotional self-expression may increase stress and encourage ill-health

ACTIVITY

Divide into pairs. Consider one explanation for earlier male death. Explain in more detail why this may help explain it and whether you think this is still as much the case as previously. Are females becoming more vulnerable in this respect?

4 A multi-ethnic society

Over the years, the number of emigrants from, and immigrants into, Britain have been sufficiently similar that net migration has made relatively little difference to the total number of people living in this country. However, immigrant groups do tend to have higher birth rates, and a younger average age, although there is some evidence that these differences may diminish over time.

Although the population size of Britain has not been significantly affected by net migration, migration has, of course, affected the ethnic composition of the population. Unfortunately, although the 1991 national census included a question on people's ethnic background, it did not differentiate between different *white* minority groups. Consequently, a major official provider of demographic information like *Social Trends*, uses the term 'ethnic minority population' to refer (incorrectly) only to non-white minorities. Given the relative difficulty getting information on white ethnic minority groups, the Activity below focuses on mainly 'non-white' minority groups.

ACTIVITY

1 In pairs or small groups, compile a list of as many of the main ethnic minority groups now living in Britain as you can (remember to include any 'white' ethnic minority groups you can think of).
2 Now try to rank the groups according to their size in descending order (that is, the largest is 1, the next largest 2, and so on).
3 Give your own estimate, as a percentage, of the proportion of the *total* population of Britain which is '*non-white*'. Compare your estimate with that of the other members of the class, and note down the range.
4 Now compare your estimates with the figures on page 82. Do they differ significantly? What conclusions, if any, do you draw?
5 Look up in an atlas the main countries of origin of members of our ethnic minorities. Produce a world map showing the national origins of our ethnic minority groups.

One reason why many (mainly white?) people imagine that the proportion of non-whites in the general population is higher than it is may be to do with the concentration of many minorities in a few geographical areas. The 1991 census showed that over two-thirds of the non-white ethnic minority population live in four conurbations: London, the West Midlands, West Yorkshire and Greater Manchester. In the South-East generally, around 10% of the population belong to a non-white ethnic minority. But in many of the country towns and largely rural parts of the country, non-white ethnic minorities form less than 1% of the population.

To counterbalance the focus on non-white minorities, it is very important to note that there is also a large number of people living in Britain today in mainly white minority groups. Most of these come from European Union countries, Commonwealth countries such as Australia, New Zealand and Canada, the USA and Eastern Europe. In 1993, the number of people from the Irish Republic living in Britain was some 466 000, with a further 302 000 from other European Union countries such as Italy, Germany and France. If these overwhelmingly white migrants from the European Union alone are regarded as one group, they constitute the second largest immigrant group in Britain, ahead of both the Afro-Caribbeans and Pakistanis. Thus, ethnic minorities are by no means necessarily non-white. Indeed, a large number of our 'ethnic minority' members are white.

Living in urban and rural communities

In the last 150 or so years, Britain has moved from being a mainly rural-based society – with most people living in villages, or in hamlets in the countryside – to one in which most people live in towns or in cities. This process is called **urbanisation**. At the same time, towns and cities have grown in size, although in recent years there has been a shift away from the cities to the city suburbs or back into the country.

ACTIVITY

How do you think living in a village is likely to be different to living in a city for a child? What are the characteristics of villages which would be significant?

Cities and villages

Some of the things which students have thought of as characteristic of village, rather than city, life include

- quiet
- children being able to go where they like, parents not having to worry
- a low crime rate
- transport difficulties
- isolation

Group	Numbers	Proportion of total population
Indian	840 000	1.5%
Afro-Caribbean	499 000	0.9%
Pakistani	475 000	0.9%
Black African & Other Black	385 000	0.7%
Bangladeshi	160 000	0.3%
Other Asian (excl. Chinese)	196 000	0.4%
Chinese origin	157 000	0.3
Other non-white	290 000	0.5
Total non-white	3 002 000	5.5%

In matters such as these, it is easy to imagine that living in a village and living in a city are polar opposites. Many sociologists who have thought about the differences between city and country living have also sometimes seen cities and villages as almost entirely opposites. Ferdinand Tönnies is one of the best known. Writing in Germany in 1887, Tönnies feared that village communities – in which people had real contact with each other – were declining. More and more people would be living in cities in which, he believed, people had contacts with large numbers of people but at a superficial and unsatisfying level.

Village society

According to Tönnies, village society is small-scale and close-knit. People who have grown up in villages have known each other for a long time, and have seen each other in a variety of roles. They have grown up with each other, have gone to school with them, have played and socialised with them, have drunk, danced, gone to church with each other, attended each other's weddings, the christening of their children, and finally have attended their funeral. They have known fellow villagers as 'whole' people rather than merely as in particular roles, and would have strong feelings about them, both good and bad. These are the characteristics of what we mean when we use the word 'community'.

City society

By comparison, cities are large, with populations which are very mixed and varied (heterogeneous). Tönnies believed that the majority of people's relationships in a city would be shallow and superficial. This is because the city was home to so many – and such varied – people. It was also because many of the contacts people would have in a city would only be with people in a particular role, and that, therefore, one would seldom get to know the whole person. The milkman, the busdriver who takes us to college or to work, the man in the newsagents, the woman who sells us a train ticket: these are all superficial and specialist contacts with people who, in a city, we may never meet again and are unlikely ever to meet in one of their other roles. We are unlikely to get to know the ticket collector as a parent, local pub-goer, husband, neighbour, person. According to Tönnies, in a village people get to know each other that intimately. In a city, Tönnies feared, people would have shallow and superficial contact with each other, and would be unable to tell each other of their concerns. So he was alarmed at what he perceived as a decline in close personal relationships and its possible effects on society.

ACTIVITY

Identify someone who has experience of living in a town or city. Find out from them how their experience of city life compares to what Tönnies wrote. Do they notice any differences?

Villages in cities and the city in the village?

Although Tönnies does seem to have been right in describing the different nature of many relationships in a city and in a village, others have pointed out that by seeing the city and village as polar opposites he ignores some of their similarities.

For instance, in many cities it is still possible to find neighbourhoods which encourage relationships like those he identified as characteristic of villages. There are still areas of cities in which people are born, live and die, and where people have known each other in a range of roles.

However, in Britain at least, areas such as these have become less common, particularly since the 1950s, with '**slum-clearance**' (knocking down poor housing) and the decline of many local industries. It is interesting how many soaps are set in such neighbourly urban communities, and perhaps no coincidence that *Coronation Street* was first introduced at about the same time as that sort of community, up and down the country, was being bulldozed to rubble and transformed beyond recognition.

However, village life too has long been changing, and in ways which may make it less like it was in Tönnies' time. Mass car ownership plus housebuilding schemes in villages have encouraged commuters and even second-home owners. Some have become 'dormitory' villages, in which it is suggested, the commuter occupants have little time left but to sleep!

Car ownership has also allowed those born locally a way out of the village and the immediate area, either temporarily or more permanently. These developments have inevitably affected the nature of life in villages, making them, perhaps, more like Tönnies' idea of the city.

Growing up in different environments

Research teams in a variety of countries have reported their findings on how young adolescents (13 to 15 years) use and regard their home territory. They have compared the young people's experiences of growing up in either an inner city, a city suburb, a city housing estate or a village.

ACTIVITY

How children see their environments

Children living in inner cities tended to see their areas as dangerous and challenging, but not boring. However, children living in city suburbs or on modern city housing estates saw their neighbourhood areas as empty and boring, and frequently complained of the lack of things to do.

When asked to draw maps of their areas, village and central city children drew more detailed, more accurate and more interesting maps than the estate children. Children from the housing estates drew plans of new housing which showed them as boringly repetitive, without much difference between the buildings. The maps of the young villagers were highly detailed. The institutions and activities of the village were shown in their rightful places along the main street and the maps were crowded with outdoor activities. Friends houses were vividly drawn; in all, they gave an impression of a well-known and well-used territory.

(From K. Lynch and T. Banerjee, 1977)

Children's need for public space

Whether growing up in an inner city, suburb or housing estate, there were very few if any places where the children could go which they could manage, control or change to suit their needs. Everything is either publicly or privately owned, even if seldom used by anyone else. In the village, however, the children did have some sense of control over space. They felt connected to the farm areas which they helped in and had access to land around the village – especially if wasteland – where they could play and dream.

When city dwelling children described their ideal place, it would have trees, open spaces and be clean. And the researchers concluded that children need public places for their private activities, especially if they are restricted at home. However, the urban environment is less likely to meet these requirements than the rural.

(From K. Lynch and T. Banerjee, 1977)

1 Under four headings – inner city, suburb, estate, village – make a list of the characteristics associated with each. Can you add any more?
2 What do you feel about the claim that 'the urban environment does not meet children's requirements'? What environment do you feel is the best for children to grow up in?
3 What are likely to be the problems for children and young people growing up in a rural setting? Assuming that you could be assured of decent and secure public funding, what projects or facilities would you recommend to help deal with the needs of rural people of different ages?

Housing policy in Britain

Before 1915, Britain had no recognisable housing policy. Private landlords controlled 90 per cent of housing with few regulations. In many cases living conditions were poor and rents high. The First World War produced a situation that could no longer be ignored by the government. They had to acknowledge the generally low standard of Britain's housing stock and profiteering of private landlords. In 1915 rent controls were introduced and the concept of a 'fair rent' emerged. Initially these controls were seen as temporary. The acute housing shortage of the period meant they remained in place for a considerable time with rent controls becoming a feature of housing policy.

The most important development in housing policy was council housing. The **Housing Act 1919** authorised local authorities to build as many houses as possible. By 1939 a million homes had been erected. The policy was received positively by the general public and politicians. It was said to improve the living conditions of the population and enhanced the well-being of society. From the end of the First World War until 1979 the private rented sector declined while owner occupation and local authority provision grew. During the 1950s the government tackled the problem of inner city slums, particularly in London. They initiated a plan of slum clearance offering the tenants new homes and jobs on the outskirts of London. Towns like Slough and Bracknell grew in this way. The 1960s and 1970s focused on issues related to funding of council housing and encouraged private provision. The Housing Finance Act and Housing, Rents and Subsidies Act 1975 were important in determining the growth of both sectors.

For over 50 years Britain's housing policy had been underpinned by the provision of council housing and a central role for the local authority. Between 1914–1938, 1 million houses were built by the local authority, between 1938–1981, 4.4 million homes were provided. During the mid 1970s the Conservative Party began to attack the existing housing policy as wasteful, bureaucratic and inefficient.

The right to buy

When the Conservative Party came to power in 1979, a review of housing policy was top of the agenda. They introduced policy that scaled down the involvement of the local authority in the provision of housing. In addition they strengthened the role of the private sector. Policy was based on the belief that home ownership was preferable to renting for the following reasons:

- home ownership increases freedom of choice and a sense of personal achievement
- home ownership improves the quality of housing: people are more likely to take pride in their homes and invest in something they own
- a reduction in local authority housing would reduce public spending
- encouraging people to buy their own homes would reduce dependency on the state and enable a better use of resources for those in 'genuine need'

This policy was criticised as being a 'tenure policy' rather than a housing policy (Donnison and Maclennan, 1985). Despite the criticisms the Housing Act 1980 reduced the central government subsidy to council housing. Large numbers of local authorities ceased to be entitled to such subsidies which meant they were unable to build new properties. Before 1979, the local authority was able to determine its own housing programme without the consent of central government. The 1980 Act requires them to submit their Housing Strategy and investment programme to central government for approval. The most controversial and radical step taken by the Act was the 'right to buy' scheme. This gave the tenants of council houses the right to buy their properties at very low cost. A reduction was made on the purchase price of the house, dependent on the length of time the tenant had lived in it. The policy proved very popular with many taking up the offer. This left a shortage of housing in the local authority sector with little opportunity for them to build new houses to replace the ones sold.

The Housing Act 1988 went a step further in reducing the power of the local authorities. It introduced the concept of **Housing Associations**. A Housing Association provides privately rented accommodation. It was envisaged that they would take over the role and in some cases the properties of the local authority. It was noted that some areas of housing were unlikely to attract private interest. These so-called 'run down' estates were to be taken over by **Housing Action Trusts (HATs)**. Their role was to improve the condition of these run down areas encouraging tenants to become active in the process. In some areas tenants organised their own HATs. The Conservative party's policy achieved its aims. In Britain in 1990 the housing stock was 22.8 million dwellings: 5.1 million (22 per cent) rented from the local authority, 0.7 (3 per cent) rented from Housing Associations, 1.7 million (8 per cent) privately rented and 15.3 million (67 per cent) owner occupation. During 1997 the Labour Government indicated its commitment to provide mortgage security for home owners and to improve the condition of rented accommodation using private finance.

Homelessness and 'housing need'

It is difficult to judge the numbers of people that are homeless in Britain. At present statistical information is limited. *Social Trends* (1990) indicated a rise in the numbers of homeless involving children during the 1980s. In 1986 the number of homeless households involving children in Britain was 87 360. This increased to 96 854 by 1988 (NCH 1989 and 1990 cited by

J. Bradshaw, 1990). The shortage of council housing has resulted in more families being accommodated in 'Bed and Breakfast' accommodation.

ACTIVITY

Aziz is 4 years-old. He lives with his mother and a sister aged 2. They live in Bed and Breakfast accommodation which consists of one room with shared bathroom facilities. The room is on the third floor and there is no lift. The family only have access to cooking facilities on weekdays and then at set times. His father and two older brothers live in similar accommodation 2 miles across town. The family would prefer to be together. They lost their council house in a fire. Their temporary accommodation is some way from the boys' school and friends. The local authority has given them priority status but can not say when a property is likely to become available or where it will be . . .

1 List the difficulties faced by this family.
2 What impact might this type of arrangement have on their lives?

The Housing (Homeless Persons) Act 1977 make it a duty of the local authority to provide accommodation for certain priority groups. This includes

- families with dependent children
- the elderly
- the sick
- the disabled
- the result of an emergency (eg fire and flood)

Such groups are deemed to be in '**housing need**'. The reasons people become homeless are many and varied. These groups are not considered '**intentionally homeless**'. For some the problems are financial (perhaps mortgage and rent arrears). For some the problems are social (for example relationship breakdown or families becoming too large for their accommodation). For some it may be related to circumstance, (for example leaving care or prison). If the local authority considers a person 'intentionally' homeless they are under no obligation to house them. Young people between the ages of 16 to 19 years often fall into this category.

Housing policy assumes that young people will remain in the homes of their parents at this stage in their lives and makes little provision for them. In order to be considered for housing young people need to prove that they are unable to remain at home. Their parents must support their case. Many parents are unwilling to admit 'irretrievable breakdown'. They fear being labeled as abusers or poor parents. The Children Act 1989 does make some provision for those leaving care and the social services department are able to help find accommodation or supported lodgings. Problems arise once young people have left care.

It is at this point that the Children Act ceases to offer adequate support to young people. Shelter (1989), a housing pressure group, estimate that over 150 000 young people experience homelessness as a result of leaving home or care. In addition housing benefit is difficult for young people to obtain.

The provision of open space

The local authority has a responsibility to provide open space and play areas. New developments are required to include recreation space in their plans. Unfortunately local authorities are often faced with a dilemma. The need to provide housing versus the need for play space. Sometimes land shortage means that the space available for recreation is sometimes built on. The **National Playing Fields Association** campaigns to preserve playspace. It also develops safety standards and regulations. Many local authorities use these standards to ensure that the playspace they are responsible for is safe.

ACTIVITY

1 Undertake a survey of the housing stock in your local area. Choose about a 1 mile radius. What type of housing is available and in what quantity (detached, semi detached, bungalow, flats, residential establishments and sheltered housing)? How much open space is there in the area? Where are the shops, churches and schools? Translate your data onto a large sheet of paper in the form of a map. What does this tell you about your local area?
2 You might consider the housing mix. Are the houses close to shops and schools? These may be in the areas where most of the people live. The larger houses might be on the outskirts of the area or not there at all. Why do you think this is?

Summary

- Britain's population began to grow rapidly from about the 1740s, when death rate began to fall, and slowed from the 1880s, with the fall in birth rate.
- Britain's population is growing slowly now, but is ageing. There are now many ethnic minority groups – white, black and brown. The non-white minorities comprise about 5.5 per cent of the population
- in the last 150 years, most of Britain's population have come to live in towns and cities
- some nineteenth century writers worried that, in cities, people's relationships would be limited and shallow
- community-type relationships can still be found in the cities, just as more impersonal relationships can be found in villages
- inner-city or village children seem to find their areas less boring than do children living on housing estates or in the suburbs
- children need access to play areas which they can freely use and over which they can have some control: village children seem most likely to have such space available
- the 1919 Housing Act introduced council housing which became the fastest growing sector until Mrs Thatcher's election in 1979, when owner-occupation private renting began to dominate as it had prior to 1919
- the Conservative governments' major policy innovations were their 'right to buy' policy for council house tenants, and their introduction of Housing Associations and Housing Action Trusts

6

Gender, race and ethnicity

Key points

- children learn gender roles from their parents, peers, school and the media
- girls are more confident than formerly and are out performing boys educationally
- discrimination can spread distrust and hatred, and seriously diminish the quality of people's lives
- among the young, different ethnic groups may be influencing each other's subcultures and sense of identity
- the state's role in ensuring equality has been to develop legislation
- it is becoming common practice for those providing services to have an **equal opportunities** policy (for example schools, colleges, hospitals and charitable organisations)
- the Children Act, 1989, contains many of the United Nations articles for the rights of the child
- the rights of children in need are protected by legislation
- alongside rights go responsibilities

The language of prejudice

A **prejudice** is a 'pre-judgment': an attitude towards, or opinion of, a person or group which is not based on, or supported by, the facts. Although prejudices can be positive, our concern is with negative prejudices which, like other attitudes, are learnt through such agencies as the family, the school and the media.

If prejudices are translated into action, so that people are treated disadvantageously because others are prejudiced against them, this is **discrimination**, and is now in many cases illegal.

Sexism and racism

These are now usually defined to include any attitudes, beliefs or theories which claim or imply that one group (either sex or 'race') is superior to another, as well as any behaviours which discriminate against, and disadvantage, people on the basis of their sex or 'race'. Racism is now taken to refer more broadly to prejudice or discrimination against any ethnic group.

What is stereotyping?

Prejudice against someone on the grounds of their sex, skin colour, class, religion, sexual orientation or whatever, invariable draws on stereotypes to 'explain' or 'justify' the negative feelings. A **stereotype** is a cluster of inaccurate, over-simplified generalisations about a group of people. These stereotypes then 'justify' the prejudiced person treating the objects of their prejudice in a negative way.

Scapegoating

For some prejudiced people, particularly those feeling threatened, stereotyping is accompanied by **scapegoating**. Scapegoating occurs when someone (or some group) feels frustrated, deprived or aggrieved at their situation or aspects of it, and blames another ethnic/racial/gender/religious group for causing the problem. By displacing their aggression onto lower status groups, they relieve some of their frustration and perhaps salvage some self-respect. However, scapegoating also encourages the creation of further myths which then reinforce the original prejudice. Because it wrongly identifies the causes of their predicament, it diverts people away from possible solutions.

Why are some people more prejudiced than others?

The extent to which individuals are prejudiced and resort to stereotyping is influenced by their socialisation in the family, in schools and in other socialising agencies. Prejudice is less likely where children get to know members of other groups, and where this contact and knowledge has been positive and unthreatening.

However, psychologists also claim that some personality types are more likely to be prejudiced than others. Particularly likely to be prejudiced is the personality type known as an 'authoritarian personality'. Such a person has a strong preference for a system in which some people control while others submit and are controlled. Often, too, they have a strong perception of, and need a sense of, a 'boundary' between members of their group (the 'in-group') and the 'out-group(s)'. They also have strong beliefs about the differences – of superiority and inferiority – between the groups.

Sex and gender

As feminists and others have drawn to our attention, both in and out of the home the roles most males and females play are still significantly different. Why that should be is controversial. One explanation which many people give is that that is how nature intended it. Men and women are built differently. Because women can have children and men can't, so women are natural mothers and homemakers, and men are naturally best equipped to deal with the harsher, more competitive world outside the home. It is their different biology which explains their different behaviours. It is widely believed, too, that nature dictates not just different roles but different psychological characteristics, such as a supposed female tendency towards dependence and lending support.

Although it may well be that biology – 'nature' – does encourage some tendencies more in one sex than the other, such as aggression in males, 'all the areas in which some biologically formed predisposition has been suggested are subject to a cultural input which *can override* the biological capacity' (Oakley, 1978). Margaret Mead's famous 1935 study of three tribes living close to each other on the island of New Guinea (see Chapter 1) has probably been quoted most frequently as evidence that males and females can be very different in different societies, and therefore that learning, rather than biology, must play the most important role (see Chapter 1).

In the Arapesh tribe both sexes acted in a way that would seem feminine to many in our society. Both were gentle, passive and unaggressive, and shared the upbringing of their children equally. Among the Mundugamor tribe, both males and females acted in ways many of us would consider masculine. Males and females were equally aggressive, with lovemaking being like a 'battle', with both sexes returning bruised and torn. Both sexes detested both childbirth and childrearing. In the third tribe, the Tchambuli, gender roles were different, the reverse of our own. It was the women who were dominant and aggressive – the practical, managing ones, who made the sexual advances and conducted the trade on which the society depended. And the men? They tended to sit around gossiping and beautifying themselves!

It is because of this and other evidence that sociologists distinguish between two words which many people now (wrongly) use interchangably: **sex** and **gender**. To put simply, sex refers to biological and physiological differences which are used to distinguish between males and females. Gender, however, refers to a society's ideas of what it thinks are the 'appropriate' characteristics – in temperament and behaviour – of males and females. In other words, gender refers to how members of a particular society think males and females should be and should behave: what members of that society mean by 'masculinity' and 'femininity'. Most importantly, in different parts of the world or at different points in time, societies can have very different notions of what they believe is 'naturally' masculine or feminine.

ACTIVITY

A Victorian view

Nature has avoided encouraging a dangerous rivalry between the sexes by giving them different talents. The man, more robust by nature, is fitted for severe labour; the woman, more delicate, is fitted for inactive occupations, and particularly for nursing children. The man, bold and vigorous, is qualified for being a protector; the woman, delicate and timid, requires protection. The man, as a protector and having solid judgment, is directed by nature to govern; the woman, conscious of inferiority, is disposed to obey. And women have more imagination and sensitivity than men.

These are not the only particulars that distinguish the sexes. With respect to the ultimate end of love, it is the privilege of the male, as superior and protector, to make a choice; the female preferred has no privilege but to consent or refuse. So it is among all nations the practice of men to court and for women to be courted: and were the most beautiful woman on earth to invert this practice, she would lose the esteem of the man whom she addressed, however by her external grace she might excite his desire.

(From the entry on 'Love', *Encylopaedia Britannica*, published 1808–1810)

1 Make a list, under the headings 'Male' and 'Female' of some of the qualities or characteristics associated with the sexes in this early 1800s view. (Don't include suggested physiological differences.)
2 You'll see that the author explained these differences in terms of 'nature'. Which, if any, of these alleged differences would *you* explain in terms of 'nature'?
3 Aside from physiological differences, do you believe there are any 'natural' differences in terms of character or personality qualities or behavioural characteristics between the sexes? If so, can you give some examples?

Learning gender roles

Ideas about what is appropriate for males and females – how to feel, what to aim for, how to behave – change over time. As the recent educational under-achievement of boys and the growing educational success of girls suggests, there have been some important changes in the last few decades in gender expectations and behaviours.

On the other hand, the evidence that males and females are still unequal in taking responsibility for the home and children – despite many more women working – illustrates how in some ways gender roles have resisted change.

1 The role of parents

As in other areas of the child's development, the child's early home and social environment help shape their view of the sexes. By the age of 2 to 3, children have learnt their sex because parents and others constantly tell them in phrases like, 'There's a good boy'. According to social psychologist R.D. Crowther, by 5 years or less, children are not only aware of distinctions between male and female roles, but they are also aware that society places a higher value on men and male roles than on women and women's roles. For many children, these impressions and conclusions develop before full-time schooling. However, even when parents try consciously to avoid passing on sex-stereotypical attitudes and behaviour, young children pick up other messages – as they are pushed down the street, sit in the launderette, or look over the bank counter – from what they observe of who does what and how the sexes interrelate.

Parents tend to have stereotyped ideas of boys and girls – how they should feel, act, look – and they begin to communicate those ideas from very early on, though not necessarily consciously. For instance, parents are more likely to engage little boys in roughish physical contact – rough and tumble, tossing and catching them, and sports. On the other hand, parents are more likely to read or tell stories to little girls. They are also likely to make more of a fuss over their daughters' appearance than their sons'.

Boys tend to find that they can get attention by demanding it. However, when girls try attention-grabbing techniques – like screaming, whining or behaving aggressively – they are more likely to get ignored. They find they are more successful in getting attention when they talk, gently touch, or use gestures.

The toys children are given are often chosen because of their sex. A telephone, rocking horse, even teddy bear, could be given to either. But girls would seldom be presented with a toy tractor, or boys with a Barbie doll. However, as Michelle Stanworth points out, in some cases research has shown that such gender-stereotyped gifts are often bought because the *child* (sometimes a very young, pre-school child) has asked for it.

There is also evidence that boys and girls are expected to make a different contribution to jobs around the house. In research conducted in the 1960s, John and Elizabeth Newson found that 11 year-old girls were more likely to be given indoor housework jobs, and boys more likely to do outdoor jobs. This early indoor-outdoor split was felt to be very significant. 'Boys are pointed out towards the world and taught (or allowed to develop) the skills needed there.' Girls spent less time out of the home and were more strictly supervised.

ACTIVITY

A happy event!

Doctor: 'It's a little boy! Say hello to mummy.'
Mother (holding baby): 'Oh, you little bugger!'
Midwife: 'It's a little girl!
Mother: She's not very pretty, is she?'

(from A. Oakley, 1978)

Treating boys and girls differently

Society puts half its children into short skirts and warns them not to move in ways that reveal their panties. It puts the other half into jeans and overalls and encourages them to climb trees, play football, and participate in other vigorous outdoor games. Later, during adolescence, the children who have been wearing trousers are urged to eat like growing boys, while the children in skirts are warned to watch their weight and not get fat. And the half in jeans runs around in sneakers or boots, while the half in skirts totters about on spike heels.

(From R. Hubbard, 1990)

1 The first extract is from research done in the late 1970s. Why those responses? Might women give the same responses today?
2 In the second extract what effects might the various 'child-rearing practices' described have on how boys and girls develop: a) psychologically, as a person; b) physically?

Masculine toys	Either sex	Feminine toys
Tractor	Teddy bear	Doll's pram
	Telephone	

3 Complete the chart above. When you have finished, what different skills or qualities do you think these different boys' and girls' toys may encourage?
4 Are the Newsons' 1960s' findings – of different tasks for boys and girls, different 'exposure' to outdoors, and different levels of supervision – still true today? Compare experiences.

PARENTS AS ROLE-MODELS

In addition to the ways in which parents treat boys and girls differently, however, children are picking up all sorts of clues about how husbands and wives, and other adult males and females, treat each other.

ACTIVITY

Are you really listening?

A number of studies of male-female conversations have found that men and women in our culture use distinctive styles of speech and also tend to play different roles when talking with one another. In a study of married couples, Boston University sociologist, Charles Derber, found that men interrupt more frequently and shift conversations to their preferred topics, while the wives are more apt to respond supportively, give more active encouragement to their husband's talk about himself, and listen better.

Women also express their thoughts more hesitantly and tentatively in conversation with men, perhaps having internalised male assumptions that what they have to say isn't very interesting or intellectually rigorous. So if the wife is direct and assertive she may be punished as 'unfeminine', but if she adopts the traditional style and role she may be dismissed as not to be taken seriously, dim or frivolous.

(From A. Kohn 'Girl talk, guy talk' *Psychology Today*, 1988)

From your impressions, do adults you know well share the conversational behaviour patterns just described? Try to test your impressions. Do some observational research on how males and females converse – both adults and young people. Note how long each talk for, who interrupts whom and whether the females seem confident of getting, and holding onto, male attention in conversation.

2 *The role of the peer group*

Although the family plays a crucial role in socialising children into gender roles, the peer group seems to have become increasingly important. Here is one not-very-flattering view of the role of the peer group for girls.

ACTIVITY

The heavy pressures to conform

What happens to the girls? By 16, it's as if someone has knocked them on the head. Their apparent maturity has been bought at the high cost of absolute conformity. Among groups of girls of this age, any oddness, any irregularity of dress, opinion, enthusiasm or behaviour casts you out of the group. The boys may have their own conventions, but they allow a far wider range of personality to be acceptable within the group.

The girls are so busy pretending to be little women that they haven't time for anything else. At 16 they can pass as adult, while boys are still boys. Because they can get themselves older boyfriends and lift themselves up into an adult world, they are prepared to sacrifice almost all of themselves in the effort. They can mimic the outward signs of adulthood more successfully. Their lives are entirely given over to boys: going to discos to meet boys, pop music to fantasise about boys, make-up and hair styles to catch boys, preferably older boys. Interests outside these narrow fields are dangerous, might expose them to ridicule, or may link them perilously with school and childhood. It isn't until later when they are older and secure in adulthood, that they can afford to allow more of their own individual personalities to grow, but by then, for many, it may be too late.

(From P. Toynbee *The Guardian*, 1978)

To what extent do you agree or disagree with Polly Toynbee's 1978 conclusion that teenage girls, more than boys, are pressurised to practice a high degree of conformity, and are so busy trying to be 'little female adults' that they fail to develop their own individuality and potential? Give as many reasons as you can to support your view.

3 *The role of the school*

Although girls have been outperforming boys academically at age 11 for many years, this is now happening at almost all educational levels (see Chapter 8). But as this is a relatively recent phenomenon, sociological explanations of underachievement by sex have, until recently, been directed at explaining the underachievement of girls at secondary and higher educational levels. The concern now is with widespread male underachievement.

Girls at school have traditionally been directed, with varying degrees of subtlety, towards subjects considered appropriate to their gender. So domestic science, childcare, cookery, secretarial courses, community care, as well as more 'academic' subjects such as human biology, social sciences, English and foreign languages were, until recently, seen as 'girls' subjects'. Maths, natural sciences, carpentry, metalwork, technical drawing were widely assumed to be 'inappropriate', and few girls could expect to compete.

It is still the case that, in many of these subjects – particularly in subjects such as childcare, community care and secretarial studies – very few boys can be found. However, people have become increasingly aware of the implicit sexism in such assumptions and the wastage it involves – both to individuals and the nation. Teachers have made conscious attempts to reverse this pattern. Policies and practices were devised and introduced to try to make the sciences more 'female-friendly' and to draw boys into supposedly 'female' subjects. Although many girls currently in secondary education still have a 'block' about maths especially, others are showing that they can equal, and in many cases surpass, the achievements of boys. Time will tell how stubborn these longstanding gender-related prejudices, fears and assumptions will prove to be.

4 The role of the media

The mass media are those forms of communication which get to a wide audience. So they include books, radio and TV, video and film, magazines and advertisements. These are all agencies of socialisation – they all play a part in forming opinions, attitudes, beliefs and knowledge. After the family, at least some of these mass media are likely to be the first agencies of socialisation with which children come into contact. Many children, from babyhood onward, are spending a substantial amount of their time watching TV and videos. So TV may be an important influence on children before they ever start nursery or begin to meet their peer group.

One of the long-established media, children's books, has often been analysed to see what messages about gender it appears to be sending out.

Children's books

In 1974 Glenys Lobban did what became a very famous study of children's books in which she analysed the sex and roles of the characters. Her general conclusion confirmed that the children's books in her study largely transmitted stereotyped role images of males and females.

In the following activity, students may like to carry out their own research to find out how children's books have changed. What images of males and females do modern children's books project? We can repeat some of Lobban's questions and methods.

ACTIVITY

Use at least three pre-school children's books per student. These should have been published within the last 10 years. Use copies of the table below to analyse the three books. If you are working in a group, you may like to collate your findings.

Table 6.1 The number of characters, their roles, and the heroes, by sex

	Male	Female	Either/unclear
Total no. of (human & non-human) characters Total no. of roles Total no. of heroes (i.e. 'good' main character)			

1 Having drawn up your first table, headed like Table 6.1 above analyse the books according to the criteria in the table. For example, the 'Total number of characters' should refer to all the books, and numbers should be written in according to their sex. At this stage include all characters, whether human or non-human (for example hobby horse, teddy bear).
2 Next, eliminate all the non-adult human male and female characters (for example, children, animals, fantasy characters) from your calculation and put your findings into a second table, headed like the one below.

Table 6.2 The number and roles of adult characters, by sex

	Adult male	Adult female
Total no. of characters Total no. of roles		

3 Try now to divide the roles of the adults into those which are mainly work-related, family-related and leisure-related, again making sure that you allocate them according to sex. Transfer your findings onto a third table, headed as Table 6.3 below.

Table 6.3 Sex roles: work, family or leisure related?

	Male No. %	Female No. %
Work Family Leisure		

4 Take from Table 6.3 the figures showing the total number of male and female adults working. Add to that the total number of jobs males and females are shown working in. Insert your findings onto a copy of Table 6.4.

Table 6.4 People shown working, by sex

	Male	**Female**
Total no. of characters shown working Total number of jobs		

5 Look at the sort of jobs males and females are depicted in. Try to divide them according to whether they are 'traditional' for that sex or 'untraditional'. Represent your findings on a copy of Table 6.5 below. When Glenys Lobban did her study of the sex role content of children's books in 1974 she concluded that 'the children's reading schemes rigidly divide the sphere of people's activity into two compartments, masculine and feminine'. She went on to say that 'the girl's world was almost entirely oriented around domestic activity and childcare. The boy's world was orientated outside the home.'

Table 6.5

	Male	**Female**
No. of traditional job roles No. of untraditional job roles		

(From L. Best, *Sociology Review*, February 1993)

6 From your research, how would you describe the presentation of males and females depicted in the children's books you have analysed? Consider their importance, characteristics, roles, and so on. Have there been significant changes since 1974?

MAGAZINES FOR FEMALES

One of the themes which runs through analyses of magazines for females, both for girls and for women, is that they frequently function as self-improvement manuals. From an early age, females seem to be getting messages that they must strive to improve: their appearance, their allure for males, their housekeeping and cookery skills, their body odour, their home decor, their sexual enjoyment, their hair texture, their fashion sense. Though there are innumerable tips and advice on how to achieve these improvements, the constant repetition of the message of the need to improve can make discomforting reading.

MAGAZINES FOR TEENAGE GIRLS

According to a study conducted by Elizabeth Davies of University College, London in the 1980s, there seems to be a link between reading some teenage girls' magazines and feeling dissatisfied with your body. She found that the more 12 year-old girls read weekly magazines – specifically, *Blue Jeans*, *Jackie*, *Oh Boy* and *My Guy* – the more they felt they were overweight, and wanted to diet.

One quote taken from *Blue Jeans* (average readership, 13 or 14 years old) helps to illustrate why.

> 'Don't forget to keep a close eye on your diet too – wintry weather doesn't mean you have to reach for the frying pan or stuff yourself with stodgy stews. There's no truth in the myth that only hot foods can keep you warm – yoghourts and crispbreads are just as good for you now as they were in the summer months.'

Davies did not expect quite such overt pressure to be slim in teenage magazines. 'It was a shock to find six of the beauty pages in *Blue Jeans* mentioning diet or exercise as a means of reducing "flab",' she said. 'Obviously, girls this age have not finished developing physically and could only be made to feel miserable about their puppy fat.'

ADULTS' MAGAZINES

Although there seems to be a wide gulf between women's magazines such as *Woman's Own* and *Cosmopolitan*, analyses of the articles, advertisements and advice columns have suggested many similarities. Relationships (especially with men), appearance, beauty, health and style tend to run throughout, and in all these areas the emphasis is upon improvement.

Most men's magazines, on the other hand, represent special interest groups: anglers, computer buffs, hi-fi enthusiasts, and men who like looking at mainly naked women. Here, masculinity is defined in terms of the pursuit of such interests. A recent trend in less specialised men's magazines is to encourage expression of maleness through 'laddish' behaviour, for example through drinking alcohol and sexual adventure. Interpersonal relationships play little part in the coverage of sex!

Yet, though femininity is still widely defined in women's magazines by appearance and relationships with men, some magazines such as *Cosmopolitan* seem to be responding to the 'laddish' approach to sex with a similar message.

ACTIVITY

From the cover of *Mizz*

'10 tricks to make him fall for you'
'Find your perfect summer love'
'Steve from Boyzone'
'Male model poster special'
'Free gift – the Body Shop Dewberry Eau de Toilette'

(*Mizz*, 1996)

Women's magazines

When women's magazines began, their focus was domestic. They provided step-by-step instruction in how to achieve perfect womanhood, in the appropriate roles of wife and mother. This included finding and keeping your man.

We're still trying to be perfect. Magazines like *Woman*, *Woman's Own*, and *Eva*, currently selling around half a million copies an issue, portray a world where women soldier on in a hell of adversity, conjuring up meals 'to tempt the family', coping with a mass of ailments, and finding release in first-person sob-stories by fellow readers so unfortunate that anyone would feel good in comparison.

When *Cosmopolitan* editor, Mandi Norwood, took over in 1995 she said that the magazine would be 'more aggressive, cutting-edge, gutsy, ballsy.' And when *Cosmo* celebrated its 25th year, it did so with headlines such as 'Plastic surgery for sexual pleasure' and 'Manhunt! Where the sharp, smart, sexiest men are – and how to take one alive!'.

However, if you flick through any mid- to upper-bracket women's magazine, like *Cosmo*, in many ways they are not so different from *Woman* and *Woman's Own*. Though more assertive and 'in your face', you once again enter a world of narcissistic, self-obsessed trivia – a menu of relationships, fashion, beauty, recipes, home improvement, and titillating (or tragic) readers' stories. They too are self-help manuals, just a little glossier.

(from G. Brown, *Independent on Sunday*, 1997)

1 Look at a number of magazines aimed at girls and analyse the interests girls are assumed to have. Is there an unhealthy concern with appearance or diet?
2 What are the characteristic and qualities of the girls represented here favourably? Are there any qualities, characteristics or interests which are either a) ignored or overlooked? or b) devalued or ridiculed?
3 Collect a range of women's (and men's?) magazines and consider a) what, if any, common themes and concerns are there? b) if men's magazines such as *Esquire* can be said to treat sex like a project to be pursued, is the treatment of sex in women's magazines similar or different? Explain why.

Gender expectations 20 years on

This section looks briefly at some of the ways in which girls' attitudes and aspirations seem to have changed or stayed much the same in the last 20 or so years.

In 1972, Sue Sharpe conducted a survey of 249 mainly working-class girls from the fourth form (Year 10) of four schools in Ealing in London. In 1991, she tried to replicate that earlier research. Ethnic minority girls were involved in both surveys.

One of the most important social changes since the earlier research has been the *change in employment prospects*, with first the loss of jobs in manufacturing industries and, more recently, the loss of jobs in many service industries such as banking. A second important change has been the *substantial increase in divorce and single-parenthood*. A third has been the relative success of campaigns to promote *attitudes favourable to sexual equality*.

JOB CHOICES

Like their predecessors in 1972, the large majority of girls wanted to work in jobs which fell into the general realm of 'woman's work'. Working with animals, air hostess, beautician and radiographer remain popular careers. However, office work, which had been the aim of 40% in 1972, had plummeted in popularity. Whereas office work was once seen as 'a nice job for a girl', who wanted a 'clean, respectable' job before marriage and child-rearing, Sharpe claims that this criterion has become old-fashioned and that girls want to avoid what is now seen as boring. Shop assistant and hairdressing jobs were also less popular. However, working with children was even more popular in the 1990s.

Other jobs which have increased in popularity, such as photography, psychology, psychotherapy, conservation, graphic design, theatre and media studies, partly reflect changes in school curricula. Though some girls wanted to become car mechanics, engineers or firefighters, that it was only a few illustrates the continuing pull of 'female' work.

Education

Girls' awareness of limited employment opportunities has meant that they are aware that they should stay in education for as long as possible to gain qualifications to improve employment chances. Whatever their feelings about being in school, only a minority now wanted to leave school at the earliest possible age of 16 years.

Changes in attitude

In general, the 1990s girls were more confident, more assertive, and more committed to sexual equality in education and employment. However, they were less optimistic about marriage. The real possibility of having to support themselves if their marriage or partnership broke down – plus their general wish not to be dependent upon or dominated by men – helped account for their almost unanimous agreement on the importance of a job or career. They were even more emphatic than the girls of 1972 that they preferred to be a girl than a boy. However, few identified themselves as feminists, which, for many, was still seen (over-simply) as rejecting men.

'Race' and ethnic group

Like 'gender' the notion of 'race' is also socially constructed. It too is an attempt, by members of a society, to impose a framework upon reality and to try to make sense of complexity. The dominant view of Western scientists of the late nineteenth century was that humanity had evolved into three or four main racial types, with many peoples somewhere between them. The three main types were represented by the Caucasians of Europe, the Mongolians of Asia and the Ethiopians of Africa, with the Caucasians being sub-divided into fair and dark varieties. These three main types were supposedly distinguished in terms of skin colour, hair texture, skull shape, but also, they believed, in terms of their natural temperament. Though they believed that they were observing and classifying objectively, we can see how Victorian scientists unconsciously incorporated many of the assumptions of their time. Inevitably, they were influenced by their experience of belonging to a great empire containing whites, blacks, browns and yellows, but with the whites overwhelmingly dominant.

Many social scientists today are very reluctant to use the term 'race'. This is partly because of these historical associations between the term 'race', supposedly a physical category, and ideas of moral and other superiority. It was such assumptions of racial superiority which, in a horrifyingly extreme form, were used to justify the large-scale murder of Jews in the Second World War.

Because many members of ethnic groups are, in broad terms, both culturally and physically different from other members of society, the term is still commonly used. However, 'races' are not distinct groups. People are different and range along a continuum, with as much variety (for instance, in skin colour) within a 'race' as between 'races'. Insofar as there remain broad physical similarities among groups, these is likely to reflect lack of sexual contact with other groups over long periods of time. As sexual contact between 'racial' groups increases, so too do the variations. However, although sociologists continue to use 'race' as a shorthand term to refer to groups sharing superficial similarities such as skin colour or hair type, they nowadays generally find it more useful to distinguish between ethnic groups, which are identified by their culture, rather than between races, which are only very loosely distinguishable on the basis of alleged physical characteristics.

ACTIVITY

A Victorian view

Table of the chief characteristics of the three fundamental human types

	Caucasian (European) (Type 1 = pale) (Type 2 = dark)	**Ethiopian (African)**	**Mongolian (Asian)**
Colour & character of skin	Whitish: 1 Florid or ruddy; 2 dusky or swarthy, both merging in some places into light olive or brown.	Blackish, sometimes almost sooty black; velvety and cool to the touch, emitting a distinct odour.	Yellowish, and almost every shade of brown. Rough in texture, often with a washed out look.
Hair & beard	1 Flaxen, light brown or red, long, wavy and silky; 2 black or dark brown, rather straight, sometimes curly. Both oval in section.	Jet black, frizzy or woolly, rather short. Sometimes said to grow in separate tufts, scant or no beard. Flat in section.	Dull, black coarse, lank, lustreless, Round in section. Beard scant or absent.
Temperament	Highly imaginative, active & enterprising; hence both speculative & practical. 1 Somewhat solid, serious & persevering; 2 fiery, impulsive but inconstant. Science, art and literature highly developed in both.	Sensuous, unintellectual, cheerful, even boisterous, but fitful, passing suddenly from comedy to tragedy. At once affectionate & cruel. Science, art & literature undeveloped.	Sluggish, gloomy, uncommunicative, passive, little initiative. But great power of endurance, sometimes passionate outbursts. Science slightly developed, art & literature moderately.

(From the entry on 'Ethnology', *Chambers's Encyclopaedia*, 1889)

A modern definition of 'race'

Race (noun); a scientifically discredited term previously used to describe supposedly biologically distinct groups of people who were alleged to have characteristics of an unalterable nature. Despite its discredited nature, the idea still exerts a powerful influence in everyday language and ideology. Many writers will not use the term except in inverted commas.

(From D. and J. Jary, *Collins Dictionary of Sociology*, 1991)

1 Pick out any of the characteristics mentioned in the table above which you think are biased, unscientific, which look like negative stereotypes. How do you interpret these ideas? Are there any patterns?
2 Try to think of evidence which seems to contradict these late nineteenth century beliefs.
3 How would you explain how people who regarded themselves as scientists could subscribe to these ideas?
4 Why, in the extract are many writers now unwilling to use the term 'race'? What do you think about its continued use?

Types of racism

Just as there is no one agreed definition of the word 'racism', so there is no one explanation for it. Some limit the term racism to refer to 'a belief that some races are superior'. Mark Halstead gives a broader definition. He suggests that the term 'racism' should be used to describe any belief or action which results in racial injustice. However, he distinguishes between different types of racism, each of which might have different explanations.

EMOTIONAL RACISM

This develops from the mix of three main factors:

- people's tendency to feel fear, anxiety, insecurity, suspicion or other threatening emotions when in the presence of people who are perceived as unfamiliar, strange or foreign
- people's psychological predispositions to want to reject, dominate, belittle, snub, ridicule, injure or hurt others (especially those perceptively 'different')
- people's ignorance about 'racial' minorities

This combination makes people particularly susceptible to myths, stereotypes and other fear-arousing ideas.

This form of racial prejudice is emotionally charged and not rational. It is therefore very difficult to change by argument or presenting facts. People who are racially prejudiced can hold inconsistent views. At different times the same person might argue the contradictory claims that 'they're all over here taking our jobs' and that 'they're all over here to live on the dole'.

IDEOLOGICAL RACISM

This uses a set of bogus religious or scientific beliefs to claim, justify or defend a group's superior position. Some, for instance, turn to pseudo-scientific theories of evolution to 'prove' the superiority of their own group.

CULTURAL RACISM

(Or perhaps, better, 'ethnicism'?) A prejudice against people on the grounds of their alleged cultural characteristics rather than their physical ones. People are critical of the alleged behaviours, 'dirty habits', and so on, of ethnic groups.

However, this variant assumes minority groups can change their behaviour, and should do, to assimilate into the 'host' community. Otherwise, they fear that cultural diversity will lead to serious social division. Diversity is perceived as a threat not as a richness.

INSTITUTIONAL RACISM

This is found in organisations like schools, the police, businesses, government agencies. These organisations do not intend to be racist but in reality often are. This is due to the failure to change satisfactorily some of the long-established practices used in the organisation, which, intended or not, disadvantage or work against the interests of minorities. For example, a government housing department may fail to take sufficient account of the special housing needs of a minority group for whom the extended family is very important.

COLOUR-BLIND RACISM

This is a belief that it is wrong to recognise, or worse, draw attention to ethnic and racial differences and wrong to treat different groups differently. This view is based on a well-intentioned wish to create a harmonious, multi-cultural society and on a fear that drawing attention to differences, or treating groups differently, could endanger equality.

However, the Swann Report of 1985 claimed that such intentional 'colour-blindness' is 'potentially just as negative as a straightforward rejection of people with a different skin colour, since both types of attitude deny the validity of an important aspect of a person's identity' (DES, 1985).

The practice of discrimination

For members of ethnic minority groups, discrimination can affect every area of their lives. Discriminatory behaviour is very varied. Violent, and frightening, discrimination from hostile whites can range from abusive harassment (being subjected to spitting, verbal abuse, racist graffiti, the dumping of rubbish, excrement through the letterbox), to beating, stabbing, arson and murder. The victims of racial discrimination can be of either sex, of any age, and of any ethnic group.

In some British cities, research shows, the fear of violence from whites limits the lives of many black and Asian people on a daily basis. Children may not be allowed out to play and must be escorted to and from school. Adults may have to take taxis to go to work or the shops.

At schools, black and Asian children suffer racially motivated bullying. In one study quoted by the Commission for Racial Equality, for instance, 79 per cent of black Caribbean boys and 70 per cent of Asian boys and girls said they had been picked on at school. The climate of fear – even terror – in which some members of ethnic minority groups live, may have some less obvious consequences. It may, for instance, help explain why there are so many black children in schools for those with 'emotional and behavioural difficulties', and why black women suffer high rates of anxiety and depression.

Non-violent discrimination

On the other hand, a lot of the discrimination which occurs is much more subtle and less easy to pin point, sometimes both for the victim and the discriminator. For instance, discrimination occurs in job opportunities, housing applications, admission to places of entertainment, and so on. Here we focus briefly on unemployment and housing.

UNEMPLOYMENT AND HOUSING

In general, blacks and Asians have significantly higher rates of unemployment than whites. This is so even when qualifications are the same. Male unemployment is particularly high compared to whites among Pakistani, Bangladeshi, African and Afro-Caribbean groups. This is particularly true among the young, who are the hardest hit.

Within the Asian communities, people from an Indian background have lower unemployment rates than Pakistanis and Bangladeshis. Yet, although

Indian employment levels are lower than those of whites, of Indians in employment over 40 per cent are in professional and managerial positions compared to 35 per cent of whites.

Afro-Caribbean groups have among the highest unemployment rates of minorities and, if employed, are more likely to work in low paid jobs, especially in the state sector, and in jobs which involve long and anti-social hours. Yet, a 1991 survey of 15 000 blacks under 35 years old found that 30 per cent had a degree or equivalent and a quarter had professional or vocational qualifications.

Black people are also likely to live in poorer housing and in 'less desirable' areas than whites. Their homes are likely to be older and more crowded. This is true for black home owners, as well as black private tenants or council tenants. Research suggests that this is largely as a result of discrimination in one form or another.

ACTIVITY

Unemployment by race

YOUNG AND JOBLESS

People from ethnic minority groups are twice as likely to be unemployed as white people, whatever their qualifications. Young people are particularly hard hit. The chart shows the average unemployment rates for 16-24 year olds between 1987 and 1989.

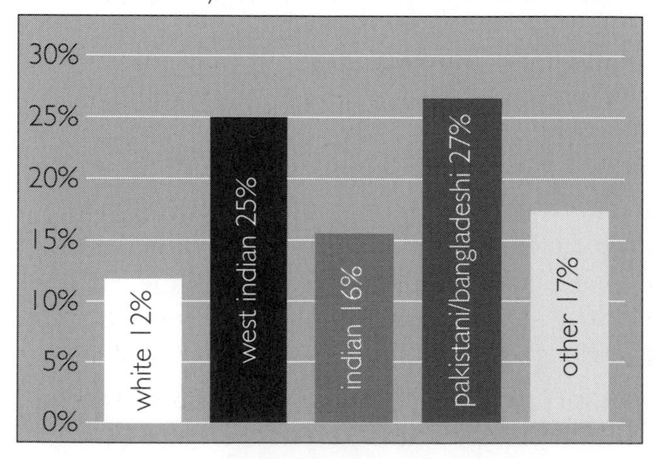

Providing evidence of discrimination

In 1988, two journalists – one black, Geoff Small, one white, Tim Marshall – decided to investigate the extent of illegal racial discrimination in housing, employment and in places of entertainment such as night clubs. They chose Bristol as the site of their study because its black population, at 4 per cent, was the British average. Their method of investigation was for the black journalist to present himself first – applying for a job, trying to rent a flat, enter a disco – and then the white journalist, with an apparently similar background and qualifications, would do the same shortly thereafter. Both filmed their experiences using a hidden camera.

They found the following incidence of discrimination:

- bed-and-breakfast proprietors – 5 out of 15
- renters of accommodation – 3 out of 16
- employers – 4 out of 10
- night-clubs – 2 out of 8

So, on the positive side, in almost every category, two-thirds or more people had not discriminated. On the negative, however, about a quarter of those studied *had* illegally discriminated against the black man.

1 Can you think of any other factors, in addition to discrimination, to explain the figures in the chart?
2 Given the experience of Geoff Small and Tim Marshall, what steps if any should the state, or organisations or individuals, take to change things?

Some consequences of discrimination

Violent discrimination spreads fear, hatred and distrust and can ruin people's lives. Non-violent discrimination also diminishes the quality of people's lives: the poorer accommodation, the less attractive neighbourhood, the inferior schooling, the higher unemployment, and so on. It can erode people's self-confidence and self-respect, and poison their relationships with members of other groups.

On a personal level, as Geoff Small pointed out, their research brought home one worrying realisation: that, in some situations, a member of an ethnic minority may never really be sure whether they are being treated fairly or whether they are being discriminated against.

'As the filming progressed,' he wrote, 'it struck me more and more that there was no real way of knowing how to interpret people's behaviour. As we went after flats . . . some of the people who were nicest to my face, who went out of their way to be helpful, were the ones who were discriminating' (G. Small, *The Listener*, 1988). That sort of uncertainty can ultimately destroy people's self-confidence and sense of self-worth. It can also make it much more difficult for members of different ethnic groups to trust each other.

The growing variety of ethnicities

Today, a majority of Britain's ethnic minorities have been born and raised in Britain. At least since they began school, many in these younger generations have had contact with other minorities as well as with whites. To a varying extent, they have been exposed to some of the cultural characteristics which the ethnic majority and minorities bring with them – the religions, the linguistic codes, the musical and dress styles, the bearing and demeanour, and the attitudes. According to various research, many of the young of all groups – including whites – are developing their own sense of ethnic identity. These identities are less straightforwardly 'traditional' than those of their elders. They are, to an extent, chosen and more of a mix than previously: a mix of some of the different ethnic identities which they see around them, or see portrayed in the media.

In the first extract in the following activity, Mac an Ghaill is talking to the Warriors, a tough group of nine students of Indian and Pakistani origins, born in Britain, who were actively anti-school, and anti-authority. They were responding to their experience of racism in the community and what they perceived as the stereotyped and racist expectations of white teachers and authority figures generally.

The second extract is from a 1995 study of young Punjabis in Southall, West London by Marie Gillespie. She found that, while there was still a strong sense of commitment to their traditional culture, many of the younger generation had partly assimilated other ethnic traditions.

ACTIVITY

The Warriors

Raj: 'When the West Indians came down to England they had much more freedom than the Indians . . . So they rebelled first, before the Indians. But now the Indians are rebelling. So we become rude boys (a West Indian

grouping) and things. We know there en't nothing for us here.'
Ashwin: 'Most of us are rude boys.'
MM (interviewer): 'Why rude boys?'
Ashwin: 'I think the main way, the main way why we call ourselves rude boys is 'coz we hate authority and school and the police. We like the music and the people.'

Asian boys at Kilby School have also identified with various white subcultural forms.

Sokhjinder: There are some heavy metal (Asians), just a few you know, that I've seen in Kilby. I've seen Teds, Elvis followers, rockers, seen a few punks . . . and there's Mods. They wear the odd earring and do their own hair.

(From M. Mac an Ghaill, 1988)

Young Punjabis from West London

Although the young Punjabis in Gillespie's study are still strongly committed to Punjabi culture and tradition, which includes arranged marriage, there were signs of change. Though about half wanted to marry within their group, 58% thought that 'going out with a boy or girl is normal' and 75% thought that 'people should be free to marry whom they liked'. However, because family and community supervision is quite strict, some visit a MacDonalds in the neighbouring borough, where they can meet members of the opposite sex. Here, they can escape the close supervision of relatives and neighbours and enjoy a welcome change in diet. Television soaps are popular, especially *Neighbours*, because they revolve around family life and gossip, and provide a way of discussing their own problems and relationships.

Especially among the Punjabi boys, Afro-Caribbean styles of music and dress enjoy high status. Black slang, expressions and gestures are sometimes copied and incorporated into their street style.

1 There are now a number of films which show how the variety of ethnic influences is contributing to the construction of young people's identities. As well as films such as 'The Buddha of Suburbia', 'Bhaji on the Beach' and 'My Beautiful Launderette', there are also widely-admired performers like Bob Marley and Apache Indian.
List some of the ethnic influences, in food, clothing, music, speech, and so on, which have influenced you and your tastes or styles, or which you see in others.
2 Do you think young people of different ethnic groups are now more or less prejudiced against others? What sort of evidence are you using?

Racism and socialisation: the early undermining of positive self-image

The age at which children begin to become aware of differences between different ethnic groups, and at which they may begin to reproduce positive or negative attitudes to different groups, has been researched in different countries over many years.

One of the most common methods of trying to investigate children's awareness of racial differences has involved using pictures or dolls depicting different ethnic groups. From that sort of research, it seems that some 25 per cent of 3 year-olds can correctly identify black or white dolls when asked. It seems that already by that age many who are able to distinguish between white and black may also have picked up an awareness of different attitudes to different groups.

For instance, from research dating back to the 1960s and 1970s, there is some evidence that, in the white-dominated, white-prestigious USA, both white and black 3 year-olds preferred playing with the white doll. It was also found that young white children were better able to identify their colour than black children of the same age, many of whom misidentified themselves as white. This higher evaluation of 'whiteness' seems to show that even children as young as three can pick up and reflect the dominant attitude in their environment towards an ethnic minority.

ACTIVITY

1 In what ways should children of different ethnic backgrounds be treated differently and in what ways should they not? For instance, should rules about school uniforms allow variations for ethnic differences? What is acceptable in morning assemblies where different religious groups are in the school? Should parents have the right to have the sexes segregated in class, or in sports or PE?
2 What experiences would help to prevent racism developing in young children? What can nurseries or primary schools do?
3 What would you do if you worked in an area where there was almost no ethnic minority group?
4 How would you cope with a nursery parent who didn't want their child to join in certain activities due to their cultural tradition?

Promoting equality through the state

The issue of **inequality** has always been a problem for social policy. In most countries of the world, people are paid differently, depending on the job they do. Some jobs have a higher status than others and are more highly paid (for example a doctor), others have low status and are low paid (for example a hospital porter). This often leads to inequality because the people in the groups with higher pay can afford more than those in the groups with lower pay. In addition, those in the higher status groups have more influence about how things should be organised than those with low status. In a country like Britain this type of inequality is accepted as 'normal'. Many politicians and academics would argue that it is impossible to make everybody equal because of the differences caused by status and pay. Others argue that it would be possible if society was willing to redistribute wealth more evenly and given equal status to all occupations.

China and the ex- USSR attempted to use communism to develop a society along these lines, but have been criticised as too authoritarian with the majority of people remaining poor. This form of inequality leads to a type of social division, which in Britain has been called class. Class has been widely discussed in a previous chapter. Some social divisions lead to a form of inequality more readily challenged by social policy. These divisions are often based on race, gender, disability, sexuality, age and religion. These groups (including class) experience their inequality as discrimination.

DIRECT DISCRIMINATION

Where a person is treated less favourably than another in the same or similar circumstances. For example:

- to refuse a child a nursery place because they are black
- to only let the boys play football

Direct discrimination can also include verbal abuse, bullying, victimisation and violence.

INDIRECT DISCRIMINATION

Where a condition or requirement is applied that will unfairly affect a particular group of people compared to others. This type of discrimination can be deliberate or unintentional. For example:

- school uniform requirements may indirectly affect some ethnic or religious groups more than others. Sikh boys having to wear a school cap or Muslim girls having to wear shorts for P.E.

Discrimination is most often expressed as prejudice and can take many forms. It can be in the form of verbal or physical abuse, sterotyping and pretending that differences do not exist.

Equal Opportunity

Equal Opportunity holds that all people should be treated with **equal regard**. This means with respect and fairness. It does not mean that we must treat everyone the same. If we did that, we would fail to respect their individuality and uniqueness. This is reflected in the legislation described below, but more so in an equal opportunities policy. All schools and early years providers must have an equal opportunities policy. A policy is a statement of intent, an equal opportunities policy states clearly how an organisation intends to provide an anti-discriminatory service.

ACTIVITY

Ask your tutor or employer to provide you with a copy of the organisation's Equal Opportunities Policy.
1 Which groups are covered by the policy?
2 Which areas of the organisation's practice are included (for example recruitment and training)?
3 How does the policy intend to ensure that these groups are not discriminated against?
4 Does the policy say how it will deal with complaints of discrimination?
If the policy you looked at was not related to child care provision, have a go at writing one. Imagine you are the manager of a private nursery school. How are you going to ensure that your nursery ensures equality of opportunity to both children and staff?

Equal opportunities legislation in Britain

Britain has developed legislation that tries to combat discrimination, making certain behaviours and practices illegal. Whilst many of the groups mentioned previously are protected by law, there are still groups that are not. There is no law as yet to protect the rights of homosexuals, lesbians or transsexuals.

Disability discrimination act 1995

This Act makes it unlawful to directly discriminate against a person because of his/her disability. Employers are required to make provision for disabled employees and service users. The disabled should not be disadvantaged because they are unable to access employment and/or services. In practical terms this may mean providing lifts, ramps, wide doors, special equipment or alternative means of communication.

The rights of children with special needs are also protected by the **Education Act 1993** and the **Code of Practice for Children with Special Needs (1994)**.

Employment acts 1973,1978,1980,1982 and 1990

These Acts introduce important protection for employees and cover maternity leave, unfair dismissal, trade union membership and conditions of service.

The children act 1989

This Act is an important piece of legislation because it makes clear that children have rights and includes many of the UN convention's articles on child right. The Department of Health (DOH) guidelines concerning registration and inspection of day care (Part III, Schedule 2 of the Children Act) includes the need for child care workers to have knowledge of and commitment to multi-cultural issues and non-discriminatory practice.

Local government housing act 1989

This Act requires Local Government to recruit people on merit and stops them making a decision to hire someone on the basis of political belief. This Act came about because the Conservative government were concerned that some local councils hired people that held the same political belief as the majority of councillors. They were worried this would affect the way policy was interpreted and services delivered.

Sex discrimination acts 1975 and 1986

This Act makes it unlawful to discriminate against a person because of his\her sex. This Act includes the European, Equal Treatment Directive. Under this Act it is illegal to treat a person less favourably than another on the grounds of sex. It covers employment and training, education and the provision of goods and services. A Genuine Occupational Qualification (GOQ) applies in cases where an employer may discriminate on the grounds of sex because of the nature of the job – for example, employing female social workers to work with teenage prostitutes.

RACE RELATIONS ACT 1976

This Act makes it unlawful to directly or indirectly discriminate against a person because of his or her race, colour or national origin. In certain circumstances it is possible to take positive action to recruit people of a certain nationality because of the nature of the job. For instance where a particular language is required.

REHABILITATION OF OFFENDERS ACT 1974

This allows individuals, convicted of a criminal offence, to be rehabilitated over a given period of time. If they do not reoffend in this period, the conviction is considered 'spent' and need not be revealed to an employer unless the person is responsible for 'vulnerable groups' (for example children and the disabled). Some sentences (normally longer ones) are never considered 'spent' and should be declared to an employer.

EQUAL PAY ACT 1970,1975 AND 1983

These Acts require employers to give equal pay to men and women in the same employment or when carrying out broadly similar work. This Act also includes the European, Equal Pay Directive.

European directives

As a member of the European Union (EU), Britain must abide by European law. In order to ensure Equality of Opportunity, the EU issues directives:

EQUAL TREATMENT DIRECTIVE

This holds that men and women should enjoy equal treatment as regards access to employment, promotion, training and working conditions. They shall not be discriminated against on the grounds of sex.

CODE OF PRACTICE

The Code of Practice protects the dignity of men and women at work and maintains that sexual harassment contravenes the Equal Treatment Directive.

EQUAL PAY DIRECTIVE

Each member state should ensure that men and women receive equal pay for equal work.

THE SOCIAL CHARTER

The social charter outlines a number of measures designed to undermine discrimination and ensure fair working practices.

Anyone can take a case of discrimination to the **European Court of Human Rights**.

Rights and responsibilities

We all have rights and alongside these rights go responsibilities. For instance we have the right to feel safe. If we have this right, it follows that we also have a responsibility to protect the safety of ourselves and others. When we drive at high speeds in a built up area we are not acting responsibly. We are ignoring the rights of others and ourselves by creating an unsafe situation. We may adopt legislation, policy, rules and/or regulations to protect the rights of individuals, groups or society.

To protect us from speeding drivers we have road safety rules in the form of legislation, the highway code and the dreaded driving test.

ACTIVITY

1 Take a sheet of paper, divide it into three. Head one column right, one column responsibility and one column protection. In the first column list those things you think of as human rights, in the second record the responsibilities that might go alongside having this right. In the last column record the ways you think this right is protected. The example above should help you.
2 Look at your list of rights. Does everyone have equal access to these rights? Which groups in **society** have less access to these rights? Why is this?

The rights of children

One of the groups you might have in your list as a result of the previous activity is children. In general society views children as dependent on adults. Adults are seen as having the right to direct the behaviour and activities of children. They have this right because they are responsible for their safety, care and education. In exercising their responsibilities adults can sometimes ignore or forget the fact that children have rights too.

To protect the rights of children, an international agreement has been drawn up called the **United Nations Convention on the Rights of the Child**. In 1991, the UK government signed the agreement. This means that British **law** and service delivery that concerns children has to meet the standards laid down by the convention. The convention is divided into a number of statements called articles.

The Children Act 1989 enshrines some of these articles in the following ways:

- **The Paramouncy Principle:** holds that the needs of the child are fundamentally important and central to any decision made about them
- **The child's best interest:** any decision made about a child should be in their best interest
- **The child's views:** children have the right to say what they think about anything that affects them: the child's age and stage of development is taken into consideration (Gillick Competency) but this does not limit the importance of their views, feelings and wishes
- **Non-discrimination:** the welfare checklist makes it clear that a child's age, sex, race, disability, opinion and family background should be acknowledged and respected. If a child is placed for adoption or is 'looked after' by the social services department these factors should be taken into account. The matching of children to families that reflect their cultural background is important as it helps the child feels comfortable and respected.

Indirectly the Act protects the rights of children in the following ways:

The welfare checklist

The welfare checklist ensures that the paramouncy principle is upheld and that any decisions made about children are in their best interest. The welfare checklist should be applied by those responsible for making decisions about a child particularly in cases of child protection. It also applies when children are involved in separation or divorce and there is a dispute about where or with whom they should live. The court uses the checklist below, when making, varying or discharging court orders.

(i) ascertain (find out) the wishes and feelings of the child concerned.
(ii) the child's physical, emotional and educational needs.
(iii) the likely effect on the child of any change in circumstances
(iv) the child's age, sex, background and other relevant characteristics
(v) any harm the child has suffered or is at risk of suffering
(vi) the capability of the parents and any other person in relation to meeting the child's needs.
(vii) the range of powers available to the court under the Children Act 1989.

(HMSO, 1989, The Children Act 1989)

Children in need

The rights of children in need are protected by imposing a duty on Local Authorities to provide services to meet their needs. A child is considered in need if:

a) he/she is unlikely to achieve or maintain, or have the opportunity of achieving or maintaining a reasonable standard of health and development without the provision of services by a Local Authority;
b) his/her health or development is likely to be significantly impaired, or further impaired without the provision of services by a Local Authority;
c) he/she is disabled.

The Local Authority has a duty to

- safeguard and promote the welfare of children within its area who are in need
- to provide services that enable children in need to be looked after by their families
- to identify the needs of children in their area and publish information about services available for them
- to provide day-care for children in need aged 5 yrs and under where appropriate (e.g. a sponsored place in a playgroup)
- to consider the needs of children in need from different racial groups and encourage persons from different racial groups to act as LA foster carers

(Source: HMSO, 1989, The Children Act 1989)

Parental responsibility

The Act acknowledges the duty of parents to adequately care for their children and for their views to be respected. Parental responsibility protects the rights of the child by acknowledging the important role of the parent. It also provides for the delivery of services that enable parents to carry out their responsibilities, particularly for **children in need**.

ACTIVITY

The United Nations Convention gives rights to children in a variety of areas. One of these is the right to protection from violence and harmful treatment. Whilst the Children Act 1989 protects children from physical abuse, sexual abuse, emotional abuse and neglect, it is socially acceptable for people in the UK to 'smack' their children.

Form three groups.

Group One: Are the Anti-Smacking League. They want to outlaw the physical punishment of children.

Group Two: Are the 'Parents have Rights' campaign. They are against having any legislation that interferes with a parent's right to punish their children.

Group Three: The local MP is bringing a **Private Members Bill** before the **House of Commons** that seeks the abolition of physical punishment against children. The MP is supported by a number of influential people (you can choose these roles).

Group One wants to make sure that they influence the content of the Private Members Bill.

Group Two actively campaigns to change the views of those in groups one and three.

Group Three responds to the views of group one and protests of group two. Role play the action between the groups. Make it as real as possible, write letters, produce posters, leaflets or banners. The final scene should be a public meeting where the groups come together and decide if they are going to support or reject the Private Members Bill.

Please remember that role play can be powerful. It is best that a tutor or facilitator is available to observe and monitor its progress. At the end of the role play you need to debrief, so that no one leaves the room feeling uncomfortable about their role or the roles of others.

Summary

- sexism and racism are learnt in contact with others and often include stereotyping (oversimplified, inaccurate generalisations) and scapegoating (blaming others for one's predicament)
- gender roles are substantially learnt: evidence from other

societies shows a wide variation in 'masculine' and 'feminine' characteristics and behaviour

- in our society, parents often put more restrictions on daughters' freedoms: girls may also be more pressured into conformity by their peers
- although children's books are now less likely to perpetrate gender stereotypes, girls' and women's magazines are often still 'self-help manuals' for relationships, appearance and domestic skills
- nevertheless, in education, girls are now commonly surpassing boys, even in traditional male subjects. Compared to 20 years ago, girls are now more confident and more assertive: most, however, still want to go into 'women's work'
- racism impoverishes people's opportunities, promotes fear and hatred, and destroys trust
- however, young people's identities are being increasingly influenced through greater contact between ethnic groups
- inequalities have always been a problem for social policy. In Britain, inequalities of wealth and status are seen as 'normal' and often government policies support them
- social divisions can lead to discrimination. These divisions are often based on race, gender, religion, age, sexuality, class and disability
- Equal Opportunity holds that people should be treated with equal regard. An equal opportunities policy states clearly how an organisation intends to provide an anti-discriminatory service: all schools and early years provision must have an equal opportunities policy
- legislation has been developed that counters discrimination and makes certain acts and behaviours illegal
- the rights of children are protected by the United Nations Convention on the Rights of Children, which Britain signed in 1991. The Children Act 1989 includes many of these rights

7

Poverty and the welfare state

Key points

- there is no agreement about how to measure poverty. Sociologists distinguish between absolute and relative poverty
- the 'welfare state' developed in part to deal with the problem of poverty
- the numbers in relative poverty increased during the 1980s
- yet, the role of the state in providing welfare services is decreasing

What is poverty?

There is no agreed definition of poverty. Most sociologists now operate with two different definitions of poverty, though each of these can be calculated differently:

- **absolute poverty** is defined as not having enough wealth or income to afford the basic necessities for staying alive: enough food, liquid, shelter, clothing. This should not exist in Western societies with a '**welfare state**'. The welfare state was intended to provide a financial 'safety net' below which people should not fall
- **relative poverty** is when you cannot afford the 'minimum acceptable standards of living' in your society (the 'minimum necessary for decency' of J.K. Galbraith) – There are important differences of opinion on what are the 'minimum acceptable standards' at any one time

The 'poverty line'

People are said to be in relative poverty if they have an income which falls below the 'poverty line'. However, there is no official definition of the 'poverty line' in Britain and it has been defined in different ways.

1 The European Union defines the poverty line as *half or less of the average national income.*

2 Alternatively, it is an income which is *low enough to qualify the person for Income Support (IS) benefits.* This is the nearest we get in Britain to an official definition of the relative poverty line. If the income of anyone – working or not working, married or single – falls below a certain level, Income Support should bring them up to the government's minimum acceptable level and, therefore, just out of poverty.

However, many studies show that people on Income Support often have considerable difficulty in making ends meet and many feel isolated and excluded from society, in large part because their income is too low and they don't have adequate opportunities to increase it.

3 Another measure is *Income Support level plus 50 percent.* The British sociologist Peter Townsend uses this measure, claiming that the amount given in Income Support is insufficient by itself to lift people out of poverty.

The payment of Income Support to people in poverty is one manifestation of the workings of the **Welfare State**. How the Welfare State came into being is discussed on page 130.

ACTIVITY

Poverty means being excluded

To keep out of poverty, people must have an income which enables them to participate in the life of the community. They must be able, for example, to keep themselves reasonably fed, and well enough dressed to maintain their self-respect. Their homes must be reasonably warm. Their children should not feel shamed by the quality of their clothing. The family must be able to visit relatives and give them something on their birthdays and at Christmas time. They must be able to read newspapers

> and retain their television sets and their membership of trade unions and churches. And they must be able to live in a way which ensures, as far as possible, that public officials, doctors, teachers, landlords and others treat them with the courtesy due to every member of the community.
>
> (From D. Donnison, 1982)

For Donnison, a person is poor if they do not have enough income to participate in the life of their community. People should have sufficient money so that they are not excluded on those grounds. Which of the items he mentions do you feel people should be able to afford in a decent society? Explain why.

Poverty means lacking 'necessities'

WHICH ITEMS ARE NECESSITIES?

(Those marked with a* are for families with children only).

1 Three meals a day for children*
2 Insurance
3 Refrigerator
4 Children's friends round for tea/a snack once a fortnight*
5 Carpets in living rooms and bedrooms
6 Two pairs of all-weather shoes
7 A telephone
8 An outing for children once a week*
9 A television
10 Leisure equipment for children eg sports equipment or a bicycle*
11 A packet of cigarettes every other day
12 Out-of-school activities, eg sports, orchestra, Scouts
13 A night out once a fortnight (adults)
14 Indoor toilet (not shared with another household)
15 New, not second-hand, clothes
16 A car
17 Presents for friends or family once a year
18 A warm waterproof coat
19 Damp-free house
20 Meat, fish or vegetarian equivalent every other day
21 Beds for everyone in the household
22 A washing machine
23 A 'best outfit' for special occasions
24 Heating to warm living areas of home if it's cold
25 A hobby or leisure activity

26 Celebrations on special occasions such as Christmas
27 Bath (not shared with another household)
28 A holiday away from home for one week a year, not with relatives
29 Enough bedrooms for every child over 10 of different sex to have his/her own*
30 A dressing gown
31 A roast meat joint or vegetarian equivalent once a week
32 Two meals a day (for adults)
33 Toys for children, eg dolls or models*
34 Friends/family round for a meal once a month
35 Fresh fruit

(From H. Frayman, 1991)

According to the researchers, if a household lacked three or more of these items they are in poverty.

1 Tick whichever of these *you* regard as necessities for a minimum decent standard of living.
2 Do a small survey of other students' views and work out the percentage regarding each different item as a necessity.
3 Then compare your responses and your findings with those reported to the researchers who originally asked the questions, shown below.
4 Do you agree that lacking three or more of these items is a reasonable measure of relative poverty in our society today?

	%		%		%
1	90	12	69	23	54
2	88	13	42	24	97
3	92	14	97	25	67
4	52	15	65	26	74
5	78	16	26	27	95
6	74	17	69	28	54
7	56	18	91	29	82
8	53	19	98	30	42
9	58	20	77	31	64
10	61	21	95	32	90
11	18	22	73	33	84
				34	37
				35	88

Percentages of those asked who classified an item as a necessity

The development of the welfare state

The development of the welfare state has been evolutionary and gradual. Derek Fraser, in his book *The Evolution of the Welfare State* (1985), charts the history of social policy from the first census in 1801. In his view the industrial revolution totally transformed social policy. The shift in population from rural to urban living and agricultural to factory occupations promoted economic and social change. The population was increasing and cities growing. New technology marked a change in the way both food and goods were produced. The combined effect was a change in the expectations of the labouring classes and the growth in importance of the business or middle classes. A number of interesting features in our history were important to the development of the welfare state that we know today. Some go even further back than the industrial revolution, although that period in our history saw one of the greatest shifts in lifestyle and social attitudes. It is this kind of shift that has the most influence on the development of social policy.

The poor law

Britain has a long history of looking after the poor. As early as the fourteenth century (1388), a labour shortage gave rise to a law. This set out how the state would provide for those out of work. In 1536 parishes were authorised to collect money to support the poor and the community were expected to take some responsibility for the unemployed, sick and disabled. Over time a number of Acts were passed that established the responsibility of society for those in 'genuine need'. The Poor Law of 1601, commonly known as the 43rd of Elizabeth, identified three main groups of poor:

- **the impotent poor**: this group comprised the aged, chronically sick, blind and mentally ill – these people were seen as poor through no fault of their own and were accommodated in almshouses and poor houses
- **the able-bodied poor**: this group were largely the unemployed. They were set to work, at a 'house of correction' or workhouse in order to instill the appropriate work ethic and enable them to provide for themselves. These places often had a brutal regime. This group were often unemployed due to a shortage of work
- **the able-bodied who absconded**: these people were deemed vagrant and idle. They were 'punished' in the house of correction. This group of people were considered unemployed by choice

The Poor Law Amendment Act of 1834 increased the use of workhouses. The workhouse test was imposed on all those seeking help. Only those without means were offered help. The means-test is still used today. It is the way we work out if people are on a low enough income to obtain benefits. The workhouse and receipt of benefit were disliked, people felt belittled and had a negative image. This is still the case for some people who claim benefits today.

ACTIVITY

How does today's benefit system provide for the poor and in which cases is a means – test applied? What schemes are available to help people find work?

Important surveys and influential figures

Every century has its important figures, politicians, experts or individuals that influence policy reform and social attitudes. One such was **Edwin Chadwick**, who campaigned about urban conditions and public health. Chadwick's report, 'The Sanitary Conditions of the Labouring Population of Great Britain,' established a strong link between environment and disease. Chadwick was convinced that environmental controls were necessary to prevent disease and 'social evils', such as crime and drunkenness. Chadwick was responsible for the provision of public sewage systems and a Public Health Act. This established the state's responsibility for the nation's health. Similarly, **Octavia Hill**, **Henry Mayhew**, **Charles Booth, William Booth** and **Joseph Rowntree**, highlighted the conditions of the poor and demonstrated that the poor could not be held responsible for their **poverty**. They maintained that lack of access to health care, education and poor living conditions played a part in the lifestyles and life expectancy of Britain's poorest citizens. The surveys and reports they published increased public awareness and drew attention to the conditions in which the working classes lived. They were influential in changing social attitudes that eventually led to policy reform.

The church and charitable organisations

The state played a minor role in providing welfare services prior to the First World War. The majority of services offered to those in need were organised by the church or charitable individuals and organisations such as Barnados and the Salvation Army.

ACTIVITY

The church and voluntary organisations continue to play a key role in highlighting issues of concern. The following extract is adapted from an inquiry called 'Unemployment and the Future of Work' (1997) produced by the Council of Churches for Britain and Ireland.

> There is a growing awareness in our society that human beings are more productive if they are valued and go through life in a spirit of learning. Churches and Christian organisations have played a large part in teaching at all levels for two thousand years . . . children should know from an early age that they are valued by society. Education and training should acknowledge and emphasis their natural gifts. It is felt that divisions in the education system will only seek to perpetuate divisions in society. For instance as part of a complete overhaul of education, tax advantages to private schools might be removed . . . more attention should be paid to providing work good enough for everyone to do . . . the aim should be to give priority in the education system to basic skills for all young people.

1 Do you think the church has a role to play in policy making decisions?
2 Research how this report was covered by the media.
3 Do you think this report is likely to have any impact on policy?

The impact of the First World War

The First World War was a watershed in social policy. It killed a great many young men and a whole generation was marked by death and mental and physical disability. The impact of this war, unlike any other, was felt by all British citizens, for it was not only the soldiers that suffered. At home coal, rent and food prices were controlled by the state and by the end of the war food was rationed. The war affected everybody and began to change the attitudes of a whole generation. Lloyd George (Prime Minister) realised that the government needed to address the conditions of its citizens in a more effective manner if they were to avoid social unrest in peacetime. A Ministry of Reconstruction was established in 1917. It aimed to bring together the Poor Law, public health authorities, education authorities and insurance commissions. It focused on four main areas:

- **Housing**: One of its first tasks was to address housing shortages. A programme of house construction offered the working class access to improved living conditions. The 'garden city' concept was introduced as many new homes were provided outside the crowded cities. **The Housing and Town Planning Act of 1919**, often called the Addison Act, gave local authorities the power to provide housing in areas of shortage
- **Health**: At this time a **Ministry of Health** was established to draw together the many different policies that influenced the health care of the nation. It attempted to provide more effective health care provision
- **Education**: In 1916 **H.A.L. Fisher** proposed changes to the Education system. The Fisher **Education Act of 1918**, established the principle that all children and young people should have access to education. It did not however provide the means for this to happen and still relied on charitable organisations and individuals
- **Poverty**: Unemployment was a problem after the war and an Unemployment Insurance Act was introduced in 1920

A severe economic depression in the 1930s forced the government to cut back on existing programmes and it was not able to support further policy reform. However the period was one in which a number of changes did take place that affected the ideology of welfare over the next 30 years.

The Second World War: a new future

The end of the Second World War is often heralded as the time when the welfare state came into being. However we have seen that Britain has a long history of welfare provision supported by the state. What made the 1940s such an important period in the evolution of the welfare state was the principle of '**universalism**' on which the social policy of the era was founded. Universalism maintains that all citizens have an equal right to good housing, health care and education. They are also entitled to social security when they are unable to support themselves financially and social services when they are unable to support themselves socially and emotionally. The introduction of the welfare state in the 1940s was successful because

- the concept of 'universalism' held that everyone has a right to free and accessible services, this idea was popular amongst the general public
- unlike other countries, Britain had been gradually introducing legislation and welfare institutions that were easily adapted. In addition, social attitudes had already changed and the people expected the government to introduce radical policy reform
- the shared experience of the war and opposition to a common enemy enhanced the feeling of community. Class divisions were seen as less important
- during the war the policy of evacuating children from inner cities to the country meant that the middle-classes had to confront and learn about the lives of the working-classes
- the government was willing to respond and political parties worked together to develop policy reform;
- the government was seen as having 'won the war' with the support of the people and there was a genuine belief that together they could 'win the peace'

Social policy and the laws passed between 1944 and 1948 reinforced the state's responsibility for welfare provision. Howard Glennerster (1995) maintains that the general public believed the welfare state would provide

- **Full employment** – a guaranteed job for all those wanting work
- **A national minimum wage** – a safety net to protect those who were unable to work through unemployment, disability or ill-health.
- **A role for the state** – central government to have clear responsibilities in key areas of welfare and the nationalisation of public utilities (water, gas, electricity, transport) and key industries (coal, shipbuilding and steele)
- **State provision** – state agencies to be established to oversee the responsibilities of the centre e.g. Local Education Authorities (LEA's)
- **Continuity** – the nation working to a common aim
- **Equal and free access** to health care and education

The main components of the welfare state

Income maintenance

There are a number of ways that we can ensure that we have enough money to pay for the things we need. We can work. In addition we can save, buy shares, take out a private pension or life insurance policy or invest in high cost items like antiques that we hope will increase in value over time. We can use this money to maintain our income in times of shortage. Not everyone has access to this type of saving. They may become unemployed, retire or suffer ill health. The state takes responsibility for maintaining their income through benefits and pensions. The term **social security** is often used to describe the way a society organises its benefit system. The system adopted by Britain in the 1940s owes much to the work of **Sir William Beveridge** (1879–1963), who is often hailed as the founding father of the welfare state. Beveridge believed that social policy had a major role in ensuring that everyone had employment. He had three main areas of interest.

FULL EMPLOYMENT

Beveridge developed the idea of labour exchanges (job centres). He believed that lack of information about job availability led to unemployment and poverty. Labour exchanges would put people in touch with jobs. In 1924 and again in 1942 he wrote reports that recommended a key role for government if full employment were to be achieved. His idea for labour exchanges was accepted and is still in place today with job centres.

SOCIAL INSURANCE

As early as 1911 Beveridge was involved in designing legislation that introduced unemployment insurance. In 1924 he wrote a pamphlet called 'Insurance for all and everything'. This contained most of the ideas that later found their way into his 1942 report. He was interested in a system that allowed workers to pay a small contribution from their wages each week in return for insurance cover. They could then claim benefit if they fell ill or became unemployed. This became known as a 'contributory insurance system'. We know it today as **National Insurance** contributions.

Beveridge's report to the government in 1942 proposed revolutionary changes and a comprehensive set of measures to tackle what were called the five giants of evil: **want**, **disease**, **ignorance**, **squalor** and **idleness**.

Beveridge's report was instrumental in the formation of a social security system that made provision for the unemployed, elderly and dependent. It included Family Allowance, National Insurance, Sickness Benefit and Pensions. Everyone would pay into the scheme and receive benefits. Some benefits were provided as of right not dependent on income, for example Family Allowance (child benefit) others were means-tested, for example social security (income support).

KEYNESIAN THEORY

In 1936 Beveridge read John Maynard Keynes' *General Theory of Employment Interest and Money* and it underpinned many of his ideas. Keynesianism held that governments could control the economy. This involved putting money into the economy during a recession thus increasing the purchasing power of consumers and raising demand. Beveridge used the ideas of Keynes when he developed the social security system. This style of economics was also used by governments to control public spending from the 1940s until the early 1970s. It became unpopular during the economic recession of the late 1970s.

Education

The reform of the education system was controversial (see Chapter 8). Before the Second World War, those who could not afford to purchase education were reliant on schools supported by charities or the church. Many church leaders were concerned that state intervention in the education of children would undermine the importance of religion and religious values. It was R.A. Butler (MP) who finally managed to persuade the church to agree to the changes. He reassured them that religion would not be ignored and would become a compulsory subject in all schools. **The 1944 Education Act** provided

- free and universal provision
- an end to all age schools
- a building programme to create primary and secondary schools in every local authority
- a school leaving age of 15 years in the first phase increasing to 16 years later on
- the right for young workers to go to college on day release schemes
- support for those going to university in the form of scholarships and grants

- religious instruction and a daily act of worship to be compulsory unless parents objected

Health

In 1943 the Ministry of Health drew up a proposal for a **National Health Service**. It said that the service would be free at the point of use and paid for out of national insurance and taxes. The **British Medical Association** (BMA) objected on the grounds that it would reduce the income of doctors. Doctors liked their independence and did not want to be controlled by local government. In 1944, the white paper 'A National Health Service' was published. **Aneurin Bevan** (MP), saw problems and knew that the BMA would need to feel safeguarded as the proposal required the nationalisation of medical services. Bevan managed to push the Bill forward focusing the BMA on the advantages for the profession to get their support. The National Health Services Act 1946 stated:

- service to be free at the point of delivery paid for out of general taxation
- services to be run on a national basis
- all citizens would register with a doctor of their choice and receive free treatment or be referred to hospital
- GPs to remain private professional people, but grouped in partnerships

PERSONAL SOCIAL SERVICES

During the Second World War, children were evacuated from the big cities to avoid the blitz (bombing). The children were sent to rural areas that were relatively safe from air attack. The evacuation of children highlighted issues of poverty, malnourishment and poor living conditions. Some evacuees and their families were treated brutally by their host families. The death of two boys led to the Monckton Inquiry (1945) which uncovered a number of administrative and professional errors. This led to a greater recognition of abuse. The Curtis Inquiry (1946) considered the plight of children at risk, which led to the implementation of the 1948 Children Act. A separate department had to be created by the local authority to look after the interests of children. A new social work profession was created with trained, specialist staff.

HOUSING

Before the Second World War, most people lived in private rented accommodation. Rent controls had been introduced at the beginning of the Second World War and were kept in place once it ended. Many private landlords found it unprofitable and left the business. This only worsened the housing shortage, as so many houses had been destroyed in the blitz. The provision of government funded housing became known as council housing. The shortage of building materials after the war meant that four/fifths of building licenses in 1948 were granted to local authorities, making council housing the fastest growing sector at the time.

A period of stability

It has been argued that the period 1945–1975 saw the main political parties working in agreement rather than opposition. This became known as a period of consensus. It was believed that both the **Labour Party** and **Conservative Party** were united in their commitment to the welfare state. Recent research suggests that the Conservatives felt uncomfortable with the concept of universalism and tried to keep a check on expenditure and the growing demand for services. Policy reform during this time was dependent not on the views of the political parties, but on economics. When the economy was stable, resources were made available. When the economy was in recession, resources were withdrawn (D. Kavanagh, 1989). The main components of the welfare state became established in the state sector and much policy formation was focused on amendments rather than sweeping changes. During the 1960s and 1970s policy began to address issues such as **race**, **gender**, **marriage** and **sexuality**.

ACTIVITY

1 How has the subject of marriage been addressed in social policy since 1965?
2 What specific areas of married life are regulated by legislation and why?
3 How has policy changed between 1965–1997?

The welfare state in crisis

During the 1970s a number of economic crises undermined the position of the welfare state:

- oil crisis
- recession
- sterling crisis (the value of the pound dropped and Britain was refused a loan)
- high levels of inflation
- decline in world trade
- high levels of public spending
- high unemployment
- growing numbers of older people entitled to pensions and services
- public sector strikes

The welfare stare had grown and the demand for services was increasing. The system was costly and the economic situation in Britain made it impossible to fund the level of service provision expected from taxation. The welfare state was criticised as bureaucratic, inefficient, ineffective and wasteful. The Labour government in power during the 1970s decided to cut back on public spending and introduce policy reforms. The Conservatives felt that Labour would not go far enough and would be unwilling to make the drastic cuts required to bring Britain out of the recession. The election of 1979 was won by the Conservatives and Mrs Thatcher became Prime Minister. She made it clear that she would cut public expenditure and look critically at the delivery of services by the welfare state.

Restructuring the welfare state

The policies of the Conservative party became known as 'Thatcherism'. Keynesian economic theory was replaced by Monetarist policies. An American economist Milton Friedman advised the Thatcher government that the way to make Britain wealthy and reduce unemployment was to cut inflation. The Conservatives developed a set of new social policies based on the following principles:

DECENTRALISATION

This reduces the role of the centre or state in the delivery of welfare services.

PRIVATISATION

This enabled private companies to own, organise and deliver services once controlled by the state, for example gas, electricity, water, railways, buses and telephone.

SELF HELP

This encourages people to do things for themselves. It also encourages voluntary organisations to become involved in service delivery.

COMPETITION

This encourages businesses to offer efficient and cost effective services if they wish to be successful and not lose custom to a competitor. It is believed that competition in business stimulates the economy and provides a greater choice for customers.

FREEDOM TO CHOOSE

This stimulates flexibility and competition in business and organisations such as schools and hospitals. It acknowledges people's right to make decisions about the type of services that best suits their needs.

ENTERPRISE

The 'enterprise culture' is based on providing services\business that promote: – Economy – Efficiency – Effectiveness – Responsiveness – Rationalisation – Community – Choice – Partnership – Participation – Self help

ACTIVITY

Look these words above up in a dictionary and note down what they mean. How do you think they apply to service delivery? It may make it easier to apply them to one area of service provision, such as a school or hospital.

Contemporary issues

The Conservative government firstly under the leadership of Margaret Thatcher (1979–1990) and later under the leadership of John Major (1990–1997), introduced sweeping changes to:

- social policy
- the organisation of the main components of the welfare state
- the role of the state in the provision of welfare
- the delivery of services

Decline or disappearance?

The welfare state has continued to evolve and change. The change in recent decades has been revolutionary. The private and voluntary sectors are becoming increasingly involved in areas of service delivery that were once the responsibility of the state. Many services provided by the state are only available for those who are defined as disadvantaged or in need. The current state system provides a 'safety net' for those most in need. It is interesting to consider how further changes in the delivery of health, education and social services may affect the structure of the welfare state in the future.

ACTIVITY

Organise a debate: Does Britain still need a welfare state?

The extent of poverty and its recent growth

Despite the welfare state's existence for some 50 years, poverty has not been defeated. Estimates of how much poverty exists depend, as always, on how it is defined.

ABSOLUTE POVERTY

Trying to cost people's basic physical needs is not easy. Even people's food needs differ according to their age, sex, occupation, body type and so on. However, from the two studies of poverty he conducted in York, in 1899 and in 1950, Seebohm Rowntree concluded that absolute poverty had fallen from 33 per cent of the city's population to 1.5 per cent.

RELATIVE POVERTY

Obviously, given the variation in definitions, estimates of the extent of relative poverty will vary. As an indication, however, Mack and Lansley estimated that about 17 per cent of the total population were living in relative poverty in 1990. Towards the end of the 1990s it is estimated that about 20 per cent of all British children now live in relative poverty.

For most of the population, their standard of living has continued to improve over the past two decades. In absolute terms, the poor today are better off than the poor in the past. Nevertheless, the number of people in poverty has grown through the 1980s and 1990s for two main reasons.

1 The most vulnerable groups have grown:

- old people
- single parent families
- the unemployed and their dependents
- low waged and their dependents
- long-term sick or disabled and their dependents

2 Benefits have fallen behind prices and average earnings, so the incomes of people in poverty have fallen even further behind those earning an income.

International comparisons

According to the authoritative United Nations' *Human Development Report*, published in June 1997, poverty in Britain has been rising faster than in any other major industrialised country. A higher proportion of old people are in poverty in Britain than in any other Western country, and our child poverty rate is second only to the United States.

Nearly a quarter of Britain's old people live in poverty, more than five times the rate in Italy and more than three times that of Ireland. Nearly a fifth of our children are poor – about twice as many as in Taiwan or Italy, four times as many as in Belgium and six times as many as in Finland. Half of all Britain's single parent families live below the poverty line.

The report adds that Britain is the only major Western country where poverty has 'increased substantially' since the early 1980s – up till then it had been falling as in every other industrialised country. The change coincides exactly with Mrs Thatcher coming to power in 1979, and the proportion of people in 'income poverty' rose by nearly 60 per cent under her leadership.

Some consequences of poverty

Poverty can affect every area of life. It is not just that parents haven't much money to spend on doing up where they live, or on food, heating and clothing. As Carey Oppenheim points out, poverty is not just about what is spent. Very importantly, it is also about what you *can't* spend on.

Children's health is affected by poverty. According to a survey of the eating habits of low-income families commissioned by the National Children's Home charity in 1991, 1 in 10 children under 5 years goes without enough to eat at least once a month. This is despite another of their findings, that 1 in 5 parents regularly denied themselves food through lack of money. The survey claims that it is not so much ignorance, but lack of money, which largely explains the unhealthy diets of poor people.

ACTIVITY

Poverty and its restrictions

Poverty means staying at home, often being bored, not seeing friends, not going out for a drink and not being able to take the children out for a trip, a treat, or a holiday.

It means coping with the stress of managing on very little money, often for months or even years. It means having to withstand society's pressure on you to consume. It affects your relationships with others. Above all, poverty takes away your 'life chances'. It steals away your chances of a life unmarked by serious sickness, a decent education, a secure home and a long retirement. It stops people being able to take control of their lives.

(From C. Oppenheim, 1990)

Poverty and overcrowding

One measure of overcrowding is given by looking at the 'bedroom standard'. The number of bedrooms required for a given family is calculated by looking at the family in terms of age, sex and marital status. It is assumed that children under 10 of either sex may sleep two to a room without overcrowding. Children over 10 may share a room with a sibling of the same sex, but a brother and sister over 10 should have separate rooms. It is also assumed that children do not share a room with their parents or other adults.

According to these criteria, in 1992 11 per cent of children were living in accommodation which fell below the bedroom standard, in other words, living in overcrowded housing. The situation was far worse for those living in rented accommodation than those in owner-occupied housing. Overcrowding applied to 21 per cent of children in privately rented accomodation, 18 per cent of those in local authority rented accommodation and only 7 per cent of children living in owner-occupied housing.

(From *Social Focus on Children*, HMSO, 1994)

Poverty and poor housing

The 1991 English House Condition Survey used two related indicators: 'unfit dwellings' and 'dwellings in the worst condition'. The latter refers to the worst 10% of all dwellings, according to the cost of repairing them. Using these, it is clear that lone parents and their children are more likely to be living in poor conditions than other family households. Eleven per cent of lone parents occupy 'worst condition' dwellings compared to only 7% of two adult and children families.

(From *Social Focus on Children*, HMSO, 1994)

Poverty and crime

According to research commissioned by the Association of Chief Officers of Probation in 1993 which studied 1, 389 young people on probation schemes, there is 'a real link between poverty and crime'.

The report continues. 'The message is clear. A significant group of people in our society, part of our investment in the future, are complete outsiders.' Only one in five had a job, 72 per cent were in poverty (i.e. less than half the average income) and more than two-thirds had 'no reliable source of income whatsoever'.

(From A. Sage, *Independent*, 1993)

1 Compile a list of all the consequences of being in poverty mentioned in the extracts above.
2 Are there other consequences not mentioned which you could add?

The causes of poverty: cultural and structural theories

Why are people poor? Cultural explanations blame the alleged *attitudes and behaviours* of poor people.

Structural explanations claim that poverty is mainly due to the *marginal positions* that some people have in society (in the social structure) and *in the labour market.*

Cultural explanations

An American anthropologist, Oscar Lewis, claimed in his 1950s and 1960s studies of poor communities in Mexico and Puerto Rico, that from birth the children there are taught a culture which effectively traps them into poverty. They learn to be resigned to their lot in life, don't take opportunities if they come, are reluctant to work, want immediate gratification, and don't plan for the future. They (unintentionally) bring their poverty on themselves.

A more recent but related view, which became popular during Mrs Thatcher's period in power (1979–90), suggests that, in countries like Britain and the United States, a whole class of people has emerged in the last few decades who share precisely these sorts of attitude and behaviour. The view is that this 'underclass' has developed largely *because of* the existence of the welfare state. The welfare state has provided people with such a range of welfare benefits that it has undermined their incentive to work, or do anything to take responsibility for themselves or their dependents. Their values are those of the scrounger and the dosser – quite different from those of ordinary, respectable folk, who value family life and hard work.

Structural explanations

Structural explanations, on the other hand, emphasise that people can be largely trapped by their situations. They are not poor because they don't want to work: indeed, they often dislike their dependence on 'handouts' (and thousands choose not to claim them for a variety of reasons). But they are poor because of their position in relation to the labour market.

- most people in poverty are excluded from the labour market or have a weak position in it
- those excluded (the old, unemployed, some sick or disabled) receive inadequate benefits or pensions (for example, according to David Piachault of the charity Campaign for Real Work, in 1990, a married unemployed claimant was getting only 27 per cent of average earnings)
- those people who are in a weak position receive low wages: that includes the unskilled, the unqualified, and groups discriminated against (women, ethnic minorities, the disabled, part-timers, the young)
- some people claim that employers want to keep both wages and benefits low. They want wages kept low in order to maximise

their profits. Employers also want to keep benefits low, so that a pool of cheap labour is always available and motivated to work: even if the wages paid are low they are nevertheless more than the benefits. Thus, new workers can always be brought in if current ones prove troublesome or too demanding

- if people find themselves in these sorts of positions, getting out of poverty can be difficult: this is so because of the 'cycles of deprivation' which poverty involves

The 'cycles of deprivation'

A child born into poverty is likely to be born with a number of disadvantages. Let's take one, fairly dramatic, type of disadvantage which some children born into poverty face. Some children born poor begin their lives homeless, or in damp, dirty, draughty, overcrowded, rented accommodation. Disadvantages like these make it likely that the child will go on to suffer from other deprivations. For example, they are more likely to suffer poor health.

Although many parents in poverty go to great lengths to ensure that their children look as well groomed as possible, some poor children will be noticably less well dressed, perhaps wearing 'hand-me-downs', and may not be as clean as other children. In time, they are likely to see other children and their parents as superior to them, as more successful, and so develop feelings of failure and inadequacy. That is likely to encourage the child to give up too easily, truant from school, fall behind, underachieve educationally, drift into unemployment or insecure, low-paid jobs, and stay – throughout their lifetime – stuck in poverty. That is one cycle of deprivation. You end as you began. No one step is inevitable, but each disadvantage makes others more likely to happen and the next generation grows up to poverty like its parents.

Of course, not all situations will be as drastic as the scenarios above, but as a general rule, a child born into poverty is more likely than most to be born into poor accommodation. They are also more likely not to be able to afford a healthy diet. That too makes other deprivations and disadvantages more likely. They are also more likely to be living in an area where the schools lack decent facilities and resources and where teachers are under high levels of pressure and there are correspondingly high levels of teacher-absenteeism and teacher-turnover.

ACTIVITY

The welfare state and the creation of dependency

The central apparent contradiction of the welfare system is that the more billions of pounds the system receives, the more people it appears to trap in poverty, crime, dependency and hopelessness. Half the population now lives in households drawing at least one means-tested benefit. (Means tested benefits are paid if the claimant's income is judged to be low). Yet state benefits paralyse self-help. They also discourage self-improvement.

(From M. Phillips, *The Observer*, 1995)

A structuralist response (1)

Many parents living on Income Support are engaged in a continual struggle to feed their children and minimise hardship – even to the extent of going without themselves. Their need to keep a tight rein on weekly spending makes them reluctant to experiment with unfamiliar 'healthy' foods that their children might refuse to eat.

Yet, far from being feckless (feeble, inefficient), there is evidence that low-income families are often resourceful in the way that they juggle bills and different sources of credit, making children their priority for any spending. The essential problem appears to be a lack of adequate income.

(D. Utting, 1995, p. 35)

A structuralist response (2)

Karen Barnes, aged 27, earns £15 a week helping to look after an elderly neighbour so that another woman can go out to work. Her husband Andrew, aged 31, brings home £170 a week as a nursing assistant in a psychiatric hospital's secure unit. They have three children, aged between four and seven. Mrs Barnes can't do more work because she cannot afford the day-care fees.

The family last had a holiday – (a week in Wales) – four years ago. Almost one-quarter of their income is taken by the rent on their three bedroom house in Preston, Lancashire. Mr Barnes relies on a lift to work as they cannot afford a car. Food and children's clothing are the priorities. 'You have to juggle the bills,' said Mrs Barnes. 'We try but it's hard.'

(From M. Halsall, – *The Guardian*, 1996)

1 Stage a debate on the causes of poverty, with some of you putting forward the view that the welfare state causes a culture of dependency and some of you taking the structuralist view.
2 Here are two examples of an initial deprivation:

- from an early age, the child is fed *a poor diet*;
- the child grows up in a poor, 'undesirable' neighbourhood, with under-resourced, low status and *second rate schools*.

Starting with one of the examples of an initial deprivation given above, list a sequence of likely consequences. Show in diagram form how the sequence of disadvantages can be drawn as a 'cycle of deprivation', so that the child born into poverty also ends up there.

3 Recent research suggests that a nursery education can help to break the cycle of deprivation. Why do you think this may be so?
4 Imagine you are a politician. What policies could you suggest which might help deal with poverty?
5 Suggest how you would fund any changes. How would you 'sell' your ideas to people who foot the bill?

The growth of child poverty

As we have seen, the provision of welfare services and social security has not made Britain immune to child poverty. Indeed, Jonathan Bradshaw (1990) in a report to the **National Children's Bureau** demonstrates that the 1980s saw an increase in child poverty and deprivation for three reasons.

1 Economic trends

Britain was in a period of recession all through the 1980s. The recession was characterised by low levels of **employment** and investment and high levels of inflation and strikes. This affected the living standards of children and their families. Whilst the 1990s saw a rise in Britain's fortunes benefit levels remain low and wages have been slow to rise for those in the lowest income brackets.

2 Demographic trends

Changes in family structure have had an impact on child poverty. The number of children living in lone parent households is increasing. In 1992, over two million children were living in poverty, 76 per cent of these in lone parent families. Jane Milner (1992) explains the prevalence of child poverty in lone parent families as the result of the different experiences of the parents – 92 per cent of such families are headed by women, many of whom were reliant on state benefits for an income. Fathers are more prosperous. They are able to remain economically active and as a consequence have access to a higher income. They are quicker to remarry and begin new families, relinquishing responsibility for the old one.

3 Social policy

A change of government policy in the late 1980s gave rise to changes in the tax system. The result was a drop in the level of tax taken from higher incomes, whilst that of lower income groups has risen. The poor in effect are paying more tax. Major changes have taken place in the benefit system since 1979. The Social Security Act 1988 replaced the supplementary benefit system with income support and the social fund. Additional weekly payments were replaced by flat rate payments and in some cases withdrawn and replaced by loans and grants. One of the aims of the 1988 reform was to provide help more effectively to low income families with children. J. Bradshaw (1990) argues that it remains unclear how effective the new system has been:

> Over two million children have become dependent on income support and there has been anxiety that the level of benefit, especially for families with children, is not adequate. This was recognised by the government in its intention to concentrate extra help on families with children in its 1986 White Paper on social security reform. It is not at all certain that this objective was achieved in practice and certainly no attempt was made to define it adequately.
>
> In addition to changes in the benefit system, children have been indirectly affected by the cuts in spending on health, education and social services. Children from deprived areas and disadvantaged families are being more keenly affected.

The impact of poverty on children

The effects of poverty on children can take many forms.

Child health

Research indicates (Carr Hill, 1988) that the height and weight of children from low income families is below that of other children. They are disproportionately affected by obesity and malnutrition. This has been linked to the nutritional value of the foods they are most likely to eat. Children in lower income families tend to eat less fresh fruit, vegetables and protein and more carbohydrates and fat. All areas of development and educational attainment appear to be affected, with children from lower income families less likely to do well in school.

Children's behaviour

Links have been made between

- truancy
- teenage conception (pregnancy)
- children's work
- juvenile crime
- substance misuse

and the income level of families. Children from lower income families appear more likely to engage in the above behaviours than other children in the same age group. We must however be very careful when considering such findings. The behaviour of children from deprived areas and disadvantaged families gets much more attention paid to it by professionals (social workers), the media and the general public. These children are very 'visible' in our society. It could be that the behaviour of children from other groups in society is similar, but defined differently or missed because our attitude to them is different.

Racial discrimination

A black child's experience of deprivation is heightened. They can become doubly disadvantaged because of racism and discrimination. Almost three-quarters of the ethnic minority population in Britain live in inner city areas in poor, overcrowded conditions. The parents of black children are more likely to be unemployed or on low incomes (J. Bradshaw, 1990).

ACTIVITY

Choose one of the areas of children's behaviour listed above and undertake a piece of topic work. Find out all you can about its history, the attitudes of society, the attitudes of the young people themselves, the reasons for the behaviour, the impact it has on their lives and the social policy that aims to address it. What recommendations would you make to tackle the issue?

The Child Poverty Action Group (CPAG)

The CPAG is responsible for publishing a number of reports on child poverty. They attempt to inform politicians, administrators and the general public about the reality of life for children that live on low incomes and benefits.

The welfare state and social security

David Whynes (1992) explains that economists use the term 'welfare state' to refer to those social services in the economy organised by the government which relate to income maintenance. Social security is available to people because they are unable to find work, are sick, disabled or are of retirement age. Those on low incomes, with a large number of dependents or high expenditure levels may also be entitled to payments. There are four main types of benefit.

MEANS TESTED BENEFITS

These benefits require the applicant to provide information about their circumstances, income and savings. Benefit will only be paid if the applicant is considered eligible. This usually means they are unable to maintain their own income with the resources they have available.

Examples: Income Support, Family Credit and Housing Benefit

CONTRIBUTORY BENEFITS

Some benefits depend on a contribution being made through tax or insurance. Whilst at work the majority of people contribute to the **National Insurance Scheme** (NI). These contributions entitle us to certain benefits if we loose our job or fall ill. **SERPS** or the **State Earnings Related Pension Scheme** is optional and provides for our retirement in the form of a pension. Many people choose to organise their own pensions and 'opt' out of SERPS.

Examples: SERPS, NI, Sickness Benefit, Statutory Sick Pay and Statutory Maternity Pay

NON-CONTRIBUTORY BENEFITS

These are benefits provided as a right and are not dependent on a means test or contributions.

Examples: Child Benefit and Single Parent Benefit

CATEGORICAL BENEFITS

These are sometimes called **circumstance benefits**. In order to receive payment, you must fall into a particular category or group. You may be disabled for instance or the carer of a disabled or terminally ill person.

ACTIVITY

Tracey is 22 years old, she has a daughter Michelle aged six and a son Rashid aged two. Tracey is a lone parent, living in a small privately rented upstairs flat on the outskirts of a large town. Tracey was unable to give the Child Support Agency any information about the whereabouts of the children's fathers and receives no support from them. Her daughter Michelle has cerebral palsy and requires constant care. She is unable to feed, dress or toilet herself. Rashid has asthma and regularly attends the asthma clinic at the hospital in the centre of town. Tracey rarely goes out and has few friends, and those she does have are in a similar situation to herself.

Think about Tracey's situation and list the possible stress factors in her life. Can you think of any solutions that may provide her with support?

Welfare to work

All the main political parties in Britain are committed to reducing the numbers of those dependent on benefits for an income. This has resulted in a number of schemes including YTS, Modern Apprenticeships, Job Seekers Allowance and Life Long Learning programmes. These schemes often target the long-term unemployed, lone parents and young people.

The Child Support Act (1991)

Whilst the Child Support Act achieved Royal assent in 1991 it was not out into practice until 1993. The Act was introduced because the government was concerned about the increasing numbers of lone parents claiming benefits. In addition the government were unhappy about the numbers of absent fathers that failed to support their children financially once they left the family home. The Child Support Act established the **Child Support Agency**. This agency is responsible for the assessment and collection of child maintenance. They undertake this duty as a right if a person is on benefit, but only at the request of those who are not.

The Child Support Act defines a parent with care as the person with day to day responsibility for the child(ren). The absent parent is the person that the child is not living with or who is having the child looked after by someone else. This means that the parents of children being 'looked after' by the local authority still have a financial responsibility for them. A qualifying child is a child with one or both parents absent. The underlying principles of the act are that

- both parents of a qualifying child are responsible for their financial support
- the duty applies whether or not the child is living with a lone parent, parents that are married or an unmarried couple
- the duty applies regardless of benefit status.
- absent parents are required to make payments of child support, worked out to a set formula contained in the act (this can not be altered or modified)
- parents with care are required to co-operate with the Child Support Agency: they are obliged to give them information about the whereabouts and circumstances of absent parents. They can only refuse if they have 'good cause' and are at risk of harm or undue stress. If they do not provide this information those on benefit could have them stopped

Children's income

Increasingly children are in 'charge' of their own money in the form of pocket money or as payment for work. Little evidence exists about the status of working children, but what is known suggests that children are working illegally. Many children are working under age or for too many hours.

Summary

- people are in absolute poverty if they cannot afford to sustain reasonably good health
- being in relative poverty means that you can't participate in community life and lack a number of items people now regard as necessities, estimated at half or less of the average income
- the main components of the welfare state are, Income Maintenance, Health, Housing, Education and Personal Social Services
- the period 1945–1975 was generally accepted as a time of stability, where the concept of a welfare state was established as the 'norm'
- a number of crises in the economy in the 1970s led to cut backs in welfare services and a restructuring of the welfare state
- the social policy of the 1980s and 1990s was based on the principles of monetarism, decentralisation, competition, self help, freedom of choice and enterprise
- the numbers in poverty have grown during the 1980s and 1990s because those in the most vulnerable groups have increased and the real value of welfare benefits has fallen
- cultural explanations of poverty blame the alleged values and attitudes of the poor, and the welfare state which is said to encourage their dependency
- structural explanations claim that poverty is mainly due to being excluded from the labour market or poorly rewarded by it, factors which increase the likelihood of suffering further disadvantages, such as educational under-achievement
- child poverty increased during the 1980s, and changes in the tax laws and benefit system affected the income levels of many families: more children are living in lone parent households reliant on benefits
- there are four types of benefit: 1) means tested 2) contributory 3) non-contributory and (4) categorical or circumstance benefits
- the Child Support Act 1988 established the Child Support Agency and a system for the assessment and collection of child maintenance

8

Education

Key points

- independent schools have an influence beyond their numbers
- Britain has seen a number of educational reforms since 1944
- pre-school education is becoming recognised as important and necessary
- the state plays a large part in the regulation, funding and delivery of education in Britain
- there are differences in educational attainment between social classes, between the sexes, and between ethnic groups

Independent schools

Some 93 per cent of all children attend schools in the state sector, but the schools of the remaining 6–7 per cent are significant beyond their numbers.

Independent schools are schools which are:

- partly or substantially outside of the state system
- mainly fee-paying (for some if not all)
- not required to teach the National Curriculum

So they include:

- the so-called public schools, and the preparatory and pre-preparatory schools which prepare pupils for them
- religious schools (for example Jewish, Quaker, Church of England, Roman Catholic)
- 'progressive' schools, with less orthodox philosophies and practices (for example Summerhill in Suffolk)

Of these, the most politically significant, by far, have been the so-called 'public' schools and the schools which 'feed' them – that is the preparatory ('prep') and pre-preparatory schools. Pre-preparatory schools generally take pupils aged 3 to 7 years-old; preparatory schools, from 7 to 13 years-old; and public schools cater for 13 to 18 year-olds, from where most go on to university.

Strictly speaking, the 230 or so traditionally male public schools are only those whose Headteacher is a member of the Head Masters Conference (HMC). In the last few years, a number have become co-educational. The 236 girls schools in the Girls Schools Association (GSA) are much less well known and influential, but the best known are Roedean in Brighton, and the Cheltenham Ladies College in Gloucestershire. Indeed, of the most important public schools, none are outside the South of England or the Midlands.

If we look at the influence of public schools, the most important are the 9 so-called 'Clarendon' schools, which include Eton, Harrow, Marlborough, Rugby, Winchester and Westminster. They are societally significant mainly because:

1 they are the schools of the wealthy;
2 they are disproportionately represented in the nation's elites (that is, society's most powerful, prestigious and wealthy groups):

- top politicians
- Church of England archbishops and bishops
- judges and top barristers
- Admirals, Generals and Air Marshals
- newspaper editors
- even (satirical) TV comedians

For much of this century Eton, the most famous school of them all, provided an average of at least one-third of the Cabinet members. Even today, more than half the Conservative party's hereditary peers went to Eton. In short, many who go to such schools and then go on to achieve high office in whatever field, are likely to have known each other for many years, sometimes since childhood, or at least to have known a relative or friend. Many then go on to university, traditionally 'Oxbridge' (Oxford or

Cambridge Universities) and continue their social contact in a variety of exclusive contexts:

- membership of London men's clubs such as White's or the Athenaeum
- special enclosures at regular social events, for example Wimbledon (tennis), Twickenham (rugby union), Ascot (horse racing), Cowes (sailing) and Badminton (horse trials)
- their children intermarrying
- professionally, through their careers

ACTIVITY

Should independent schools be allowed?

1 If it were possible, should the *public schools* be abolished? What are the arguments for and against abolishing them?
2 Do you think that there should be *any* schools allowed outside the state system? What sorts of schools, and why? Give your reasons.

Changing policies in England and Wales

Although the children of the wealthy (especially males) were traditionally educated by private tutors, and more recently at public schools, it is only since 1870 that free, state education has been provided in England for ordinary people. Ten years later, education up to the age of 10 years was made compulsory, thereby preventing children up to that age from working, and making them more expensive to have and to keep.

However, although changes were made to the educational system throughout the twentieth century, it was not until 1944 that a serious attempt was made to ensure that bright working-class children could get a good academic education. Before 1944 they would have had to win a scholarship to a grammar school, schools which were mainly stocked with middle-class children who paid for their education. We look below at some of the main changes to education in England and Wales from 1944 onwards.

The 1944 Education Act

This represented an important social policy reform. The evacuation of children during World War Two had highlighted the level of illiteracy and ignorance amongst the general population. The education available before and during World War Two was shown to be ineffective. This Act made it a duty of the Minister of Education to provide a national educational system that was available to all children aged 5 to 15 years. Fee paying was abolished and the primary and secondary model of delivery established. Children who passed the 11 Plus exam went to grammar school, those that did not went to secondary modern or technical schools.

Comprehensive education

In the 1960s the **Labour Party** won the battle to scrap the 11 Plus exam. They introduced the Comprehensive System of education merging grammar, secondary modern and technical schools into one. Children were educated together in the same school regardless of academic ability or social status. The **Conservative Party** was opposed to Comprehensive Education and has continued to try and reintroduce grammar schools ever since. The general public's acceptance of Comprehensive Education as the standard form of education has made this difficult.

The 1988 Education Reform Act

The Conservative government's 1988 Education Reform Act intended to move schools away from a widespread pattern of comprehensive schooling to one of greater diversity and competition. The Act brought about a number of important educational changes.

1 It introduced a National Curriculum of subjects that must be taught in all state schools. From 5 to 16 years all state school pupils were required to study the 'core' subjects of English, maths and science, and take PE, plus, up to at least the age of 14, technology, history, geography, art and music, and, at secondary age, a foreign language. The National Curriculum is discussed in more detail below.

2 Teachers were required to carry out an assessment of pupils' achievement levels and progress by administering Standard Attainment Tests (SATs) in the core subjects to children at the ages of 7, 11 and 14. All schools were then required to publish their SAT results and, in the case of high schools, their GCSE and 'A' level examination results. Local schools could then be ranked in a 'league table' based on test and exam results.

3 It introduced Grant Maintained Schools (GMSs) and City Technology Colleges (CTCs). In so doing, the government (intentionally) reduced the role and influence of LEAs.

- Grant Maintained Schools are primary or secondary schools which have chosen to opt out of LEA control and be financed directly by central government. They are no longer governed by the LEA but by the school's governors and headteacher. They take all the decisions about the employment of staff, how to spend their budget, and can select up to 50 per cent of the school's pupils, based on criteria they decide for themselves.
- City Technology Colleges (CTCs) are also directly funded by central government, with some financial support from private industry. They teach the National Curriculum, but – like the secondary technical schools of the 1944 Act – put a particular emphasis on maths, science and technology. By 1994 there were only 15 of these, mainly located in the larger cities.

In introducing these changes the government hoped to:

1 improve the standards of education in schools by introducing competition between schools for pupils and resources;
2 allow parents to choose which school their child attends;
3 enable parents to make an 'informed' choice of school, by requiring schools to publish their SAT and exam results. Schools whose SAT and exam results were good would then attract parents to send their child to them and would be rewarded by extra funding;
4 encourage 'successful' schools to flourish while forcing 'unsuccessful' schools either to improve or to close through lack of parental support;
5 increase parental influence in schools. This was to be achieved by increasing the power of governors and increasing parental representation on governing bodies.

In their response, the National Union of Teachers (NUT) argued that these changes could have a number of undesirable consequences, including:

- schools in poorer areas, where children are less likely to achieve academically, become labelled as 'bad' schools, and that parents' support be reduced, making the schools poorer still

- popular schools becoming crowded and class sizes increased
- community undermined, as children travel long distances to school rather than attend a local school
- the division between the able and less able be increased

The NUT also argued that:

1 By not including information about pupils' ability levels when they first arrive at school, the published 'league tables' of schools' results does not show the effectiveness of the school in improving children's performance.
2 Parents do not really have a 'free' choice of school place

- in GM Schools, the schools also do the selecting
- in LEA schools, the limited number of places available make it impossible for everyone to have their first choice
- LEA entry policy is usually geared to matching local children to local schools, making it difficult for parents to choose schools outside their local area

However, along with other misgivings about the 1988 Act, one of the most basic was this: although for some pupils Grant Maintained Schools and City Technology Colleges have increased diversity and choice, by returning to selection in GMSs, we are in danger of returning to the days of grammar, technical and modern schools, and a secondary system of education largely divided according to social class.

The National Curriculum

The National Curriculum was intended to promote in pupils the development of 'lively inquiring minds, with the ability to question, argue and apply themselves to tasks'. It aims to provide pupils with knowledge and skills over a range of topic areas but focuses particularly on the acquisition of basic skills such as literacy and numeracy. In addition it aims to raise educational standards by setting achievable targets for learning.

The national curriculum applies to all pupils of compulsory school age attending state or grant maintained schools. The curriculum is organised in Key Stages.

Key Stage	Pupil Age	Year Group
1	5 to 7 yrs	1–2
2	7 to 11 yrs	3–6
3	11 to 14 yrs	7–9
4	14 to 16 yrs	10–11

At each Key Stage attainment targets are set. Attainment targets are a list of things that children can be expected to do at a certain age and are tested by SATs.

Initially the National Curriculum did not find favour with teachers. One of their main concerns was that it was too rigid and did not allow for flexibility and innovation. Teachers felt the increased amount of paperwork would take valuable time away from lesson preparation and other classroom tasks directly related to the learning process. These concerns were acknowledged by Sir Ron Dearing in his review in 1995. More 'free' time was made available to teachers and the content of the curriculum cut back. There is still some argument as to the usefulness of SATs and dispute over the value of publishing such results.

ACTIVITY

1 Research Key Stage 1.
2 Consider the attainment targets at Key Stage 1 for Numeracy, Literacy or Science and choose one.
3 Design a piece of topic work for a Year 1 group that follows a theme, for example, transport, work or animals. Plan at least 3 activities. Write a brief report that says which attainment targets are being met and how the activity stimulates child development.

The Education Bill 1997

The Labour Party's 1997 **Election Manifesto** made it clear that education was its number one priority. They said they would:

- increase spending on education
- have 'zero tolerance' of poorly performing schools
- guarantee quality nursery education for all 4 year-olds
- focus on standards in primary schools

The Labour Party won a resounding victory in the 1997 election and outlined their proposals for education reform in the Education Bill (1997). The Bill contains a number of proposals which include

- the reduction of class sizes to 30 or under for 5, 6 and 7 year-olds
- grouping children in classes according to ability
- the DfEE to give a strong lead and help raise school standards
- LEAs given greater powers to deal with poorly performing schools
- changes to the National Curriculum with a stronger focus on literacy and numeracy – literacy summer schools and homework clubs
- integrate where possible children with special needs into mainstream schools
- improved representation of parents, as governors and on LEAs

Pre-school provision

Informal networks – including families, friends and neighbours – provide the majority of care for pre-school children in Britain, particularly those under 3 years. These networks are becoming more fragile. People move around more and do not necessarily live near family members who could help with child care. Women go out to work, reducing the number available at home that can offer to care for the children of other family members or friends. Most parents prefer their younger children to be cared for by someone they know. Patricia Hewitt and Penelope Leach, in *Social Justice, Children and Families* (1993), cite a British Social Attitude Survey. Mothers were asked to imagine their ideal form of child care. Top of the list was time for themselves or their partners, so that they could combine parenting with work. Over half of the employed women said they would prefer to work only whilst their children were at school. In their ideal world, social and economic arrangements would allow parents to combine parenting and work. Unfortunately employment patterns are based around traditional notions of the working day being 9am – 5pm and the working year about 46 to 48 weeks. The ideal expressed in this survey is not available and would require significant changes to policy for it to become a reality.

The majority of parents are reliant on some form of pre-school provision.

- Childminder
- Day Nursery
- Private Nursery
- Nannies and 'au pairs'
- Workplace Nursery
- Play group
- Nursery Schools and Classes (LEA)
- Before and after school clubs

The recent government interest in pre-school provision is linked to concerns about **demographic trends** and the needs of the **labour market**. A decline in the number of school leavers, coupled with skill shortages and difficulties with recruitment, has led to a recognition that women will be needed in the labour market. The **Department of Employment** in 1990 predicted that 4 out of 5 new jobs would go to women. If women are needed by the labour market, the issue of child care becomes a concern for economic policy. In addition, the level of provision for under 5s in Britain is one of the lowest in Europe. All the political parties have struggled with this issue, largely due to the high costs involved in providing the comprehensive service needed.

The needs of the labour market are one thing but the needs of the child must be far more important. The National Children's Bureau in 'A Policy for Young Children' (1990) maintain that 'all children should have access to good quality pre-school experiences, that are appropriate to their stage of development'. It has long been recognised that young children benefit from social interaction with their peers and the play opportunities provided by pre-school provision.

ACTIVITY

1 List the benefits of pre-school provision for under 5s.
2 Choose three countries that are member states of the European Union (other than Britain) and compare their level of provision with our own.

In 1989 The **Rumbold Committee** made a report to the then Education Secretary, Kenneth Baker (Conservative), on Education Provision for the

Under-5s. Later the same year the Conservative Government announced a five-point programme for developing child care provision:

1 amendments to the Children's Bill 1988 (it became the Children Act 1989) to improve the registration requirements for day-care;
2 guidance to be issued to LEAs and School Governors on the use of school premises for holiday and after school clubs;
3 encourage providers to consider the need for a voluntary accreditation scheme to provide information about availability of child care facilities;
4 support the voluntary sector;
5 encourage employers to utilise the tax relief available to provide child care.

All of the above measures were addressed, some with little success. Few employers provide workplace nurseries and an accreditation scheme does not seem to have emerged. Also in 1989 calls were made to improve the training of those working with under 5s. More teacher training places for this age group were to be made available and a framework of qualifications would be developed (NVQ). Specialists in this area have been involved in the development of 'desirable outcomes' for under 5s.

The Nursery Education Voucher Scheme

The Nursery Education Voucher Scheme underpinned Conservative policy on pre-school education. In its guide to the Nursery Education Voucher Scheme, the DfEE described nursery vouchers as a way of giving parents greater control of the funds available for their child's place in pre-school education. It sought to give parents purchasing power and the power to choose a high quality nursery place that suited the needs of their child. The Nursery Education Voucher Scheme began to operate throughout England in April 1997. The parent of every 4 year-old was eligible to receive a voucher worth up to £1100. They could be used for up to three terms of nursery education in validated provision. A registered provider had to agree to

- meet the desirable outcomes (initially work towards)
- publicise information for parents
- provide places for children with Special Educational Needs and follow the SEN Code of Practice
- provide in the first two years three sessions per week and thereafter five sessions per week (a session represents a half day or not less than 2.5 hours)

Many small providers in areas where the number of pre-school children was low, were concerned about the impact of the voucher scheme. Some private nurseries and playgroups were particularly concerned that schools would increase the level of nursery education they provided or take children into reception class at 4. Some LEAs did change their entry policy and are providing a greater level of service to 4 year-olds. The General Election in May 1997 saw a change of Government and the **Labour Party** decided to scrap nursery vouchers altogether and replace them with a new Nursery Education Scheme.

THE FUTURE OF NURSERY EDUCATION

Things that stay the same

- providers that have been validated for vouchers can receive funding for places taken by eligible 4 year-olds (those that had vouchers) until March 1998
- providers must continue to meet desirable outcomes
- providers must continue to take note of the Code of Practice for children with special needs
- nursery inspections will continue

Things that will change

- a plan must be draw up by the LEA in consultation with all local interested parties and an Early Years Partnership established:
- the plan must show how a good quality place can be provided for all eligible 4 year-olds whose parents want one

How places will be funded

- the government will provide £366 per term for five sessions
- the LEA is responsible for finding places for eligible 4 year-olds and this may include playgroups and private nursery schools as well as LEA nursery classes

The Future

- LEAs should set targets to extend provision to 3 year – olds
- an Early Years Education partnership should be established in every LEA. This group is responsible for drawing up and monitoring the developmental plan
- a qualified teacher should be involved in all early years settings. The level of involvement has yet to be decided
- provision for Children with Special Needs should be integrated into mainstream settings wherever possible
- a network of 25 centres of excellence will be established as models of good practice

(From DfEE guidelines circulated May 1997)

Desirable outcomes

Desirable outcomes are 'goals for children's learning'. Like the National Curriculum they are divided into topic areas. They are designed to address the needs of 4 year-olds.

PERSONAL AND SOCIAL DEVELOPMENT

This outcome focuses on how children learn to play, co-operate with others and function in a group.

LANGUAGE AND LITERACY

This outcome covers aspects of language development and communication, providing the foundations for literacy.

MATHEMATICS

This outcome considers aspects of mathematical understanding and provides the foundation for numeracy.

KNOWLEDGE AND UNDERSTANDING OF THE WORLD

This outcome focuses on children's understanding of their environment and other people (History and Geography). It also provides for learning about the technical world (IT).

PHYSICAL DEVELOPMENT

This outcome focuses on the child's physical control, mobility, awareness of space and manipulative skills.

CREATIVE DEVELOPMENT

This outcome focuses on the development of the child's imagination and ability to express ideas and feelings in creative ways.

(from: The Schools Curriculum and Assessment Authority. 'Nursery Education, Desirable Outcomes for Children's Learning, HMSO, 1996')

ACTIVITY

Find out more about desirable outcomes. Choose one topic area and devise a curriculum plan that shows how you would meet this outcome in a playgroup setting.

OFSTED

The 1992 Education Act saw the development of the OFSTED

Inspectorate. Its role is to ensure the quality of provision in pre-school and primary school care and education. OFSTED is responsible for nursery inspections focusing on SCAA's desirable outcomes in pre-schools and the National Curriculum in primary schools.

Lifelong Learning

The idea that education only takes place in schools, colleges and universities between the ages of 5 and 22 is now accepted as unrealistic. The demands of new technology and work make it necessary for people to keep updating their skills or learn new ones. Learning takes place throughout life. All of the major political parties are committed to promoting adult education and training. A number of schemes are being developed to enable adults to return to education or training. Employers are being encouraged to assist workers and provide some financial help.

Children with special needs

The **1944 Education Act** addressed the needs of children with special needs and defined 11 categories of handicap. It required local authorities to provide education for children with special needs. The term 'special need' was not applied at that time and the service provided for children was largely based on the separation of children with special needs into 'special schools and residential institutions'.

The 11 categories of handicap were described as:

▶ deaf	blind	partially blind
▶ partially deaf	delicate	diabetic
▶ epileptic	speech defective	physically handicapped
▶ maladjusted	educationally sub-normal	

ACTIVITY

Consider the language used above, and the fact that there are some terms here we would not use today because they promote a negative image of children with special needs. Make a list of those terms and say what you think is negative about them. What makes the remaining descriptions acceptable?

The **Education Act 1970** included severe mental handicap. These definitions were common until the 1980s. In 1978 **Mary Warnock** was commissioned to undertake a review of educational provision for 'children and young people with disabilities of body or mind'. The **Warnock Report** recommended that

- where possible these children should be integrated into mainstream schools
- the categories of handicap removed and replaced with special educational needs (SEN)
- a child's special educational needs (SEN) defined as mild, moderate or severe
- the term Specific Learning Difficulties (SLD) applied to children that had difficulty in particular tasks, for example reading or writing.

These recommendations were incorporated into the **1981 Education Act**. The next leap forward was the **Code of Practice on the Identification and Assessment of Children with Special Educational Needs**, and was the result of the **Education Act 1993**. The Code of Practice was introduced in 1994 and gives guidance on the identification and assessment process and clearly defines the steps that should be taken to ensure that, where necessary, a child receives a Statement of Special Educational Need. The statement is a legal document that sets out the nature of the child's individual needs and the services available to ensure those needs are met.

ACTIVITY

Refer to the Code of Practice on the Identification and Assessment of Children with Special Needs. This can be obtained from the DfEE. You should also find a copy in your local library.

1 Find out what the five stages in the statementing process are.
2 Research the roles and responsibilities of the professionals involved in supporting children with 'special needs'.

3 Find out how effective policy on the integration of children with special needs has been in your local area.

The role of the state in education

After this overview, what then is the role of the state in education? According to Michael Hill (1996) the state has three main roles: regulator, funder, and planner and provider.

Regulator

As a regulator, the state does not leave decisions about education entirely to parents. Legislation makes education compulsory for children aged 5 to 16 years. The **National Curriculum** regulates the content of education and **OFSTED** inspections maintain standards and quality.

Funder

In the main, the education service is funded by the state. The ways in which schools are funded is complicated and depends on their status, for example **grant maintained** or under **Local Education Authority** (LEA) control. LEAs receive funding from central government. They then use it to provide education. Local Management of Schools (LMS) is a system of funding where the LEA gives money directly to schools who then decide how to spend it. LEAs will put some conditions on how the money can be spent. Grant maintained schools receive their funding directly from central government. The private sector is still relatively small in Britain, but provision in this area has been supported by government policies over the last 20 years. In some cases schools may be funded by the church or a charitable organisation.

Planner and provider

The state is responsible for making sure that education is available to children aged 5 to 16 years. It takes a lead role in developing policies that affect the way education is organised, for instance the National Curriculum and the Education Bill 1997. However the last 10 years have seen changes in the way that education is provided, particularly for the over 16s. The role of the LEA has been cut back. Colleges of Further and Higher Education, and universities, have been given independent status and are now businesses in their own right. Similarly some schools are opting out of LEA control, by becoming grant maintained.

Differences in educational attainment

It has been recognised for many years that some groups do better in education than others. This section considers the differences between different social classes, between males and females, and between ethnic groups.

1 Social class and educational attainment

In broad terms, academic achievement and social class are linked. On average, the higher a child's class of origin the higher their final educational qualifications. The lower the child's social class, the more likely they will end up with none.

This link between social class and educational attainment has remained constant over all the years that it has been researched. Despite the many post-war attempts to encourage working-class success – for example the 1944 Act, comprehensives, the expansion of the university system, student grants – there has been little change to the traditional class-related inequalities in educational achievement.

At every level – from nursery to university – middle and upper-class children tend to do better than working-class children. Very significantly, this is even so when one compares middle and working-class children *of the same measured intelligence quotient* (IQ). If you take children of the same measured IQ at the age of 7, by 11 the middle-class children are likely to be doing better. So middle-class success can't be explained simply by saying that they are 'brighter' than working-class children. The phenomenon occurs even when they aren't.

To try to explain these differences, we look first at factors primarily to do with **1** the *home and family* and **2** the *school*.

Home and family

Material factors

In general, working-class families have a lower income and less wealth. With money in shorter supply, and little grant support for post-16 year-old students, working-class parents are more likely to pressurise their children – and particularly their girls – to leave education and seek work and an income.

Working-class children are likely to live in smaller houses, without a comfortable place in which to work, away from the noise and distraction of other family members.

Working-class parents are also less able to afford a range of educational experiences, such as given by books, toys and travel.

CULTURAL FACTORS: PARENTAL ENCOURAGEMENT

According to the findings of a famous study of children's progress over many years by J. W. B. Douglas, the crucial cultural factor in academic success is parental encouragement. Though important for both working and middle-class children, encouragement was generally higher in the middle-class. In part, this may reflect the greater familiarity and confidence of middle-class parents with education and academic study.

Working-class parents, on the other hand, may provide less encouragement partly because they have more mixed feelings about education and about their children succeeding educationally. For working-class parents, educational success can draw their child into an alien and unfamiliar world – perhaps one associated with 'snobs' or 'not for the likes of us' – into which it is difficult for the parents to follow and feel comfortable. For middle-class parents, their child's educational success confirms their middle-class position and the likelihood of the child remaining in a similar social world themselves.

CULTURAL FACTORS: 'TRADITIONAL' VALUES AND ATTITUDES

Certain values and attitudes – particularly associated with the traditional working-class – may also make academic success less likely. Barry Sugarman (1970), for example, suggests that, like their parents, working-class children are more likely to be *fatalistic* (accepting their situation and doubting their ability to change it), *present-oriented* (not making long-term plans or setting goals) and concerned with *immediate gratification and pleasure*. In other words, working-class children are less likely to work hard at school to achieve the distant reward of a well-paid job in the future.

According to Sugarman, if working-class parents socialise their children into such values and attitudes, this probably represents a realistic response to the types of jobs traditionally available. As manual workers, (and even more so as unemployed), they are used to having less job security (encouraging *fatalism*), have no career structure in their jobs and so less opportunity to improve their position (hence less need of *long-term planning*), and are used to having less surplus income to invest (so encouraging *immediate gratification*).

In another study, Paul Willis (1977) found some manual workers passing on values and attitudes to their children which were even more likely to discourage educational success. In this case, the mainly semi-skilled factory 'shop floor' workers passed on values and attitudes to their boys which encouraged them to create at school a 'counter-school culture' very much like the 'shop-floor culture' of their fathers and their mates at work. At work or at school, both fathers and sons opposed and challenged the values espoused by those in authority over them, and of their conformist peers – whom 'the lads' in school dismissed contemptuously as 'ear'oles'.

Although 'the lads' expected that the jobs they would get would be 'dead-end' and in many ways boring and unpleasant, nevertheless they looked forward to them because of the wages and their future acceptance into the world of 'real men'. The sort of job they wanted had to have a masculine ethos, and as few 'ear'oles' as possible. It would be one 'where people are not "cissies" and can "handle themselves", where "pen pushing" is looked down on, and which can pay good money quickly' (Willis, p. 96). Their attitude in school ensured their failure. But the macho male culture which ensured academic failure allowed them to take pride in their resistence to authority and solidarity with their mates, and perhaps helped them survive the types of jobs they acquired.

CULTURAL FACTORS: THE USE OF LANGUAGE

According to Basil Bernstein (1970), language is an important factor in explaining why working-class children don't do as well in education. In general, middle-class children and their parents use language in ways which are more precise and better express ideas: exactly the qualities required in education.

According to Bernstein, in England there are two types of speech code – the **restricted** and the **elaborated codes**. While middle-class children can use both, working-class children are likely to be limited to using the restricted code and this affects their educational success. The restricted code involves short, often unfinished sentences. It's a sort of verbal shorthand. Understanding the restricted code often depends on knowing what's being talked about, that is knowing the context. For instance, if you pass someone you know in the street who just says, 'Nice, isn't it?', what do you say? It could refer to all sorts of things. But because of the context – you're both outdoors, the sun's shining and the sky is blue – you assume that the reference is to the weather, and you can simply reply, 'Lovely'. Because both sides know what's being referred to, such an exchange can be entirely adequate and effective. In education, however, in writing essays and doing exams, children need to be able to describe and explain things in such a way that the reader doesn't need to know the context. If they can't, they are unlikely to do well educationally.

The second type of speech is the elaborated code. Someone using the elaborated code, as now, tries to 'spell out' the meaning taken for granted in the restricted code, so that the reader or listener doesn't have to guess at what is being referred to. It provides details and background information. Because meanings in the elaborated code are made more explicit, sentences tend to be longer and more complex, and use a wider range of vocabulary.

According to Bernstein, the middle-class use both the elaborated and restricted codes, depending on the situation, whilst the working-class (or at least the lower working-class) is limited to the restricted code. In their attempts to help children understand, teachers must mainly use the elaborated code. While this may feel perfectly familiar to a middle-class child, however, it may strike a working-class child as artificial and alien. They may resent both their difficulty in using such language forms and the pressure on them from teachers to do so.

ACTIVITY

'Spelling it out'

In one famous experiment, children were asked to write a story based on four pictures. Here are two examples.

Three boys are playing football and one boy kicks the ball and it goes through a window. The ball breaks the window and the boys are looking at it and a man comes out and shouts at them because they've broken it. And a woman looks out and tells them off, so they run away.

'They're playing football and he kicks it and it goes through the window and they're looking at it and he comes out and shouts at them because they've broken it and then she looks out and she tells them off so they run away.

(From B. Bernstein, *New Society*, 1970)

Counter-school culture

The 'lads' specialise in a caged resentment which always stops just short of outright confrontation. Settled in class, there is a continuous scraping of chairs, a bad-tempered tut-tutting at the simplest request, and a continuous fidgeting about, which explores every permutation of sitting or lying on a chair. During private study, some openly show disdain by apparently trying to go to sleep with their head sideways down on the desk, some have their backs to the desk gazing out of the window, or even vacantly at the wall. A continuous hum of talk flows around injunctions not to and everywhere there are rolled-back eyeballs and exaggerated mouthings of conspiratorial secrets.

(From P. Willis, 1977)

Living for the present?

Joey's view: We wanna live for now, wanna live while we're young, want money to go out with, wanna go with women now, and uh think about five, ten, fifteen years time when it comes, but other people, say people like the ear'oles, they'm getting their exams, they'm working, having no social life, having no fun, and they're waiting for fifteen years time, when they've got married and things like that. I think that's the difference. We are thinking about now, and having a laff now, and they're thinking about the future.

(From P. Willis, 1977)

1 In small groups, analyse the differences between the two stories in the first extract.
2 Explain with reference to all three extracts the ways in which educational success is made more or less likely.

Schools

Although family and class background seem to be the main factors which influence how well children do in education, the school can still make a difference. In a study of London primary school children's achievements in maths and English, children who were otherwise similar in terms of class, ethnicity and gender were found to achieve differently at different schools. Schools which seemed most 'successful' shared a number of characteristics:

the head gave purposeful leadership, teaching was challenging and stimulating, the classroom atmosphere was businesslike, and teachers tended to praise and reward rather than criticise and punish.

However, while good schools can boost children's achievement levels, they do so for both working and middle-class children. Thus, they do not remove the class gap in educational achievement and they cannot sufficiently compensate working-class children for their disadvantages.

Dividing children into streams (that is placed in the same group for all subjects) or sets (divided for particular subjects) has also been said to affect the educational success of working-class children. Working-class children are more likely to be placed in lower streams or sets, and children in those groups tend to make slower progress and achieve less than they are capable of.

There is also some evidence that teachers may have lower expectations of pupils they perceive as working-class. Teachers may overestimate the ability and motivation of middle-class children and underestimate those of working-class backgrounds. So teachers may make greater efforts with those they regard as able and motivated, may unconsciously award higher marks, may be more likely to allocate them to a higher stream or set, and so on.

ACTIVITY

Schools can make a difference

Dog Kennel Hill primary school and Grange primary school are both in the London borough of Southwark. In both, about a third of the pupils speak English as a second language and about half the children are eligible for school meals – a key indicator of social background. Yet, while almost 50 per cent of the 11 year-olds at Dog Kennel Hill primary achieved the standard expected for their age in English and mathematics, at Grange primary only 8 per cent did so in English and none in mathematics. However, governors and the head teacher accepted that the school had underperformed. And according to David McElroy, the school's new head teacher, 'Although the school is in a significantly socially disadvantaged area, we do not consider this an excuse for underachievement'.

(From J. O'Reilly and C. Norton, *The Sunday Times*, 1997)

But neighbourhoods matter too

Teyfant primary school, set amid the high-rise flats and prefab council houses of the Hartcliffe estate on the southern fringe of Bristol, is among the worst performing primary schools in the country according to the government's league tables.

With its local factories now shut, almost 70 per cent of its predominantly white inhabitants are unemployed. About 75 percent of the families on the estate are on benefit. Some 25 per cent of the parents themselves have literacy problems and most had their first child before the age of 21. Also, theft from the school has been a big problem. In one month in 1993 there were 22 burglaries, including a ram-raid. 'Criminals would watch from the high-rise blocks with binoculars,' said Gus Grimshaw, the head teacher. 'If a new video or a computer arrived they would be in that night to carry it away, sometimes still in its packaging.'

Over the past year, however, Teyfant has become what it describes as a community school, opening its doors for parents to return to the classroom for literacy and numeracy lessons. And 'There has not been a break-in for 18 months,' said Grimshaw. Not all the news is good news, however. Already, five of the 52 pupils who left Teyfant last year have been expelled from their secondary schools.

(From J. O'Reilly and C. Norton, *The Sunday Times*, 1997)

1 How do you think each school could improve their pupils success levels?
2 Are there other ways (beyond that mentioned in the Tayfant extract above) in which schools could get involved in their communities? How would any changes be resourced?

2 Gender and educational attainment

Although class differences in educational attainment remain stubbornly persistent, in achievement related to gender there has been recent and spectacular change. Females have long since outperformed males at primary level, especially in areas involving language skills. For instance, even in the 11 Plus exam under the old tripartite system in the 1950s, females were already outperforming males. More recently however, at GCSE level, females have increased the overall lead they have had for a number of years across a range of subjects. Now, they are even achieving more top pass grades than boys in science, finance and computer studies, and achieving similar results in maths – subjects once regarded as 'male strongholds'.

In the 1990s, however, girls are also outperforming boys at 'A' level and beyond into university degree level. For instance, by 1992 more females than males were gaining 3 or more 'A' levels. Through the 1990s, girls have continued to extend their lead in traditionally 'feminine' subjects such as English, English literature, modern languages, history and biology. Significantly, however, they have also been catching up in both mathematics and the sciences, with females who take the exams in those subjects now more likely than boys to 'pass' in mathematics, physics, chemistry and technology.

So, while boys who are behind at the age of 11 have traditionally been expected to catch up, given their later maturity, the evidence of the last few years suggests that boys tend not to catch up but instead fall further behind, with the gap widening during the teen years.

How can these reverses be explained? There is now a significant body of evidence that male and female attitudes to educational attainment have changed. Why that might be is considered after a brief review of the research findings.

Changes in attitude and behaviour of male and female pupils

While it does seem to be the case that female attitudes to educational attainment – and to maths and science in particular – have become more positive and more confident, male attitudes and behaviours seem to have suffered a corresponding deterioration.

Research conducted in the 1990s confirms that, compared to boys, girls are more motivated, more ambitious, more likely to want to stay in education and less likely to want to leave school and start a family. In general, girls work harder, are more prepared to do schoolwork at home and spend longer on it, value qualifications more and have given more thought to their futures.

By contrast, boys – and especially working-class boys – appear to be experiencing low self-esteem and poor motivation, with lower levels of concentration and self-discipline. They read less easily, are more reluctant to write, and understand less of what they read. In groups, they set themselves lower attainment norms and are more likely to discourage hard work and academic achievement. Despite underachieving, many seem relatively unconcerned about it.

There are two main explanations for these changes. The first is to do with policies which have aimed to make traditionally 'male' subjects such as maths and sciences more 'female-friendly'. The second concerns changes in male and female roles beyond the school.

1 Correcting gender-bias in schools

Until recently, research suggested that girls in co-educational schooling often experienced a decline in their self-esteem and settled for lower career ambitions than their ability would suggest. Consequently females were under-represented in higher education and thereafter in the more prestigious jobs. Female underachievement was nowhere greater than in maths, and in sciences such as physics and chemistry (though not biology).

In a conscious response to this, however, came a number of equal opportunity initiatives, intended particularly to encourage girls into areas traditionally dominated by males. Although such national projects as 'Girls into Science and Technology' and 'Girls and Technology Education' seem to have had some limited direct effect, they may have had a bigger indirect effect by encouraging teachers to reconsider how science has been taught and the importance of making it more 'female-friendly'. Additionally, a growing awareness of equal opportunity issues has encouraged schools generally to reappraise teaching methods and materials for sex-bias and consider how to increase girls' interest and involvement in education.

2 Changes in adult gender roles

The changes in male and female attitudes to education and attainment discussed above seem to have been more affected by experiences beyond the school than by specific educational policies. For instance, two-thirds of women now work, and almost two-thirds of them are in full-time employment. At the same time, unemployment is hitting males particularly hard and the trend is expected to continue. While traditionally male jobs in engineering, construction and manufacturing continue to decline, new 'female' jobs in service industries and information technology are expected to be created. There is also evidence of the 'feminisation' of work, with women being employed in preference, as employers increasingly value such qualities characteristically associated with females as communicational skills, teamwork and flexibility.

Additionally, separation and divorce have become common and girls are seeing adult females having to cope in what was once 'a man's world', and often providing a positive role model by doing so competently and successfully. Significantly, perhaps, girls seem generally more optimistic about the future.

ACTIVITY

Socialisation into gender roles

Recent research suggests that the most influential factor in the higher achievement of girls is parents. Between two and four years old, children, who are wanting to please their parents, are picking up ideas of what the parents want them to be good at. Giving them clues, parents generally spend less time reading to boys, buying them books and talking about books. On the contrary, fathers spend more time with boys doing other things, such as sporting activities. Already, by the age of six, therefore, many children have ideas about how the sexes differ: e.g. 'Boys don't work hard.' By their teens, many (particularly working class) males have a clear idea that 'It's not a macho thing to work (at school)', 'You want to have a laff', 'You want to stand out'.

(from *Panorama*, BBC 1, 1994)

The influence of adult role models

The authors of recent research into the underachievement of males relate their findings to the gender 'regimes' which the young people encounter in their homes and communities. With more women working, girls are increasingly likely to have working mothers providing positive role models. And at least some of the girls studied, exposed to the image of woman as organiser, responsible for home and family and wage-earning, displayed similar characteristics themselves, i.e. being highly organised with school work and homework. However, according to Harris *et al.*, the dominant stereotype of the male in the working class communities they examined was highly 'macho'. Typically, this involved a disregard for the authority of organisations and an enjoyment of the active company of other males. Some boys were already fulfilling such a stereotype in their approach to school, showing little regard for working steadily, and dissociating themselves from the demands of the school.

(From J. Clark, *Sociology Review*, 1996)

In favour of single-sex schools

> Sir, The advantages to girls of single-sex education are well recognised. However, concern is now surfacing about the underachievement of boys. The relentless spread of coeducation may have contributed to this by polarising the sexes, suggesting to boys that academic achievement is 'girlie' and encouraging them in laddishness, to differentiate themselves as much as possible from their female classmates. So single-sex schools are possibly good for boys as well as girls. Yours faithfully, J. Lang, President, Girls' Schools Association
>
> (From a Letter to the Editor, *The Times*, 1997)

1 In small groups, identify some of the different factors mentioned which help explain the current differences in gender-based educational success.
2 Now try to evaluate some of these different factors which help explain differences in gender-related educational success.
3 Make a list of any other relevant factors you can think of, and say why they are relevant.

How to help boys succeed

Although the evidence for male underachievement is now quite comprehensive, and the causes of it much discussed, there have been relatively few suggestions as to what, in practical terms, could be done to boost boys' achievements.

One of the few attempts to provide practical advice comes from Professor Ted Wragg (1997).

ACTIVITY

Professor Wragg's 'ten point plan'

1 **Start early** Encourage boys to attend nurseries, to make an early start on language activities and learn to behave well in class.
2 **Help at home** More fathers should help at home, especially with reading and writing, so language is not seen as a 'female' activity.

3 **Give special support early** Schools or other agencies must provide early specialist help for the many boys who make a slow start to reading.
4 **Appeal to boys' interests** Wherever possible boys' reading should appeal to their interests and likes, such as humour, adventure and sport.
5 **Improve boys' behaviour** Work on improving boys' behaviour so that they concentrate better and distract others less. Trying hard at school should come to be seen as normal, not 'swottish', effeminate or 'uncool'.
6 **Raise awareness of boys' underachievement** Parents, children and teachers need to be more aware of boys' underachievement, and of how early it can start.
7 **Use new technology** Many young boys like using new technology and often concentrate more when they use it.
8 **Involve boys in their own learning** Boys must be directly involved in improving their own performance, setting themselves targets, improving relationships and knowing when to ask for help.
9 **Identify secondary pupils 'at risk'** As well as supporting young children falling behind, secondary school boys likely to be 'at risk' when they leave must also be identified and helped.
10 **Redesign Key Stage 4** 14 to 18 year-olds need to be able to mix 'academic' and 'vocational' modules to meet their individual needs and interests.

(From T. Wragg, *Times Educational Supplement*, 1997)

1 Working in small groups, select two or three of Professor Wragg's proposals and suggest practical ways in which the aims can be achieved.
2 How would you enlist parents' support in a catchment area where many parents are not noticably supportive of education?

3 Ethnicity and educational attainment

From a number of studies, it seems that children in the United Kingdom who come from different ethnic groups do achieve differentially in education. On average, some groups do better and others worse. However, the evidence is not straightforward and both the evidence and the interpretations are argued over.

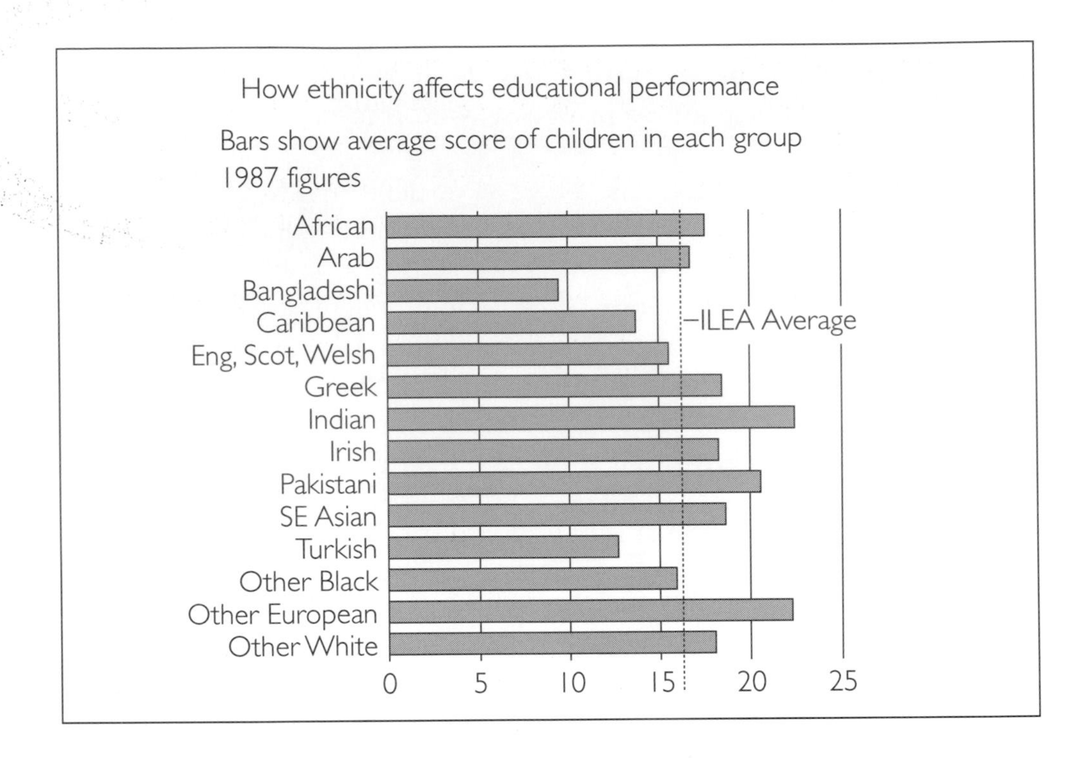

Explanations of differential ethnic attainment

How do sociologists try to explain these variations in educational achievement? There are three main types of explanation, each of which can offer insights.

Structural explanations

In the first approach, explanations focus on material factors to do with wealth, income and social class. In this view, just as class must be taken into account in explaining differences in attainment within the white ethnic majority, so it is quite misleading to compare the achievements of different ethnic groups while ignoring the class composition of the groups. For instance, children from Indian backgrounds have generally done far better in British secondary school exams than Bangladeshis. But Indian parents in this country also have higher educational and social class levels than adults from a Bangladeshi background. So too do those of another high-achieving group – from Hong Kong.

Cultural interpretations

A second interpretation stresses possible subcultural differences between ethnic groups. So, the relative success of some ethnic groups such as Jews, Indians or Pakistanis, is seen to reflect a cultural background which encourages and supports high levels of achievement. It is argued that among such ethnic groups a high value is attached to education by both family and community. Similarly, there is a general ethos of hard work, supported by a tightly-knit community with a sense of tradition and high levels of self-esteem and motivation, all of which encourages educational success.

Such an interpretation implies, of course, that less 'successful' groups, such as Afro-Caribbeans, lack the values, and family and community encouragement, to achieve in education. Yet there are problems with that analysis. First, it is interesting that, in the United States, those of Jamaican background are noted as high achievers. This throws up some interesting questions. Are Jamaican-Americans of a different class profile to British-Jamaicans? Or is American society somehow more supportive?

A second challenge to the idea that the Afro-Caribbean culture mitigates against educational success is the evidence that, in their early years, Afro-Caribbeans' levels of attainment are often high. It is mainly during secondary education that Afro-Caribbean performance – as conventionally measured by school and educational authorities – slumps. Indeed, according to many Afro-Caribbeans, there is a traditionally high value attached to education, which helps explain early Afro-Caribbean attainment. For instance, according to Heidi Safia Mirza of London's South Bank University, whose own parents came to Britain from Trinidad 30 years ago, early literacy and numeracy among Afro-Caribbean children 'reflect the motivation and investment of Caribbean parents in education. Like their parents before them, they devote incredible amounts of time to helping their children to read' (quoted in Hymas and Cohen, 1994).

Explanations focusing on racism

In a third approach – not necessarily denying the insights of the two interpretations above – advocates emphasise how crucial *racism* can be in affecting educational, and other, success: both the *experience* of racism, of being on the receiving end of it, and of how different ethnic groups may have *responded* to it.

In this view, it is by focusing attention on the prejudice and discrimination suffered by different ethnic groups, and perhaps on their responses, that the relative frequency of Afro-Caribbean children's subsequent underachievement can be understood. Thus, Afro-Caribbean underachievement is interpreted by many primarily in terms of the prejudice and discrimination which they encounter at school. Additional to, and intermixed with, such prejudice and discrimination may be more or less genuine cross-cultural misunderstandings.

For instance, though black pupils may come to secondary education relatively well qualified, they are up to 4 times more likely to be suspended from secondary school than whites. This seems in part due to the stereotypical expectations of some white teachers, who expect blacks to misbehave. According to David Mallen, the Inner London Education Authority's education officer, while 'Asian children are considered thoughtful, hardworking and capable, these are not the sort of qualities associated with Caribbean children' (quoted in Hymas and Cohen, 1994). It can also be partly due to white teachers misinterpreting the body language of blacks as hostile, arrogant and defiant. David Gillborn, a researcher at London's Institute of Education: 'A typical example could be three black kids grouped on a staircase, which might be regarded as threatening by the teacher. My research suggests that translates into different treatment of black pupils by white teachers' (quoted in Hymas and Cohen, 1994).

It is controversial why Afro-Caribbean students' experience of racism seems to result in their being significantly more disadvantaged than some other non-white groups, also subjected to prejudice and discrimination. It has been suggested that some Asian groups have traditionally responded more passively to racism than blacks, and sought instead the solace and support of their own well-structured community. It may also, or alternatively, be that white teachers' expectations of Asian students – whatever the attitudes and behaviours towards them of white schoolchildren – have been higher and more positive, seeing them as predisposed to education and achievement, and more accepting of authority.

ACTIVITY

'Young black pupils at the top of the class'

Black children are outperforming pupils from all other races at the age of five in the most important skills of reading, writing and arithmetic, new research reveals. The study of more than 6,000 five year olds shatters the stereotype that Afro-Caribbean children are 'trapped' by underachievement and low aspirations from birth.

The study, by Birmingham education authority, reveals that black children start school with the best grasp of the basics and maintain their lead until at least seven. Afro-Caribbeans were almost twice as likely as five-year-olds from other ethnic groups to be classed as above average in mathematics tests. White and Indian pupils were behind but on a par, followed by Bangladeshis and Pakistanis. In reading and writing, the proportion of pupils a year or more ahead for their age were: black 4.6 per cent, white 3.6 per cent. Thirty per cent of all Birmingham pupils were average or above for their age, but 32.1 per cent of the Afro-Caribbeans.

Similar results are revealed in National Curriculum tests for seven year-olds in English and mathematics – a phenomenon academics attribute to the value placed on a good education by many black families.

(From C. Hymas and J. Cohen, *Sunday Times*, 1994)

Extracts from a 1985 study of two midlands comprehensives, by Cecile Wright

The study found that Afro-Caribbean students entered the two schools with reading ages on a par with or higher than those attained by the Asian and white groups. Yet they finished up with only one child in each school entered to take five or more 'O' levels.

Despite their generally higher attainment levels on entry, Afro-Caribbean students were seen by staff as less well-behaved and less cooperative and this led to many being placed in lower ability streams. In one school, nearly 20% of Afro-Caribbeans compared to 7.7% of Asians and no whites were placed in remedial groups. In the other school, Afro-Caribbean students in the lower ability stream had the highest average performance of all three groups in the sample. Even when there was a clear case for reallocation to a higher stream, teachers were extremely reluctant to make the change.

Afro-Caribbean students encounter, or believe they encounter, racial prejudice and discrimination from teachers. By about the third year in the secondary school they respond with lack of interest in their work and with disruptive behaviour.

(From B. Passmore, *The Times Educational Supplement*, 1985)

1 Consider the extracts above. What evidence do you find for any of the sociological explanations of the educational performance of black pupils?
2 What would be the most important thing to change to encourage greater educational success among black pupils?

Summary

- the most significant independent schools are the public schools, which provide a disproportionate share of the nation's elites
- 'post-war' education reform began with the 1944 Education Act, which upheld the principles of free and assessable education for all
- the 1988 Education Reform Act introduced the National Curriculum, which aimed to raise educational standards by setting achieveable targets for learning
- the requirements for Children with Special Needs have been addressed through a Code of Practice introduced in 1994
- the voucher scheme was replaced: LEAs are required to draw up developmental plans in consultation with interested parties in an Early Years Partnership and provide a plan to show how the LEA will ensure a good quality place for all 4 year-olds whose parents want one
- working-class underachievement in education is explained in terms of material factors, and cultural factors which include less parental encouragement, use of the restricted language code, some traditional values and attitudes, as well as school-related factors
- females have overtaken males at almost all educational levels. Male underachievement seems to reflect less positive attitudes, which may in turn be due to gender socialisation and changes in adult gender roles
- some ethnic minority groups outperform the white majority, but Bangladeshi and Afro-Caribbean attainment is relatively low: factors which may help explain this include class background, attitudes to education and racism

9

Child health

Key points

- children's death rate has fallen dramatically this century
- children's health has also generally improved, though some diseases now affect more children
- there are class differences in children's risk of death and ill-health, due to structural and cultural factors
- females live longer than males but appear to suffer more sickness
- health-risk behaviour also varies by sex
- the most common children's disability is behavioural
- the role of the state in the provision of health care is to act as funder, planner and provider of services
- good health is reliant on more than medical provision

Trends in child mortality

Technically, 'child mortality' refers to the death of children under 6 years old. But, for convenience, the way it is used here refers to the death of any child, that is up to 16 years old.

A child's expectation of life or **life expectancy** means, roughly, how long on average babies born in their year can be expected to live. During this century people's expectation of life in Britain and the West has risen. In 1900 at birth British females could be expected to live on average to about 50 years old, and males to about 46. Born in 1994, females could expect to live about 78 years, and males about 72. However, the figures are misleading. The 1900 figure is pulled down by the relatively high number of young deaths. If people born in 1900 survived into adulthood, they stood a fair chance of living into their 60s or even beyond.

The improvement in children's death rate this century has been impressive and quite comprehensive. Babies are now less likely to be born dead (stillborn), to die within the first month (neonatal mortality), die within the first year (**infant mortality**) and they *are* more likely to make it to adulthood than they were at the start of the century. In 1901, for instance, 149 in every thousand babies died before their first birthday. By 1992, this had fallen to just seven. But at every age, from birth to old age, people nowadays are more likely to survive.

What are the main causes of child death today?

One major change in child mortality compared to a century ago is that children today are much less likely to die from *infectious diseases*. Major killers of the last century, such as tuberculosis, measles, scarlet fever, whooping cough, mumps, pneumonia, and so on, are now seldom fatal (though they are by no means 'beaten' and there are some worrying signs of a 'comeback' in some cases).

Nearly 4100 children under 15 died in the United Kingdom in 1992. By and large, children die for different reasons to older people. Of babies who died before their first birthday, the major killers were *congenital disabilities* (about 25 per cent of the total) and another 25 per cent were *cot deaths* Remarkably, five years earlier, cot deaths had been three times higher.

Technically known as 'Sudden Infant Death Syndrome' (SIDS), cot death happens when an otherwise healthy infant dies suddenly, usually in their cot. SIDS peaked in 1988 and then declined, falling most dramatically between 1991 and 1992 when cot deaths halved. This is thought to be because of the success of a medical campaign to have babies placed on their backs for sleeping, room temperature kept between 16 and 20 degrees Centigrade, not over-wrapping the baby, and keeping the baby away from cigarette smoke.

As children get older, they are less likely to die. However, children are more likely than adults to die through *accidents* and *injury*. They are more likely to die from *road accidents*, the cause of 71 per cent of deaths among the 10 to 14 year-olds. Although road fatalities (but not injuries) have declined in recent years, this is thought to be partly due to the dramatic fall in the number of children allowed out on the roads.

Children are also more likely to die through *home accidents* involving fire, drowning, cycling, or through poisoning. In fact, with road and other accidents combined, Britain has the worst rate of child casualties in Western Europe.

One child in 600 still develops *cancer* before the age of 15. But fewer children die – and those that do generally live longer before dying. Cancer now accounts for about 1 in 5 deaths between ages 1 to 14, a rate which has fallen by 43 per cent over the last 20 years. Leukaemia is the most common type, accounting for about 3 in every 10 cases.

A further major cause of death among children and young people is suicide. This appears to have been increasing through the late 1980s and into the 1990s, although the increase may partly reflect coroners' current tendency to record deaths as suicides, rather than an actual increase.

Child morbidity (sickness or ill-health)

In 1995 the Office of Population Censuses and Surveys (OPCS) brought together data aimed at answering the question, 'Are our children healthier?' While there seems no doubt that this was the case during the century as a whole, the survey found that, even since 1970, children have been getting healthier.

Very significantly, over the century, *infectious diseases* have declined dramatically. Last century, they were the main cause of childhood death. But even between 1974 and 1992, measles fell by 91 per cent, whooping cough by 86 per cent and tuberculosis by 57 per cent. Experts believe that these improvements reflect the widespread immunisation of children and improved diagnosis and treatment.

Easy to overlook, but a dramatic improvement nevertheless, is in children's dental health. In 1983, 42 per cent of 15 year-olds had active tooth decay, but by 1993 this had fallen to 30 per cent. There are, however, big differences between the countries of the United Kingdom. Among 15 year-olds in 1993 the incidence of active tooth decay was as follows: Scotland 46 per cent, Northern Ireland 44 per cent, Wales 32 per cent and England 27 per cent.

However, some other diseases have been increasing. They include:

- respiratory (breathing) diseases
- obesity
- eating disorders
- stress

Respiratory diseases

These now account for 1 in 3 visits to GPs. Overall, during the past 20 years, childhood asthma has doubled. It now affects about 1 in every 7 children. Even more striking: between 1962 and 1985, hospital admissions for asthma for young children (0 to 4 years) increased 13-fold. For those aged 5 to 14 years it increased 6-fold.

Weight problems

These have increased. According to a Royal College of Physicians report about 5 per cent of children are now overweight. But the proportion increases with age. The 1993 *Health Survey for England* found that 44 per cent of men and 32 per cent of women were overweight. On top of this, however, a further 13 per cent of men and 16 per cent of women were identified as 'obese' (seriously overweight).

Eating disorders

It is very difficult to be sure to what extent eating disorders have increased or merely become more 'visible'. However, the founder of the National Centre for Eating Disorders, Deanne Jade, believes that, among teenage girls, eating disorders are at unprecedented levels. She estimates that one in every 100 girls will become anorexic – refusing to eat for fear of becoming fat – with even more becoming bulimic – bingeing and then vomiting to avoid weight gain.

Jade is alarmed that so many girls are learning – often before reaching their teens, and often from their mothers – that they need to be thin to be loved and so must diet. She estimates that one-third of 9 year-old girls have already dieted, and that by age 15 the proportion has risen to 75 per cent.

Ironically, of course, those dieting are often not the overweight or obese. In a mid-1980s survey for BBC2's *Brass Tacks*, half the dieters they interviewed were either the right weight or underweight for their height. Most of the 'unnecessary dieters' were female.

Stress

It seems that stress among children may also have increased. There are many causes of stress. For females especially, however, one factor is negative self-perception, which again can manifest in eating disorders, as mentioned above.

ACTIVITY

Self-dissatisfaction, stress and eating disorders

> Women not only agonise about their overall weight but also about specific parts of their bodies. In Elizabeth Davies's adolescent sample, about one-third were displeased with their busts; a slightly greater number with their waists. Though, at age 12, 75% of the girls were perfectly happy with their hips, by 18 this had plummeted to 38%, just over one-third. And unfortunately, there's more to come.
>
> When the girls were asked which parts of their body they found most distressing, upper thighs, buttocks and stomachs were the top-rankers. Among 12 year olds, between 10% and 20% were *already* worried about these. Among 18 year olds the proportion more than doubled.
>
> *Cosmopolitan* has decided not to print diet plans because of the increased rates of anorexia in young girls. But you still can't open an issue without falling over the thousands of super-slim leggy models.
>
> (Maryon Tysoe, *New Society* c. 1984)

1 What do you think of *Cosmopolitan*'s decision to ban diet plans, while retaining 'super-slim' models?
2 Do you think that such magazines encourage dissatisfaction among girls with their appearance?
3 Why do you think that eating disorders have increased, especially among girls?

Inequalities of children's health

1 Health and social class

Much sociological research uses this six-class scale.

Social class		Examples
I	Higher Professional	Doctor, lawyer, architect
II	Middle Managerial	Manager, teacher, social worker
IIIN	Routine non-manual	Clerk, secretary
IIIM	Skilled manual	Electrician, carpenter, plumber
IV	Semi-skilled manual	Postal worker, cash till operator
V	Unskilled manual	Labourer, porter

Inequalities in health between the social classes start at birth or even earlier. Using a social class scale such as the above, it is possible to see that many inequalities in health show what is called a social class gradient. What this means is that, in general, as one moves from Class I to Class V there is a growing likelihood of children:

- being born dead (*stillborn*)
- having *low birth weight* (that is under 2,500 grams/5.5 lb)
- *dying* in their *first year* of life
- being *disabled*
- suffering an *accident* or *injury*
- suffering *chronic* (longstanding) *illness*
- suffering *anxiety*
- exhibiting *behavioural problems* (for example hyperactivity, conduct disorder and school absenteeism)

Why are so many health differences linked to children's social class position? Most explanations mention a combination of structural and cultural factors.

STRUCTURAL EXPLANATIONS

Structural explanations focus on people's positions in the social structure, their class, occupation, ethnic group, and so on. They stress the disadvantages suffered by people in low power, low status groups:

- lack of capital and a low income
- poorer quality accommodation – likely to be damp, overcrowded, inadequately heated, poorly ventilated, and, if living in a city . . .
- polluted inner city living
- less nutritious diet – many studies have shown that poorer people often have a poorer diet because of insufficient money to spend on the relatively expensive, 'healthier' foods, rather than because of ignorance
- these and other disadvantages also increase the incidence of stress-related disorders, eg mental ill-health, heart problems

CULTURAL EXPLANATIONS

Cultural explanations stress that attitudes and values are important:

- there is a lower incidence of **breastfeeding** in lower classes – less nutritious diet. In the United Kingdom in 1990, 62 per cent of babies were breastfed at birth. **Socio-economic group 1**: 86 per cent mothers likely to breastfeed. **Socio-economic group 5**: 40 per cent mothers. In Scotland, **socio-economic group 1**: 84 per cent; **socio-economic group 5**: 28 per cent. In Northern Ireland: 81 per cent and only 18 per cent
- **smoking** – **socio-economic group 5** males 3 times more likely to smoke than males in **socio-economic group 1**
- children less likely to be **immunised**

However, the extent to which such behaviours as smoking and not having children immunised are due to cultural factors – such as lack of knowledge, or different attitudes to these activities – or more material factors is controversial. For instance, living in poverty, in poor housing in a threatening neighbourhood, can be highly stressful. It is perhaps not surprising that people living in such areas are more likely to smoke than are, for instance, middle-class lecturers and lawyers living in spacious houses, in leafy suburbs, and holidaying abroad twice a year. In such situations, smoking may be seen as an understandable – if misguided – response to stress rather than as a sign of not 'caring', or of irresponsibility, or of ignorance of the dangers.

2 Health and gender

On average, males live less long than females and, at almost any age, males are more likely to die. Nevertheless, women are more likely to report sickness, consult a doctor and be hospitalised. In particular, women seem more likely to suffer from chronic (long lasting) illnesses, and are more likely than males to be diagnosed neurotic, psychotic or depressive.

More boys than girls die at every age between birth and age 16. Girls are rather more likely than boys to die of congenital abnormalities and diseases of the nervous system or sense organs. Boys are rather more likely than girls to die of Sudden Infant Death Syndrome ('cot death'), injury and poisoning.

HEALTH-RISK BEHAVIOURS

Smoking is the largest preventable cause of death as well as being a major cause of ill-health. Although boys start experimenting with smoking earlier than girls, by the age of 14 girls are more likely to have tried smoking than boys. In 1992, 18 per cent of 11 year-olds in England had smoked at some time. By age 15, 64 per cent had smoked. Of the 15 year-olds who had smoked, 23 per cent were 'regular smokers' with another 10 per cent 'occasional smokers'. Since at least 1982, more girls than boys have been either regular or occasional smokers. Statistically, of those regular 15 year-old smokers who don't give up, one in four will be killed by it.

By contrast, alcohol drinking among under 16 year-olds is higher for boys than girls. Among 11 year-olds, 30 per cent of boys and 19 per cent of girls had alcoholic drinks at least a few times a year. Among 15 year-olds, the figures had risen to 87 per cent for the boys and 84 per cent of girls. It was found that 36 per cent of 15 year-old boys drank at least once a week, compared to 30 per cent of the girls.

Illegal drug use also varied between males and females. Among young people aged between 14 and 25 in 1982, cannabis had been used by 41 per cent of males and 25 per cent of females, amphetimines by 13 per cent of males and 6 per cent of females, 'magic mushrooms' by 12 per cent of males and 4 per cent of females, and acid/LSD by 11 per cent of males and 7 per cent of females. When all illicit drugs were included, some 45 per cent of males and 26 per cent of females between 14 and 25 years had used at least one.

ACTIVITY

Has smoking a special allure for females?

Despite three decades of hard-core medical evidence, smoking for women is still imbued with sex appeal and a sense of sophistication. Smoking for women is bound up with self-image. In social situations it makes a woman feel more powerful, with her cigarette acting as a distancing device, a prop that says, 'I'm cool, I'm different, don't get too near.' This was a pose immortalised by classic film noir idols like Lauren Bacall, whose smoking symbolised her entry into a hard male world.

Most women are in conflict about their smoking habits. Aside from the sophisticated aura, many feel that on a practical level they have to smoke to keep their weight down. This is largely illusory: a third of women who give up actually lose weight. Slim models cheerfully flashing cigarettes, however, do little to destroy this assumption.

Smoking for women is also a time-honoured way of coping with stress, allowing them to contain anger or frustration instead of expressing it. But the more popular picture is of female smokers looking cool and composed, so cigarettes seem like a form of personal emancipation.

(From L. O'Brien, *The Guardian*, 1989)

1 Identify what the appeals of smoking for women are said to be. What do you think of the suggestions made?
2 Do you agree with the implication of the extract, that smoking 'means' something different for females and for males? If so, what?

Disability and special needs

According to a 1985 survey, there are an estimated 360 000 British children under 16 years-old with one or more disabilities. These included problems of:

- locomotion (moving around)
- seeing or hearing
- intellectual functioning
- consciousness
- disfigurement

More boys than girls had disabilities – among 5 to 9 year-olds, 4.5 per cent of boys and only 3 per cent of girls.

The most common type of disability in all age groups is *behavioural*. This sort of disability – and some others such as in locomotion, personal care, continence and communication – seems to increase with age. Behavioural disability among the 0 to 4 year-olds was 1.3 per cent; among the 5 to 9 year-olds 2.3 per cent and among the 10 to 15 year-olds 2.4 per cent of all children. However, some of these apparent increases could be due to the disability being identified as the child goes to school.

ACTIVITY

The person behind a 'disability of disfigurement'

Dear Miss Lonelyhearts, I am 16 years old now and I dont know what to do and would appreciate it if you would tell me. When I was a little girl it was not so bad because I got used to the kids on the block makeing fun of me, but now I would like to have boyfriends like the other girls and go out on Saturday nites, but no boy will take me because I was born without a nose – although I am a good dancer and have a nice shape and my father buys me pretty clothes. I sit and look at myself all day and cry. What did I do to deserve such a terrible fate? Ought I commit suicide? Sincerely yours, Desperate

(From N. West, quoted in Goffman, 1963)

Disability as a 'stigma'

How do children who are blind, disfigured, stutterers, or otherwise 'abnormal', and treated more or less as social outcasts, maintain a semblance of dignity and self-esteem in the face of their humiliation? The American sociologist, Erving Goffman, uses the term **stigma** to help us understand how children with disability, for instance, may try to come to terms with their condition and the experience of rejection and humiliation which they are likely to have suffered.

A stigma is an attribute or characteristic which makes someone different from, and less desirable than, the 'normal'. A stigma carries with it some disgrace, shame or embarrassment, and results in what Goffman calls a 'spoiled identity'.

In his book *Stigma* (1961), Goffman examines some of the strategies people use in their attempts to cope. Some learn how to pass off their stigma in public or try to prevent the sneers and looks of others by joining in 'normal' society. If they can find them, others withdraw into the security of 'worlds' where their defects are considered normal. This may be limited to the family. Some may even fight back and try to encourage people to change their view of them and treat them equally, if necessarily differently.

(From 'Great ideas: Erving Goffman on stigma' *New Society*, 1985)

1 Goffman says that people with a disability may develop a sense of 'spoiled identity'. In what ways do you think the writer in the first extract has a spoiled identity?
2 In what ways may 'normal' people encourage a sense of stigma and spoiled identity among people with a disability?
3 What other conditions than disability can you think of which are stigmatised?
4 How do other stigmatised people cope? Do they adopt the coping strategies Goffman mentions? Are there others?
5 Can children be taught not to stigmatise others? How would you attempt it?

The role of the state in health care

The role of the state in health care is similar to the areas described in Chapter 8 in the discussion on education and social policy.

FUNDER

The state funds health service provision from taxation. The ways in which it distributes these funds are many and complex. Some services are funded centrally. That is, the government pays for them directly. Others are funded indirectly through Regional Health Authorities and NHS Trusts.

PLANNER

The state is responsible for planning the overall structure of the health service. A great many reorganisations have taken place between the first Health Service Act in 1946 and the 1990 National Health Service and Community Care Act. The initial aims of the 1946 Act were fulfilled. It brought together all the health services under one central ministry – The Ministry of Health. It nationalised the hospitals and GP practices.

In 1974 the health service was reorganised. The main aim of this reorganisation was to bring community health and hospital services under district management. It was hoped that the new structure would achieve a more balanced distribution of resources. In reality the system was found to be inefficient with lines of communication many and complicated.

In 1982 a new, simpler management structure was introduced. In 1983 Sir Roy Griffiths chaired the Management Inquiry and introduced a more business-like approach to the management of the health service. He suggested that cost-centred budgeting (service providers being responsible for deciding how to spend the money available to them) would involve practitioners (consultants, surgeons and doctors). This would make them more aware of the cost of treatment and the choices that have to be made about service delivery. Griffiths also introduced performance review and performance related pay.

In 1988 the Prime Minister (Margaret Thatcher) called for a review of the NHS. The White Paper 'Working for Patients' recommended yet further changes to the management and budgetary structure of the NHS. Those using the services of the NHS like fund holding GPs would 'purchase' services from the NHS Trusts. The public feared that the National Health Service was slowly being dismantled and would eventually disappear. These fears made the changes in the 1990 Act unpopular.

The Regional Offices have overall responsibility for the health service. They are responsible for the planning and management of capital expenditure (buildings and equipment) and the appointment of some specialist staff. The District Health Authorities (DHAs) are responsible for the management of the hospital and community services (except GP practices). They are required to enter into a contract with the local NHS Trusts and specialist units to secure services for the patients in their area. The Family Health Service Authorities (FHSAs) are responsible for non-fund holding GPs and pay them to provide services to local people. They also administer dental, optical and pharmaceutical services. The NHS Trusts are responsible for service delivery. Fund holding GPs are able to purchase treatment for their patients directly from service providers, such as NHS Trusts and specialist units.

PROVIDER

Good health does not depend solely upon direct medical provision. The achievement and maintenance of good health depends on the following:

- adequate income
- satisfactory housing
- safe water supply and system of waste disposal
- the avoidance of accidents
- an unpolluted environment
- a safe life style
- satisfactory relationships
- a nutritious diet
- avoidance of stress

(From: Michael Hill, 1996)

At present health policy ensures that everyone has access to health care. This promotes the 'good health' of the population and well-being of society generally. Services are delivered in a variety of ways. Primary health care services are those that offer treatment of some kind. They are the front line services and include hospitals and specialist services such as burns units and VD clinics. Secondary health care services are those that offer some sort of preventative treatment or service such as GPs, health visitors and community nurses. Tertiary health care services are those that try to maintain good health by providing information and advice on keeping healthy. These services are often referred to as health promotion.

Child health promotion programmes

The aims of such programmes are to

- promote positive health and development
- prevent illness, accidents and abuse
- recognise and eliminate any problems affecting development, behaviour and education
- encourage early detection of any risk to health or development

Child health programmes need to be flexible if they are to meet the needs of individual children and their families.

ACTIVITY

Visit your local Health Promotions Unit. They will be able to provide you with a range of information on the promotion of child health and development. Choose a topic that interests you. It may be keeping safe in the sun, bullying or safety in the home. Using the information you have been given design a poster that would convey this message in a simple, colourful and visual way. It should be suitable for children aged 4 to 6 years.

Monitoring child health and development

In order to ensure the developmental progress of children and early identification of any problems, the growth and development of children is regularly monitored. Many methods have been devised that enable health visitors, doctors and other professionals to monitor the developmental progress of children.

- The neonatal examination that takes place as soon as possible after birth: it is primarily a physical check to ensure that the baby is intact and that the vital organs are functioning properly.
- The six to eight week check is carried out by the GP. Parents/ carers are asked about the child's, feeding, sleeping, and toileting habits. The GP looks to see how responsive the baby is to light and sound. The baby is measured and weighed.
- The six to nine month check is carried out by the GP or Health Visitor. They observe the baby's visual behaviour, hearing and vocalisation. They also monitor the baby's physical development and motor ability. They are weighed and measured.
- The two-year check is carried out by the health visitor often in the child's home. The height and weight are measured. Both hearing and sight are monitored. The health visitor checks out the child's physical, social and behavioural development. They do this using normative development charts. If a child is developing at a rate significantly below that typical for their age group the health visitor will monitor their progress more closely and discuss with the GP.
- The 4 to 5 year check is carried out by the GP and health visitor. They observe their gross motor skills, manipulative skills, communication skills, vision, hearing and behaviour. The GP

makes sure that the heart and lungs are functioning normally and that the testes have descended in little boys. Weight and height are measured.

- The eight-year check is carried out by the school nurse. It is a general review of development and includes the measurement of height and weight. A vision test is also administered.

In addition, children are immunised against a variety of infections that may adversely affect or delay their development. It is usually the responsibility of the health visitor to maintain growth charts and a record of the child's progress from birth to 5 years. Thereafter the task is passed on to the school nurse.

ACTIVITY

Find out the immunisation schedule of children aged 0 to 15 years.

Summary

- the fall in child death rates is largely due to our reduced vulnerability to common infectious diseases
- children's health, including dental health, has generally improved but some diseases have increased: respiratory diseases, obesity, eating disorders, stress and probably suicide
- children from lower socio-economic groups suffer higher levels of mortality and morbidity
- structural explanations include living in poor quality accommodation, in polluted areas of cities
- cultural explanations note the lower incidence of breastfeeding and child immunisation, and a high incidence of smoking
- boys are more likely to die than girls at every age
- females live longer than males but women suffer higher rates of chronic diseases and psychiatric illness
- boys are more likely than girls to have disabilities
- behavioural disabilities – the most common type in all age groups – seem to increase with the age of the child
- the structure of the NHS has seen a number of changes since 1946, the most recent and far reaching in 1990

- at present the health policy of the UK ensures that everyone has access to health care which is free at the point of service delivery
- the health and development of children is maintained through health promotion programmes, developmental checks and immunisation

10

The early years

Key points

- the idea of childhood is not universal
- some historians claim that young children were often treated with indifference, and worse, until relatively recently
- steps to protect children were taken in the nineteenth century, and the twentieth century was expected to be 'the century of the child'
- there is now concern however that children are less able to remain children and that childhood may even be disappearing

Introduction

What is a child? At first glance, it seems obvious. Children are biologically and psychologically immature human beings. They are not just smaller than us, they are much more naive, much less knowledgeable, much less worldly and much less experienced. They need a long period of growth – both physical and mental – before they can start to become ready for adult society.

Because this seems so self-evident, it comes as a surprise to realise that this is very much a modern view. For, although children are everywhere, the idea of 'childhood' – as a separate age status in which the person is expected to behave distinctively, and unlike adults – is not universal.

As Steve Wagg points out:

> Like so many vitally important aspects of social life, childhood is *socially constructed*. It is, in other words, what members of particular societies, at particular times and in particular places, say it is. There is no single

> universal childhood, experienced by all. So, childhood isn't 'natural' and should be distinguished from mere biological immaturity.
>
> (From S. Wagg, *Sociology Review*, 1992)

The experience of childhood varies greatly between cultures. As Ruth Benedict concluded from her 1934 survey of anthropological studies, there are often big differences between small-scale and industrial societies in how children are treated and expected to behave. The sexuality of children is one such area. In one influential Western view of children, which can be traced back to the eighteenth century French thinker Jean-Jacques Rousseau, children are seen as more or less angelic innocents, with a natural, unworldly goodness which adults may worship and idolise. But among the Trobriand Islanders, for instance, Malinowski found active, and active acceptance of, child sexuality. Thus, he found that children commonly

> . . . indulge in pastimes in which they satisfy their curiosity about the appearance and function of the sexual organs, and receive a certain amount of positive pleasure. Genital manipulation and oral stimulation of the organs are typical forms of this amusement.
>
> (From B. Malinowski 1957)

The adults' response, he noted, was typically one of 'tolerance and amused interest' and 'easy jocularity'.

Some historians of childhood have argued not just that different societies have different expectations of childhood, but that, whereas the biological stage of infancy is universal, in some societies the idea of childhood as a separate age status has not even existed.

That was the case, according to the French historian Philippe Ariès (1973), in medieval Europe. Ariès notes, for instance, that until the thirteenth century, there are no pictures of children as children, 'but only men on a reduced scale'. For as soon as the child could live without the constant support of their mother, nanny or cradle rocker, they were expected to behave like an active, participating member of adult society, and they were treated accordingly. This extended to every area of social activity, from joining in the many games that adults played (for example puppetry, card games, snowballing, hide and seek and blind man's buff), to practising skilled crafts, to playing their part in the many festivals, feasts and celebrations which made up so much of the medieval year.

But by the sixteenth century in Europe, however, the child is being gradually distinguished from the adult, and seen as a source of amusement and relaxation because of their sweetness and simplicity. By the end of the sixteenth century, for the first time, and only for male children of the upper classes, the child began to be dressed not like the adult, but in a distinctive outfit reserved for his age group. As Ariès remarks, 'The adoption of a special childhood costume marked a very important date in the formation of the idea of childhood. Custom thereafter dictated that childhood, henceforth recognised as a separate entity, should also have its special costume'.

However, although European society in the late 1500s gradually began to perceive childhood as distinct, and came increasingly to expect children to behave differently from adults, how they thought of children is still very far removed from how we like to think of children today.

Traditional attitudes to children

According to some historians, in some countries such as England and France, most mothers and fathers probably felt little if any love for their babies and very young children until as recently as the nineteenth century. This is thought likely to be the case throughout much of Europe where, according to the American historian Edward Shorten (1976), 'mothers viewed the development and happiness of infants younger than two with indifference'. Or with worse than indifference.

According to Ariès, until about the sixteenth century, very small children were seen, even by their parents, as hardly being people. Their birth or death was a matter of chance, depending entirely upon God's will; they barely possessed their own souls and, in the brief time that they may have lived, they gained little adult sympathy or compassion.

As evidence of parental indifference, Shorter refers to a number of practices which clearly don't support modern notions, either of maternal 'instincts' or of paternal love. One common practice of parents, for instance, was to use the cradle as a benumbing instrument: the parents used the cradle for violent rocking in order to bring sleep to the child by knocking it out. It also wasn't uncommon to refer to the baby as 'it', or 'the creature', to forget their child's age, to forget how many children they'd had, or to give to a newly born baby the name of one recently dead.

Undoubtedly poverty encouraged many apparently unloving practices, but poverty isn't sufficient to explain them away. Babies and children frequently just weren't wanted. It was common, for instance, in eighteenth century Western Europe, for babies to be sent away from home immediately after their baptism, to be wetnursed for two or more years. Among the well-to-do in France, for example, large numbers of babies were boarded out. Poor women in rural areas, on the other hand, might send their babies away and then take in the nursling of a wealthier family to make money. Parents seldom visited the children they had sent away. Given that many of the wetnurses lived in desperate poverty in rural hovels, however, this was perhaps just as well.

Those who didn't send away their babies often left them by themselves for long periods of time, 'stewing in their own excrement for hours on end' (Shorter, 1975). Sometimes they did so near a fire, where the tight swaddling clothes in which they were bound accidentally caught alight, or sometimes the babies were attacked and eaten by the barnyard hogs. In some areas, neither parent would attend a child's funeral if they died at less than 5 years old. The death of children was commonly received with little obvious concern and, after the third or fourth child, was widely perceived as a blessing, both for the parents and for the child, who could thereby get straight to heaven (provided they had been baptised) without having to endure life's misery. Some parents would simply leave their babies to die in the gutters, and it was common to come across dead children in either town or countryside.

ACTIVITY

Captions for photographs giving evidence of common nineteenth century experiences

a) Babies abandoned in a New York tenement.

b) Infants abandoned at a French foundling hospital were left in the revolving box provided and were admitted into hospital when the bell was rung.

c) A Spanish wet nurse is seen leaving her own child to nurse another woman's baby.

(All taken from E. Shorter, 1975)

On the death of a child

In the Middle Ages, no one thought of keeping a picture of a child, whether the child had lived to grow to adulthood or had died in infancy. If it lived, childhood was just an unimportant phase which didn't justify recording. If it died, the child wasn't worthy of remembrance. The general feeling was that one had several children in order to keep a few.

It may be that the child who had died too soon in life was buried almost anywhere, much as we today bury a domestic pet, a cat or a dog. He was such an unimportant little thing, so inadequately involved in life, that nobody had any fears that he might return after death to pester the living.

The feeling of indifference towards a too fragile childhood is not really very far removed from the callousness of the Roman or Chinese societies which practiced the exposure of new-born children. There is nothing about this callousness which should surprise us; it was only natural in the community conditions of the time.

(From P. Ariès, 1973)

The routine tormenting of children?

According to the journalist Colin Ward, the evidence gathered from the past reveals, not just an indifference to children, but an automatic callousness towards the young. Whether they were among the vast number reared in penal institutions for the sin of being orphaned or handicapped, whether they were 12 year old workers destined for long hours of hard labour, or even whether they were among the children of the rich parked at eight years old in boarding schools, hardship and brutality seem often to have been deliberately imposed.

Folklore is full of tales of country children who dared not return to their father or their employer because some task had been bungled or an animal lost. They were found shivering and weeping or frozen to death, or may even have committed suicide out of despair.

One favourite trick of adults was to count the sheep and pretend that one was missing. At the Kentford Junction on the road from Bury St Edmunds to Newmarket there is a wooden cross, periodically renewed, recording 'Joseph the unknown gypsy boy'; a memorial to a boy who

hanged himself having been told, just to tease him, that one of the flock was missing. He was also reminded that he was bound to be accused of sheepstealing, punishable by death, so he took the law into his own hands.
(From C. Ward, *New Statesman and Society*, 1989)

1 Summarise the evidence that parents in the past have generally been relatively indifferent to their younger children.
2 Do you think that the way parents in the past commonly behaved to their younger children should be called 'cruel'? Justify your answer.

'The century of the child'

In 1890 a Swedish feminist, Ellen Key, published a book called *The Century of the Child*. In her optimistic view of the coming twentieth century, children's parents would be physically healthy and mutually loving. The mother would be ever-present at home, bringing up the children and providing a caring and protective environment for what were increasingly seen as civilisation's greatest asset – its children.

Steps to create a protected childhood had already been taken in most Western societies in the late nineteenth century. Child labour had been controlled by law and the worst manifestations of it made illegal. Compulsory, free education had been established. Child homelessness and the problem of street children, which so troubled Dr Barnado, had been eased. Moreover, dramatic falls in infant and premature death had been achieved, thanks largely to better sanitation and higher standards of living. This encouraged parents to have fewer children, more confident in the belief that they would be looked after by a surviving child in old age. So children had fewer siblings and the children were closer in age.

Changing theories of parenting

Additionally, in the early years of the twentieth century, science was increasingly called upon to provide directions in the raising of children, and the emerging profession of psychology arose to fit the bill. Yet, for much of the first 30 years of the century, the rules which the 'experts' advised parents to apply encouraged a greater distance between parent and child.

The dominant philosophy was **behaviourism**, which claimed that children could be trained to behave by the systematic use of rewards and punishments. The advice internationally was consistent. 'The rule that parents should not play with the baby may seem hard, but it is without doubt a safe one' (the United States Children's Bureau, 1914). 'There is a sensible way of treating children. Treat them as though they were young adults. Never hug and kiss them, never let them sit in your lap' (American psychologist, John Watson). 'The leading authorities of the day all agree that the first thing to establish in life is regularity of habits. The establishment of perfect regularity of habits, initiated by "feeding and sleeping by the clock", is the ultimate foundation of all-round obedience' (Truby King, 1937). As Hugh Cunningham points out, this hardly looks like 'the century of the child'.

In the 1930s, however, a shift to a less behavioural parenting took place. An increasingly influential Freudian psychoanalysis drew attention to the dangers of suppressing children's will and emotions. People also linked such repressive forms of child-rearing with the fascism which was coming to prominence in Germany and elsewhere. Together, these perceptions gave way to a more enjoyable, more easygoing and more 'intuitive' type of parenting whose most famous advocate was the American child psychologist Dr Spock. After the Bible, his book, *The Common Sense Book of Baby and Child Care*, published in 1946, became the century's bestseller.

In 1951, an ex-army psychiatrist, John Bowlby, produced a report on the psychological effects of separating young children from their homes which, when published in 1953 as *Child Care and the Growth of Love*, also became a bestseller. Bowlby argued from the psychoanalytic insight that children's early experience can have an important and lasting effect on their personality and behaviour as adults. From that 'surely reasonable proposition' (Oakley, 1981), Bowlby went on to claim that, from the evidence of his own researches and that of others, the child's mental health would almost certainly be damaged by the prolonged loss of his or her mother's care. It is 'essential for mental health' that children experience with the mother a 'warm, intimate, continuous relationship', which the feminist Ann Oakley interprets as requiring the mother's 'more or less continual presence'.

Children were defined by Bowlby as 'deprived' if they

- lived with a mother who had an 'unfavourable' attitude to her child

- lost their mother through death, illness or desertion
- were removed by medical or social agencies to live with strangers

According to Bowlby, a major cause of deprivation was what he called the failure of a child's 'natural home group'. By that, however, he included the following, any one of which was a potential cause of child deprivation: his list included as indicators of 'failure of the natural home group' divorce, illegitimacy, maternal employment and other factors.

Although Bowlby's become the single most influential theory of child development in Britain's post-war years, his views were criticised by the anthropologist Margaret Mead as 'a new and subtle form of anti-feminism' (quoted in Oakley, 1981). According to other critics, Bowlby failed to consider a number of important questions which would have affected his findings. For instance: What was the cause of separation? Who else was the child separated from? What do 'normal' mothers do for their children in the way of play, stimulation, and so on (Oakley, 1981). Margaret Mead argued that, far from 'an exclusive and continuous relationship between mother and infant' being the natural and universal arrangement, it is only possible 'under highly artificial urban conditions'.

Although Bowlby later modified his ideas, Oakley concluded that Bowlby's success and great influence was because his message fitted the spirit of the times. It was another manifestation of 1950s' reaction against women in a period that saw women in a highly traditional home-centred role and was already very child-centred. For Margaret Mead it was 'a new and subtle form of anti-feminism in which men – under the guise of exalting the importance of maternity – are tying women more tightly to their children than has been thought necessary since the invention of bottlefeeding and baby carriages' (quoted in Oakley, 1981).

ACTIVITY

Do you depend for your guidance on 'maternal instinct' or the 'expert'?

One of the greatest problems women face in becoming mothers today is the double expectation: both that child rearing comes naturally and that it must be learned from experts. Mothers are told both that they must follow experts' advice, and that, because of their 'instincts', they are their own experts. As Dr Spock puts it, 'Trust your own instincts, and follow the directions that your doctor gives you.'

Suffused with guilt because they do not naturally know how to help a baby take the breast, how to make a 7 year old go to bed or how to counsel a rebellious teenager through her first love affair, mothers receive from experts the clear message that there is a scientifically correct way to bring up children. And whatever vices their children have as adults are to be attributed, one way or another, to faulty mothering. However, Catch 22 is that the experts themselves are in a quandary about what the 'right' way is.

(From A. Oakley, 1981)

Do you believe that there is a 'right way' to bring up children? What do you believe are the dominant ideas of our time about how children should be brought up?

Is childhood disappearing?

If the dominant vision in the first part of the twentieth century was of an optimistic 'century of the child', the closing years of the century seem to be dominated instead by a gnawing unease. Our relatively recent ideas of childhood as a time of protected innocence seem increasingly difficult to sustain. Instead, the talk now is of the possible death of childhood. Children, many now fear, are no longer able to be simply children, and childhood as a time of separate, sheltered interests is coming to an end. It isn't that childhood is no longer seen as important, but people are afraid that childhood cannot remain protected. What are the arguments?

ACTIVITY

Exposure to adult concerns

The overriding contemporary belief about childhood in the 1990s is that it is lousy and may well be producing vicious young people. Neil Postman put the case powerfully in 1994 in his book, *The Disappearance of Childhood*, arguing that childhood as we have come to think of it is coming to an end, thanks largely to the increasing representation of adult concerns through the mass media. Film and television, Postman claims, are everywhere, and are everywhere dominated by adult interests in sex, violence and consumption. Young people's continual exposure to such adult concerns is eroding the distinctions that once allowed them to remain special, to be children.

(From G. Bedell, *Independent on Sunday*, 1996)

The disappearance of age differentiation

Technology, in the form of television, video and now home computers, has revolutionised children's leisure time. BBC television went live in 1936 (having broadcast on radio since 1922). Initially there were no programmes specifically for children, but when television returned after six years of war, it was with a Mickey Mouse cartoon.

More recently, there has been an increasing recognition and targeting of children as powerful consumers, and this has been marked by a boom in TV-linked merchandising. Significantly, there has also been a disappearance of age demarcations – the news delivers graphic detail to all ages; many controversial children's shows, like *Power Rangers*, are watched by children as young as 3 or 4 and by teenagers; daytime soaps like *Home and Away* and *Neighbours* are watched by under 10s, teenagers and adults; and shows aimed at adults, like *The X Files*, attract huge adolescent audiences.

(From D. Holder, *Independent on Sunday*, 1996)

Little change in children's favourites

There is a general assumption that what children watch today is more violent than what previous generations watched. In fact, it depends when and what they watch. Pre-school television has changed very little and even television for the under-12s features many of the same old favourites. With four terrestrial channels now catering generously to children, however, plus cable in many areas, children are exposed to much more television in terms of quantity and thus to more variation in terms of quality. Children's favourites are not always popular with parents. 87% of 11–15 year olds in a recent survey said that they watch films rated unsuitable for their age, and 45% said that they watched these films 'a lot'.

(From D. Holder, *Independent on Sunday*, 1996)

The growth of children's rights

> In some ways the 'century of the child' has lived up to its billing, but in unanticipated ways. In legal processes and family disputes, adults try to discover and respect children's views in ways unimaginable at the beginning of the century. Statements of the rights of children now emphasise not only their protection but also their right to some degree of decision making and self-determination.
>
> (From H. Cunningham, 1995)

1 Summarise the arguments in the first two extracts. Can you develop more arguments *in support of* the claim that childhood is disappearing?
2 Summarise the arguments in the second two extracts. Can you develop more arguments *against* the claim that childhood is disappearing? After relaying the two arguments to each other, what are your conclusions?

What is happening to childhood?

In his 1982 book *The Disappearance of Childhood*, the Californian Neil Postman proposed the view that childhood as we had known it this century was coming to an end. In his view, it had already become increasingly difficult to distinguish between children and adults in terms of their values and behaviours. For instance, they were no longer particularly distinctive in their tastes, styles and their interests: there were now few special games, foods, or clothing for children. Moreover, like adults, children had high crime rates, suffered from alcoholism and drug use, and lacked a sense of shame over sex. Like the ancient Greek Socrates, Postman lamented that the children also showed little respect for their elders.

Postman's originality, however, was in his explanation for these supposed changes. In brief, childhood as we knew it is dying because we are moving from a print culture to a visual culture. In his reading of history, the idea of childhood had emerged following the invention of the printing press and the mass production of written materials became possible. Reading became a valued skill.

However, learning to read involved more than just learning the skill. Learning to read also developed certain qualities in children, such as persistence, the ability to sit still, and the ability to delay gratification. But visual culture, such as film, TV and video, requires none of these qualities, so children are unlikely to learn them.

Visual culture is not just a medium of communication; it is also embedded with commercial values which, particularly in video, are beyond parental and adult control. So children are exposed to (often very dubious representations of) sex and violence. They are also exposed, Postman notes with concern, through advertising and elsewhere, to a materialistic conception of the good life, which suggests that happiness can be bought by consumption, and turns children into egocentric consumers.

This century's shifting roles for children – from wage-earner to consumer, from contributor to family income to major focus for family expenditure – have been accompanied by a gradual collapse of adult authority. In Britain, Cunningham thinks it began among the middle-classes when the difficulty of hiring nannies and servants forced mothers into closer contact with their children and the contact became less formal. However, it accelerated as parents became more affluent and were able to give children pocket money and more material goods. Already by the 1930s, for instance, children were a substantial market. In the midst of the Great Depression in 1933, the Disney empire was selling $110 million of merchandise, much of it models of such cartoon characters as Donald Duck and Mickey Mouse. (In a 1940s survey of British towns, it was reported that 'school children in the poorer districts had far more pocket money than those of the better class' and that they spent it 'largely on sweets, ice-cream and comics', the sweets being 'often of the most wretched quality' and the comics 'poor to a degree' (quoted in Cunningham, 1995).

But according to Cunningham, the collapse in adult authority is also reflected in a trend to parents 'giving in' to children's demands. This tendency was increasingly encouraged by a range of social pressures to 'give in', including the calculated layout of supermarkets, with sweets carefully located at eye level in the queue.

However, Cunningham argues that the 'shift in the balance of power' from adult to child was not simply economic. It was also emotional. Parents increasingly looked to children for emotional gratification. The tendency to 'give in' also manifested in a reluctance to be as disciplining – as well as remote and rigid – as many had found their parents to be. By the 1960s, and for many earlier, parents wanted a more companionate relationship with their children than they felt their parents had had with them.

This may not look like 'the death of childhood'. However, according to Cunningham, the century which opened with a vision of children as powerless and dependent, has seen both the decline of parental authority and children's successful demand for earlier access to the adult world and their rejection of the prolonging of childhood into the late teens. But whereas the ending of childhood by 14 is the return to the norm of earlier centuries, the difference is that children by that age then were economically productive. Now they are not, and many will have a further seven or more years of non-productive dependence. Little wonder, he concludes, that 'adolescence has come to be seen as a time of stressful contact between parents and children' (Cunningham, 1995).

Summary

- the biological stage of infancy is universal, but childhood – as an age status in which one is expected to behave in certain ways – is not
- Ariès claims that it wasn't until the sixteenth century in Europe that children were seen as having different characteristics to adults
- some historians claim that, until perhaps the nineteenth century, the treatment of children was, in today's terms, often callous and cruel, for child death often provoked little obvious concern
- in the nineteenth century, free education, improved child mortality rates, limitations on child labour and an attack on child homelessness began to create a more protected childhood: the twentieth century was expected to be 'the century of the child'
- however, early (behaviourist) 'child rearing experts' advised parents to act in a distanced manner to their children
- such methods largely gave way, from the 1930s, to less repressive child rearing practices
- many people are now concerned that childhood is disappearing, as children are exposed to adult interests in sex, violence and consumption and an alleged collapse in adult authority
- others, however, claim that childhood is still protected, with children now generally better treated and more considered than ever

11

The later years

Key points

- though the biological event of **puberty** is universal, '**youth**' is a social construction, and so varies in different societies
- distinctive groupings of youth may have emerged in the eighteenth century but youth as a 'universal' age status in the West emerged after the Second World War
- sociologists distinguish between commercially-driven youth culture and the more seriously **deviant** youth sub-cultures
- youth sub-cultures appear to provide solutions to problems typically faced by some young people
- different youth sub-cultures attract young people of different social classes, but have generally been male dominated
- youth sub-cultures generally accentuate what are otherwise 'subterranean values'

The social construction of youth

In the previous chapter we distinguished between the biological stage of infancy and the social stage of childhood. Here, we distinguish between

- **puberty** – a universal biological phenomenon, although the average age at which it occurs in both sexes varies in different societies
- **youth** or adolescence – which are, in contrast, social constructions

This distinction is illustrated, for instance, by a society such as the Bemba of Zambia, in which there is no concept of youth as an age status. Individuals move directly from childhood to adulthood – though usually after having undergone an important traditional ritual. In other societies, although a period between childhood and adulthood may be recognised, their assumptions about it are very different from ours.

In those societies, the gap between children's and adults' behaviour is usually small. Children work alongside adults and share much of their daily lives, so children's and adults' behaviour are much more similar than in our sort of culture. Thus, compared to what 'youth' is expected to involve in our society, their period of 'youth' requires much less giving up of 'childish' things and having to adjust to quite different adult concerns. In such traditional societies, children's and adults' activities and concerns are similar, and behaviours which in our society are assumed to be inevitable aspects of puberty, such as self-concern, mood swings and social awkwardness, may not occur.

The confusing nature of youth in the West today

In Britain and the West, however, things seem particularly confused. At a self-identity level, youth is perceived to be a time of confusion, of emotional upheaval and social embarrassment. As societies, we too seem confused, about the rights and responsibilities – even about the 'boundaries' – of youth.

For instance:

- when does youth start? Does youth begin with puberty? Does childhood end with puberty? Does it depend on one's years? One's experience? As asked in the previous chapter, are children any longer distinct from youths?
- when does youth end? Is it with the attainment of adulthood, or can one be a youth beyond the age of 18?

In physiological terms, of course, in many societies, adulthood begins with puberty. In the West, it depends upon *chronological age* (18 years). The rights which come with adulthood are not given because the body is mature, but because a person has attained a particular age. So adulthood in Britain is not 'tailored' according to individuals' biological development, as it is among the

Bemba of Zambia or among orthodox male Jews, whose initiations into adulthood happen with puberty.

In the West, even the legal age for adulthood isn't straightforward. People get different legal rights and obligations – all associated with adult status – at different ages. Our uncertainty about the beginning and ending of youth may help explain the nature of youth in the West: among other things, its emotional 'storm and stress', and its dilemmas between independence and dependency, and between childishness and maturity.

ACTIVITY

The Bemba: no youth

Among the Bemba people of Zambia, the initiation ceremony which moves a female child into adulthood takes place after her first period, which itself is marked by a separate 'puberty rite'. The puberty rite may involve ceremonial washing of the girl and isolation indoors before her return to the community. The girl then waits until it is convenient for her coming of age ceremony to begin.

This ceremony is composed of many individual rituals, including the physical testing of the girl through various ordeals, her social isolation as a form of ritual separation and the singing of ritual songs. The ceremony lasts for over a month and ends with the girl's change of status being marked by the end of her social isolation. The girl is bathed, dressed in new clothes, brought out of the hut and placed on a new mat outside its door.

The girl sits in silence in front of the villagers, who throw small presents on to the mat. At the end of the ceremony, girls are considered ready for marriage, and often a marriage ceremony follows immediately.

(From quotation in J. Pilcher, *Sociology Review*, 1995)

The West: extended youth

In modern society maturity is staggered. And the time between puberty and full financial responsibility for oneself and one's dependents (often late 20s) is scattered with ambiguous indicators of maturity: sexual maturity, finishing school, leaving full-time higher education, entering paid employment, taking on a mortgage, marriage, parenthood. All these important passages are strung out over an extended time scale.

> There is thus a substantial stretch of the life-cycle in which a person experiences partial independence but few responsibilities except for the self. This period of adolescence is thus an interlude of relative freedom from the all-defining roles of dependent childhood behind and full maturity ahead. In all classes, the adolescent is expected to rebel a little, especially the boy, and to be a bit wild and irresponsible before settling down. The folk sayings legitimise the youthful pursuit of pleasure: 'You're only young once'; 'Enjoy yourself while you're young'.
>
> (From B. Martin, 1983)

1 How do you think the experience of Bemba girls might affect their experience of the post-puberty years?
2 Find out the legal ages at which young people in our society are given the following rights and responsibilities: criminal responsibility, motorbike riding, joining the services and killing the enemy, drinking alcohol in a pub, voting, standing as an MP. What other rights and responsibilities are age-related?
3 What are the arguments for the against awarding a young person in Britain all their 'adult' legal rights and responsibilities at the same time?
4 Should there be a formal coming of age ceremony in Britain today? Does the current widely practiced type of celebration have any significance other than enjoyment?
5 If any of these, or other, changes were introduced, could it change the experience of being a young person in Britain today? Is that a desirable goal?

The emergence of 'youth' in the west

The emergence of 'youth' as an age status – of groups of people with a sense of identity, in some ways distinct from adults and children – can be traced back to at least the eighteenth century. However, it is only since the Second World War that very substantial numbers of young people, in all social classes, have developed styles, tastes and identities which are distinct from those of adults and children (though that does not mean that the styles and tastes are shared among themselves). Though a number of factors can help explain this historical process in the West, we focus here on two:

1 the gradual spread of education across the classes;
2 the relative affluence of post-Second World War young people.

1 The spread of education

According to the French historian Philippe Ariès, 'youth' began to emerge as a separate category at different times among different classes. In each case, however, young people came to be separated from adults and brought together because of the recognition that children needed to be educated and that schools would need to be established for that purpose. This process of segregation tended to encourage among the young a common sense of identity. This process of separation happened among the:

- **upper-classes** from the eighteenth century onwards, especially among those sent away to boarding schools
- **working-class** in late nineteenth century and the provision of mass, compulsory education
- **middle-class** in the latter part of the twentieth century, with the expansion of higher education

The consequences are that:

- more young people extend their education
- the age of biological maturity has been falling, but the period of dependence (on parents and/or the state) has been extended, and adulthood postponed
- this extra time of dependence and limited responsibility is mainly spent in the company of large numbers of their peers, with minimal close contact with, supervision by, or influence from adults
- an increase in social distance between adults and youth
- new tastes, fashions and behaviours, which can emphasise and symbolise youth's sense of separateness, can easily spread

2 The greater affluence of the young

Before the Second World War young people, and even children, dressed much the same as their elders, and largely shared their other tastes. By the late-1950s, however, young people's styles, tastes and fashions had diverged noticably from those of their elders. This was made possible by the greater affluence of young people over that period.

According to some estimates, between the late 1930s and the late 1950s, young people's earnings grew at twice the rate of that of adults. It would be an exaggeration to say that young people in the 1950s were well off: many were not. But the growth in jobs and a general rise in earnings meant that many young people – including the mainly middle-class young still at school – had uncommitted money (that is money left after paying for their necessities).

The greater affluence of young people, coupled with their increasingly lengthy segregation in schools, encouraged the development of distinctive tastes. Responding to, and encouraging, distinctive styles and tastes, a whole range of industries developed specific goods and services aimed particularly at young people. Young people's sense of identity and differentiation from adults were catered for and boosted by a range of goods – records and record players, bikes and motor bikes, clothes, cosmetics and films – and services, such as hairdressing, any and all of which, to varying degrees, would scandalise their elders.

Youth culture and youth sub-cultures

Although there are differences in how sociologists use and define some of the relevant terms, those trying to understand the norms, values, tastes, behaviours and so on of contemporary young people have often found it helpful to distinguish between the idea of a youth culture and that of youth sub-cultures.

The term **youth culture** has been commonly used in two main ways:

1 To refer to the idea of a *common 'culture'* supposedly shared by young people. Nowadays, however, sociologists are clear that there is no one such homogeneous youth culture whose norms, values, styles, beliefs and so on are shared by all, or even most, young people.
2 It can refer instead to the *commercial market of goods and services* produced by the youth-oriented leisure industries, which has developed from the 1950s. These include the youth-oriented mass entertainment and style industries, with over £1000 million a year spent on musical recordings, fashion, cosmetics, magazines and so on. In these terms, buying a Top 20 CD, *Just 17* magazine, brand-label jeans and wearing a baseball cap is all part of commercially-driven youth culture.

It is useful to be able to refer to a 'youth culture', to encompass all the commercially produced goods and services aimed at young people. But it is clear that young people are *not* one homogeneous market, and that 'youth culture' has many facets, each of which are aimed at, and will appeal to, different groupings of young people. Indeed, which aspects of the youth market young people dip into has been found to be strongly influenced by their age, social class, sex and ethnicity.

Although 'rebelliousness' and the denigration of 'straight' adults is built into many aspects of youth culture, it is a mainly superficial rebelliousness. Thus, disagreements with parents in the main are to do with matters of style and personal freedom (for example when the offspring has to return home after an evening out).

Youth sub-culture, on the other hand, is used to refer to the more seriously rebellious and subversive groupings which, though influencing many 'conventional' young people, perhaps especially in terms of style, only actively involve a minority of young people. More than most young people, they are likely to be, in various ways, seriously critical of 'straight' society and conventional life styles, often including those of conventional youth culture.

What are the appeals of youth sub-cultures?

According to Mike Brake, all youth sub-cultures offer:

- a range of cultural elements – such as styles, values, and belief systems – which allow individuals to *develop an identity* outside the identity provided by home, school or work
- a *meaningful way of life during leisure*, which is apart from the worlds of school or work
- *solutions to particular problems* experienced by *particular groups* of young people

What, then, are the different types of youth sub-culture, and what problems do they attempt to resolve?

Although particular youth sub-cultural 'movements' – such as the Teds, the skinheads and the rockers – have differed in terms of specific styles and tastes (for example in speech, music and clothing), Brake suggests that there are some 'traditions' or themes which they share. This is because many of the underlying key values of these specific movements are very similar. There are, then, different sub-cultural traditions among young people, into which particular groups or movements can be 'fitted'. Some of these values which they share, for instance toughness, set them apart from other youth 'movements', such as the hippies. However, there are other values which they share which also seem to be shared by other, apparently very different, deviant youth sub-cultural groups – such as the hippies – and distinguish them all from the wider society.

Brake suggests that there are four main 'traditions' among young people:

- respectable or straight
- delinquent
- bohemian or cultural rebel
- politically militant

Very importantly, the different traditions are distinguished from each other partly by class. The last three sub-cultural traditions Brake identities as deviant. That is, they have values or norms which are significantly different from, and challenge, those of the wider society.

However, the reasons why some young people become actively involved in one sub-cultural tradition rather than another is influenced by their class, gender and ethnic positions. This is because, in Brake's view, different groups of young people face different types of problem, depending largely on factors such as their class position. So, the different sub-cultures offer some different 'solutions' to the problems typically experienced by different groups of young people.

1 Respectable youth

Most young people engage in somewhat rebellious behaviour for some of the time but pass through the teenage years without serious crisis, and without abandoning important cultural goals, such as marriage, family, academic achievement, and 'respectable' employment. Although they will be involved in aspects of commercial youth culture and may well be influenced by one or more youth sub-cultures, they remain fairly conventional. This majority draws from all classes.

Most young people, of middle and working-class backgrounds, manage to find 'solutions' to their problems as adolescents, or just live with and through their problems, without significant involvement in deviant sub-cultures. The hopes and aims of most are in accord with tradition – marriage, children, home, job, security and a 'good' standard of living.

2 Delinquent traditions

This sub-cultural pattern has included members of a number of different groups, such as teds, mods, rockers, skinheads, greasers, 'soccer hooligans' and Hell's Angels. They are generally working-class and particularly involve young males. Traditionally, the males have been involved in violence, toughness, vandalism, theft and heavy drinking. The females, who often appear to play a secondary, dependent role, are more likely to come into contact with the authorities on the grounds that they are 'beyond parental control' and involved in 'unacceptable' sexual behaviour.

A common problem facing mainly urban working-class youth is the limited likelihood of success at school, and of attractive opportunities beyond it. Early educational experience often involves first being put into the lower streams of an educational system which divides children according to 'ability'. Later, if able to find work at all, it has traditionally been in occupations which are 'meaningless, poorly paid and uncreative' (Brake, 1985).

The 'solution' the sub-culture offers is 'to infuse into this bleak world a period of intense emotion, colour and excitement during the brief respite between school and the early days of working and settling down' (Brake, 1985).

3 Bohemian/cultural-rebel traditions

This sub-cultural traditions has included the hipsters and beats of the 1940s to 1950s (for example Jack Kerouac, Allen Ginsberg), the late 1950s to early 1960s 'beatniks', the late 1960s 'hippies' and, going further back, perhaps some of the nineteenth century romantics such as the opium-taking poet Samuel Coleridge.

Members of such groups typically wish to be expressive, creative, spontaneous, poetic, sensitive, experimental, emotional rather than rational, and are often prepared to use drugs to explore altered states of mind. They tend to be middle-class or have middle-class educations. Their 'problems' are similar to those of the politically militant, and these are discussed below.

4 Politically militant

Included within this tradition are groups whose major motivation has been politically committed action and achieving political change. They may be radical ethnic groups, anti-war groups, anti-capitalist or anti-imperialist groups or, more recently, animal rights or environmental groups. Often regarded as 'extremist', the tradition has included groups like the American Black Panthers, the Black Muslims, the American Weathermen, the Campaign for Nuclear Disarmament (CND), the British Angry Brigade, the German Red Army Faction, the Animal Liberation Army and others.

Both the 'bohemian' and 'politically militant' type groups tend to recruit from the same sections of society – from the well-educated sons and daughters of well-to-do liberal middle-class parents, though Jock Young the British sociologist found that the 'radicals' were more likely to include middle-class young from working-class backgrounds as well. One of the 'problems' of people in their position is that, being reared in materially comfortable surroundings, they may not greatly value such possessions – especially seeing what their parents have gone through to get them, and doubting that their accumulation of possessions has brought their parents, or others of that age group, much happiness or contentment. Among environmentalists, the material benefits of modern society are not seen as compensating for, or justifying, the accompanying damage to the environment.

Among the 'solutions' proposed by bohemian groups are group living, and cooperative ways of meeting their own needs cheaply, including sharing skills and resources, to try to stay clear of the sort of competitive, money making jobs and businesses that their parents are involved in.

For political radicals, 'solutions' are less to do with 'opting out' and more concerned with trying to encourage people to organise politically and wrest power from established groups and institutions.

ACTIVITY

The class should divide into two groups, Group 1 and Group 2. Groups 1 and 2 should sit apart. Those in Group 1 **only** should read both of the following two extracts.

Group 2 **only** should turn **directly** to the extract on page 227 and read that. When everyone has finished their reading, members of each Group should work together in small groups, agreeing their answers to the questions which follow. Each small group should choose a notetaker to record their agreed answers.

Soccer hooligans

Last week, a decade after the first wave of football violence, the latest lot of unsavoury louts was apprehended in Amsterdam and Rotterdam. None of the measures taken to dissuade the original bunch of troublemakers has deterred the most recent band. Put them on a list of banned people and they change their names. Segregate them on the pitches and they take their fighting to the bars. All they have learned from legislation is how to avoid it. They have become more shameless, insulting and devious, and are proud of it. While these louts thumb their noses at the authorities, they are applauded by their peers.

As a parent I believe every adolescent in the country should be required to perform some form of compulsory community service, and particularly some of the more unsavory of society's tasks, such as clearing away the carnage after road accidents and emptying old people's bed pans, and doing so alongside people from very different social backgrounds.

(From G. Roberts, *Sunday Times*, 1993)

The breakdown of respect and order

1. Today, insubordination to parental authority, leading to insubordination to all authority, is very general.
2. Our young people have no idea of discipline or subordination.
3. We have been for some years in an undisciplined state. It is impossible to govern people without the exertion of parental authority.
4. He has learned no definite moral standards from his parents, is contemptuous of the law and is easily bored.
5. Children brought up in the last thirty years have nothing like the same reverence for or submission to their parents. This is the chief cause of the increase in crime.
6. Over the last twenty years or so, there has been a revulsion from authority and discipline.
7. In the past twenty five years or so we have cast aside the word discipline and now we are suffering from it.
8. The morals of children are tenfold worse than formerly.
9. There has been a growing spirit of independence in the children and a slackening of control in the parents.

Having read the two extracts above, agree answers to the following questions in small groups:

1 About how long has football violence been with us?
2 How has the behaviour of hooligans changed since it first emerged?
3 Bring together from both Items and briefly summarise the explanations of juvenile delinquency given.
4 What solutions are proposed?
5 What are your thoughts and opinions about any of the above?
When you are agreed, choose a representative who will shortly express your findings to members of Group 2.

This Item should be read only by members of Group 2

A sub-culture of the 1890s

The word 'hooligan' made an abrupt entry into common English usage during the hot summer of 1898, following an excessively rowdy August Bank Holiday celebration when hundreds of people were brought before the courts on charges of assault, disorderliness, drunkenness, robbery and attacks on policemen. Thereafter, 'hooligans' were regularly described as engaged in pitched battles among themselves, wrecking coffee stalls and pubs, or robbing and assaulting old ladies.

Although the name 'hooligan' may have been borrowed from a then-notorious London Irish family, the London Irish probably weren't particularly significant in the disturbances. But the term stuck to describe what we would now call a youth sub-culture. Bell-bottom trousers with a buttoned vent in the leg, colourful neck scarves, a distinctive style of cap, boots 'toe-plated with iron and calculated to kill easily', ornamental leather belts with designs worked in metal pins, a haircut with a 'donkey fringe': this was the London 'hooligan' style. In other cities youths with the same clothes and the same street-fighting habits were known and feared by different names. In Manchester there were 'Scuttlers', in Birmingham, the 'Peaky Blinders'.

Victorian cities pulsed with rowdy and violent street life. There was 'holding the street' for example. Youths blocked their home street to all strangers, kicking and beating all who tried to pass through. Or there was the 'Scuttle', described in Manchester in 1890: a pitched battle of some

600 youths, waged with the buckle ends of belts, stones and powerful catapults, knoves and iron bars. Or a free fight in the Old Kent Road, August 1898, with up to 300 people in a kicking contest.

And the law then was irregular and informal, with very few arrests and sometimes none at all from these disturbances. Street crime then was all too commonplace and trivial to cause any special concern.

Their explanations of hooliganism still sound very familiar today. It was used as evidence of the break-up of family life and the decline of parental authority, especially the mother's. It was explained as due to the law being too lenient, to floggings not being tough enough, to Board School discipline not being sufficiently strict. And just as television is believed to explain the 'recent' phenomenon of hooliganism, so in the late 19th century the music hall was blamed, and when the silent movies arrived, so too were they!

(From G. Pearson, *New Society*, 1983)

Having read the extract, agree answers to the following questions:

1 How long has hooliganism been with us?
2 In what ways are there historical similarities and continuity in the behaviour of hooligans?
3 What explanations of hooliganism have historically been offered?
4 What are your thoughts or opinions on any of the above? When you are agreed, choose a representative to express your findings to Group 1.

Matza's theory of 'subterranean values'

Although the different youth sub-cultural traditions – such as the delinquent and the bohemian – appear very different, David Matza suggests that, beneath the striking surface differences, the different sub-cultural traditions share and emphasise similar key values. These values manifest differently, in the different norms of behaviour of the various youth sub-cultural traditions. However, the values that youth sub-cultures seem to share and accentuate are not values which are alien to either 'respectable' youth or 'respectable' adults. But for the 'respectable', they have a time and place, and that is in leisure time. Matza calls them 'subterranean' (underground) values, because they only legitimately surface out of working hours. What youth sub-cultures do, Matza suggests, is seek to elevate these subterranean, leisure time values into a full-time life style.

Values which apply to the formal work situation		Values considered legitimate during leisure time; also characteristic of youth sub-cultures
Planning, postponement of pleasure	vs	Lack of planning, pleasure-seeking, spontaneous, present orientated
Conforming to rules imposed from above	vs	Self-expression, rule breaking, freedom (of dress, to travel, and so on), 'doing your own thing'
Acceptance of routine, repetition, predictability	vs	Seeks new experience, range of experience, excitement
Work performed to achieve additional rewards, eg income, status, power	vs	Activities done for their own sake, or for what they do to, or for, one, for their direct effect
Hard work seen as a virtue. 'Workaday' values would include: competitiveness, being a 'realist', materialism	vs	Disdain for work and workaday values cooperative, non-competitive, not ambitious, group or community orientated

ACTIVITY

The rockers and their bikes

Completely opposite to their cultural enemies of the early 1960s, the mods, rockers are bikers or greasers. With their black leather jackets, studs, boots and jeans, they were violently, studiedly working class, butch 'wild ones' – anti-domestic and anti-authority. They were mainly low paid, unskilled manual labourers, while the mods were semi-skilled, white collar workers. The rockers were either free-spirited 'easy riders' or 'greasers' less involved with the cult of the motor bike. Their love of the motor bike – itself a symbol of freedom, mastery and intimidation – was in line with their masculinism and rejection of deferred gratification.

They were a kind of motorised cowboy outlaw (as with the Hell's Angels), loners and outsiders linked by the camaradie of the bike. Their sexism showed in a contempt for women, the traditional ties of responsibility and respectability.

(From Brake, 1985)

The hippy use of drugs

The importance of drugs lay in the way they facilitated passing through a great symbolic barrier. On the straight side of the barrier was the world of personal responsibility, grey colours, lack of style, on the other side was the world of freedom, lack of responsibility, stylishness.

Less: That's the whole point, you know, drugs give you the opportunity to change your consciousness, give you new insights. 'Straights' use alcohol to blot out, to lower the level of consciousness, and they use smoking to lower the level of neurosis, and, you know, dope is used to increase one's perceptions of one's surroundings. In other words, visual perception is heightened possibly, and definitely audio-perception.

One crucial aspect of this yielding to experience is the total preoccupation with the 'now'.

Robin: 'Dope' has meant a certain amount of freedom. I believe that one must live in the present, you know, this instant, now, experiencing now for what it is, because it is.

(From P. Willis, 'The cultural meaning of drug use' in S. Hall and T. Jefferson 1976).

Make a list of the apparent differences between the rockers and hippies. Now try to make a list of similarities. Are there any 'subterranean values' which they share? How do the same values show in their behaviour?

The role of the female

In many of the studies of youth sub-cultures, girls are either virtually invisible, are on the margins of the group, or appear only in a stereotyped role. Youth sub-cultures, in short, have been overwhelmingly male dominated, though females have featured more in some than others.

TEDDY GIRLS: 1950S

According to McRobbie and Garber, there were small groups of girls who saw themselves as Teddy Girls in the 1950s, who went with the boys to the cinema or dancing, and who seemed to revel in relaying tales of the violence of their male mates. But most working-class girls could not have participated.

First, girls' wages in the 1950s were not as high as boys' and they were required to spend them differently. Teddy boy culture involved escaping from the family into the street and café, as well as evening and weekend trips into town. Although the Teddy girls would go out, either individually with a boy friend or as a group of girls accompanying a group of boys, they would be much less involved in just 'hanging about' on street corners. Girls would spend much more time at home, and in preparing to go out. For their working-class parents, it was acceptable for boys to 'have fun while they could', but for girls the major injunction was not 'getting yourself into trouble'. But while boys were allowed to 'sow their wild oats' and then reform and settle down, for a girl to become known as one of the wild oats which had been sown was 'drastic and irreversible' (McRobbie and Garber, 1976).

FEMALE MODS: EARLY TO MID 1960s

Much more than was the case with the earlier Teds, or the contemporary rockers, among the mods of the 1960s, girls were a visible part of the scene. Although there were a variety of mods and mod styles, 'mainstream' female mods were elegantly dressed, with cropped hair and whitened, deadpan faces and, like the males, were almost obsessively careful about their appearance. The 'mainstream' male mod wore 'a suit, neat, narrow trousers and pointed shoes' (Brake, 1985). For this, he was scorned by the arch-rival rockers as effeminate (a sentiment typically expressed less sensitively)!

Unlike the assertively working-class rockers, the mods – both male and female – were likely to be employed in routine white collar, office or retail jobs. Many of the girls worked in relatively new jobs, as secretaries or in the boutique, cosmetic and clothes trades: jobs which, though apparently 'glamourous' were mainly routine and dead-end, with few career prospects and few wage increases. Yet the jobs had glamour and status and 'a touch of dressing-up and going to work "in town" about them, at least in the big cities' (McRobbie and Garber, 1976).

For both males and females, the smart, 'respectable' style, and the 'cool', detached behaviour could be more easily sustained among adults, both at home, school and work, without provoking their direct displeasure in a way that a more aggressive style probably would.

The greater involvement of girls in mod sub-culture is thought to be partly due to the more 'feminine' nature of mod style, and a relative absence of otherwise prevalent harshly sexist attitudes among the males. It may also be due to the relative lack of dependence on a male or males: 'mod girls could just be "around", without necessarily being coupled with any one mod boy: she could "be a mod", in a mod couple, in a crowd of other mod girls, or even alone' (McRobbie and Garber, 1976). Longer term, however, they remained orientated towards marriage and the family.

FEMALE HIPPIES: LATE 1960S

'Hippies' were a very diverse, but largely middle-class, collection of groupings. In Britain, however involved and committed they became, many came to the sub-culture as 'A' level or higher education students. Yet females still seem to have been largely contained within mainly traditional female images and roles. 'The stereotypical images we associate most with hippy culture tend to be those of the Earth Mother, baby at breast, or the fragile pre-Raphaelite lady' (McRobbie and Garber, 1976). In music, females barely featured except as singers. But even there, the images available were limited. 'The few women who made it usually fit either the gentle, lyrical, introspective image such as Joni Mitchell, or the aggressive, butch, whiskey-sodden type such as Janis Joplin' (McRobbie and Garber, 1976).

FEMALE SKINHEADS: 1970S

The skinheads of the 1970s were a similarly 'hard', male-orientated, working-class sub-culture, who also attracted a relatively small band of female associates. If anything, they seem to have played a role closer to that of their boyfriends than did the Ted girls. For whereas the Ted girls looked and acted quite differently to their boyfriends, the female skinheads dressed, looked and acted like the males, including regularly attending football matches – a crucial activity for skinheads – and participating actively once there.

ACTIVITY

1 How would you explain the position or role of females in any of the sub-cultures described?
2 Do a piece of research to try to identify whether people are aware of any youth sub-cultures today. If they are, how do they identify them and what are their characteristics? How do the roles of male and female compare?

Summary

- youth is a social construction: it does not exist in a society such as the Bemba, and in societies where it does, it can be much less of a problem phase than in the West
- youth in the West may be difficult partly because its boundaries and nature are confused, arbitrary and unclear
- youth as an age category emerged from the eighteenth century as different groups of young people were largely separated from adults, and brought together in large numbers, by the evolving education system
- 'youth culture', developing from the 1950s with young people having uncommitted money, refers here to the commercial market of goods and services aimed primarily at the young: it challenges 'adult culture' mainly on issues of style and taste, or young people's personal freedoms
- three main deviant youth sub-cultural traditions were identified: the delinquent, bohemian and politically radical, each attracting members of a particular social class
- despite their differences, deviant youth sub-cultures seem to share an enthusiasm for lifestyles in which subterranean values are central: among 'straights' such values as seen as more appropriately limited to leisure time
- in most sub-cultures, girls have seemed marginal or playing a stereotyped role, with the mods of the early 1960s a relatively rare exception – nevertheless, even their longer-term goals remained, rather stereotypically, marriage and family

Bibliography

Abel-Smith, M. and **Titmuss,** K. (eds) (1974) *Richard M. Titmuss: Social Policy An Introduction.* London: Allen and Unwin.
Aries, P., *Centuries of Childhood* (Penguin, Harmondsworth, 1973).
Banting, K. C. (1979) *Poverty, Politics and Policy.* London: Macmillan.
Bedell, G., 'A Kind of Innocence', *The Independent on Sunday* (September 1996).
Bernstein, B., 'Education cannot compensate for society', *New Society* (February 1970).
Best, L., 'Dragons, dinner ladies and ferrets: sex roles in children's books', *Sociology Review* (February 1993).
Brake (1985) *Comparative Youth Culture.* London: Routledge and Kegan Paul.
Chamber's Encyclopaedia (1889).
Clark, J., 'Gender and Education Revisited', *Sociology Review,* Vol. 5 (April 1996).
Cunningham, H. (1995) *Children and Childhood in Western Society Since 1500.* Harlow: Longman.
Donnison, D. (1982) *The Politics of Poverty.* London: Martin Robertson.
Encyclopaedia Britannica (1808–1810).
Fraser, D. (1985) *The Evolution of the British Welfare State.* London: Macmillan.
Frayman, H. (1991) *Breadline Britain 1990s: The Findings of the Television Series.* London Weekend Television.
Glennerster, H. (1995) *British Social Policy Since 1945.* Oxford: Blackwell.
Goffman, E. (1963) *Stigma.* Harmondsworth: Penguin.
Gough, K. (1959) 'Is the family Universal? The Nayar Case' in Bell and Vogel (eds) *A Modern Introduction to the Family.* London: Collier Macmillan.
Hall, D. (1994) *The Child Surveillance Handbook* (2nd edition).
Handy, C. (1989) *The Age of Unreason.* London: Century.
Hewitt, P. and Leach, P. (1993) *Social Justice: Children and Families.*
Hill, M. (1996) *Social Policy: A Comparative Analysis.* Englewood Cliffs: Prentice-Hall.
Holder, D., 'Now and then: an index of childhood' *The Independent on Sunday* (1996).
Hornby, W. F. and Jones, M. (1993) *An Introduction to Population Geography.* Cambridge: Cambridge University Press.
Hymas, C. and **Cohen,** J. 'Young black pupils top of the class in 3Rs', *The Sunday Times* (December 1994).
Jary, D. and J. (1991) *Collins Dictionary of Sociology.*
Kavanaugh, D. (1989) *British Politics: Continuities and Change.* Oxford: Oxford University Press.
Key, E., *The Century of the Child* (1900).
Kohn, A., 'Girl talk, guy talk' *Psychology Today* (February 1988).
Lynch, K. and **Banerjee,** T., 'Growing up in cities', *Society Today* (March 1977).
Malinowski, B., *The Sexual Life of Savages,* (Routledge and Kegan Paul, London, 1957).
Martin, B. (1983) *A Sociology of Contemporary Cultural Change.* Oxford: Blackwell.
McRobbie, A. and **Garber,** J. (1976) 'Girls and Subcultures' in S. Hall and T. Jefferson (eds) *Resistance Through Rituals,* London: Hutchinson.
Mead, M. (1935) *Sex and Temperament in 3 Pimitive Societies.* London: Routledge and Sons.
Murray, C. (1990) *The Emerging British Underclass.* IEA.
Norton, C. and **O'Reilly,** J., 'Inner city children fail basic 3Rs test' *The Sunday Times* (September 1997).
Oakley, A., 'What makes girls different from boys?', *New Society,* 21 (1978).
Oakley, A. (1981) *Subject Women.* London: Fontana.
Oppenheim, C. (1990) *Poverty: The Facts.* London: Child Poverty Action Group.
O'Reilly, J., (see **Norton,** C.).
Parton, N. (1985) *The Politics of Child Abuse.* London: Macmillan.
Passmore, B., 'The educational and vocational experience of 15–18 year old young people of ethnic minority groups', *The Times Education Supplement* (25.10.85).
Pearson, G., 'From Hooligans to Heroes', *New Society* (30.1.83).
Pearson, G., 'Hooligans and youthful crime: "Permissiveness" and "tradition"' *Social Studies Review* (March 1988).
Perrott, E. (1972) *Looking into Organisms.* London: John Murray.
Phillips, M., 'The Observer Essay', *The Observer* (1995).
Pilcher, J., "Growing up and growing older: the sociology of age', *Sociology Review* (September 1995).
Postman, N. (1982) *The Disappearance of Childhood.*
Roberts, G., 'Community Service: a cure for louts', *The Sunday Times* (1993).
Sage, A., 'Poverty "helps push young into world of crime"', *The Independent on Sunday* (1993).

Sharpe, S. (1994) *Just Like a Girl: How Girls Learn to be Women: The 70s to the 90s*. Harmondsworth: Penguin.
Shorter, E. (1976) *The Making of the Modern Family*. London: Collins.
Small, G. (1988) *The Listener*.
Spiker, P. (1985) *Social Policy: Themes and Approaches*. Englewood Cliffs: Prentice-Hall.
Spock, Dr. (1946) *The Common-Sense Book of Baby and Child-Care*.
Sugarman, B., 'Social class, values and behaviour in schools' in **Craft**, M. (1970) *Family, Class and Education*. London: Longman.
Toynbee, P., *The Guardian* (1978).
Tyson, M., 'Shaping Up', *New Society* (c.1984).
Utting, D. (1995) *Family and Parenthood: Supporting Families, Preventing Breakdown*. York: Joseph Rowntree Foundation.
Wagg, S., 'I blame the parents', *Sociology Review* (April 1992).
West, N., 'Miss Lonely Hearts', *New Directions* (1962).
Whynes, D. (1992) *Welfare State Economics*. London: Heinemann.
Williams, F. (1994) *Social Policy: A Critical Introduction*. Cambridge: Polity Press.
Willis, P. (1977) *Learning to Labour: How Working Class Kids Get Working Class Jobs*. Farnborough: Saxon House.
Wilson, A. (1985) *Family*. London: Tavistock.
Wolterek, H. (1965) *What Science Knows About Life: An Exploration of Life Sources*. Massachussetts: MIT Press.
Wragg, T., 'Oh Boy!', *The Times Educational Supplement* (1997).

Index